£1·50

Judith Anderson.

Traditional Buildings and Life
in the Lake District

Traditional Buildings
and Life
in the Lake District

SUSAN DENYER

LONDON
Victor Gollancz Ltd/Peter Crawley
in association with
The National Trust
1991

Also by Susan Denyer

AFRICAN TRADITIONAL ARCHITECTURE
(Heinemann Educational Books Ltd)

First published in Great Britain 1991
in association with The National Trust
by Victor Gollancz Ltd/Peter Crawley
14 Henrietta Street, London WC2E 8QJ
Designed by Harold Bartram
Map by Malcolm Porter
Plans and Diagrams by Martin Higgins

British Library Cataloguing in Publication Data
Denyer, Susan,
 Traditional buildings and life in the Lake District.
 1. Cumbria. Lake District. Housing
 I. Title
 363.5094278

ISBN 0-575-04552-3

Photoset in Great Britain by
Rowland Phototypesetting Ltd, Bury St Edmunds, Suffolk
Printed and bound by
Butler & Tanner Ltd, Frome, Somerset

Contents

Preface 7

Acknowledgements 9

1 A Cabinet of Beauties 11

2 Domestic Interiors 18

3 House Plans 54

4 Animals 73

5 Crops 111

6 Barn Plans 133

7 Construction: Materials and Techniques 148

8 Looking Forward 192

Glossary 199

References 201

Index 205

Townend, Troutbeck, c.1890.
'Ivy muffling them in a sober green mantle, even to the chimney tops.' Townend was the home of the Browne family, certainly from the early seventeenth century (and maybe from much earlier) until 1944. It is now open to the public and remains largely as the family lived in it, complete with furniture, books and domestic utensils. It is a remarkably complete example of a prosperous yeoman farmer's house.

Preface

To MANY people, the most familiar image conjured up by the name 'the National Trust' is of an organization that looks after the stately homes of England. This is not an image that would have been recognized by the Trust's founders back in 1895. Until the late 1930s, the Trust owned only two great houses – Barrington Court and Montacute, both in Somerset – and was deeply concerned that it lacked the means to furnish them adequately. Only with the introduction of the Country Houses Scheme initiated by the Marquis of Lothian in 1937 did the Trust turn its attentions to great historic houses, and then they began to arrive thick and fast.

The first historic building acquired by the National Trust in the year of its foundation gives the clue to what the founders, Octavia Hill, Canon Rawnsley and Robert Hunter, would have felt justified the charity's subtitle of 'Places of Historic Interest or Natural Beauty'. The tiny medieval priests' house in Alfriston, Sussex, was saved for posterity by purchase at 10 pounds. The Alfriston Clergy House was what might be described as an example of vernacular architecture. This is a term that can rouse puzzlement in the uninitiated – in architecture, as in linguistic terms, it signifies native or peculiar to a particular locality.

The Trust owns many thousands of vernacular buildings, and has for the past eight years spent a lot of time and effort in making detailed vernacular surveys through its regional offices. These surveys have often been carried out with the help of the Manpower Services Commission, and the Trust is very grateful to all who have contributed to the undertaking. Much of the information to be found in this book is based on research carried out for the vernacular survey in the Trust's North-West Region, where Susan Denyer is the Historic Buildings Representative.

Traditional Buildings and Life in the Lake District is the first volume in a series in which it is hoped to look at vernacular architecture in every part of the country – the National Trust looks after properties in England, Wales and Northern Ireland, but not Scotland, which has its own National Trust and, indeed, its own most successful Small Buildings Scheme. However, it is fitting that the series begins with the Lake District for it is here that the Trust owns a large and representative number of small, traditional buildings. The Lakes are the heartland of National Trust philosophy: Canon Rawnsley was inspired to help to found the Trust in order to save the hills and lakes of his homeland from the twin perils of industrial development and the pressure of too many visitors. He in turn inspired his friend, Beatrix Potter, who had bought the farmhouse of Hill Top at Near Sawrey with the earnings from her famous children's books, to buy up hill farms that came on to the market and to bequeath them to the National Trust. Beatrix Potter's interest in the traditional life of the Lake District was a vital ingredient in preserving so much for us to enjoy, as you will see in this book.

It is the Trust's policy to preserve these farms and their traditional way of life if at all possible, even in these hard economic times. Thus most of the buildings referred to in the text are still working farms and ancillary buildings, so they cannot be visited in the same way as the stately homes now in the Trust's care. So, please enjoy the photographs that we have reproduced of many of these fascinating buildings, rather than try to view them at first hand!

Margaret Willes
The Publisher
The National Trust

Note: The majority, but not all, of houses and farm buildings mentioned and illustrated in this book belong to the National Trust. An entry does not, therefore, necessarily imply ownership by the National Trust.

Acknowledgements

MANY PEOPLE have been involved in the National Trust's surveys, from which this book has drawn so much information. First and foremost I would like to record the names of the main members of the Vernacular Survey Team in the Lake District from 1983 to 1988 – Martin Higgins, Jeremy Lake, Sheila King, Gary Corbett, Simon Greene and Tim Whittaker – all of whom carried out detailed field surveys of buildings and wrote analytical reports. Tim Whittaker also worked on the photographic survey, as did Robert Thrift and David Pearson.

The extensive archive research for all the farms was carried out by Janet Martin and was written up into individual farm histories. Martin Higgins has kindly redrawn some of the survey plans, specially for this volume, and he has also produced the explanatory drawings.

Since 1987 a Landscape Survey Team has been at work recording all the man-made features in various valleys within National Trust ownership. The survey work is currently being carried out by Neil Stanley and Arnold Webster, together with a team of volunteers, and Bill Bevan is responsible for the archive research. He was helped with this for a year by Sarah Lewery. For two years Nick Steenman-Clarke researched the history of some of the National Trust woodlands.

Many people have made helpful comments on the text and I would particularly like to thank Ronald Brunskill for reading and commenting on the whole text, and Angus Winchester and Raven Frankland for reading and commenting on particular chapters. My especial thanks go to Janet Martin for her help, not only in reading and commenting on the whole text but also for providing me with much archival information and for many enjoyable and valuable discussions over the last few years. Thanks also go to the tenants of the National Trust who have tolerated the attentions of more than one survey team over recent years, to Pippa Dineen who patiently typed the whole text and last, but certainly not least, to my family for encouragement and help both with the content of the book and with the workings of the wordprocessor.

The opinions expressed here are entirely my own; the book has been written in my spare time and not as an employee of the National Trust. The views put forward may not, therefore, necessarily be those of the National Trust.

Despite all the help that has been given, any omissions or short-comings in this volume remain solely my responsibility.

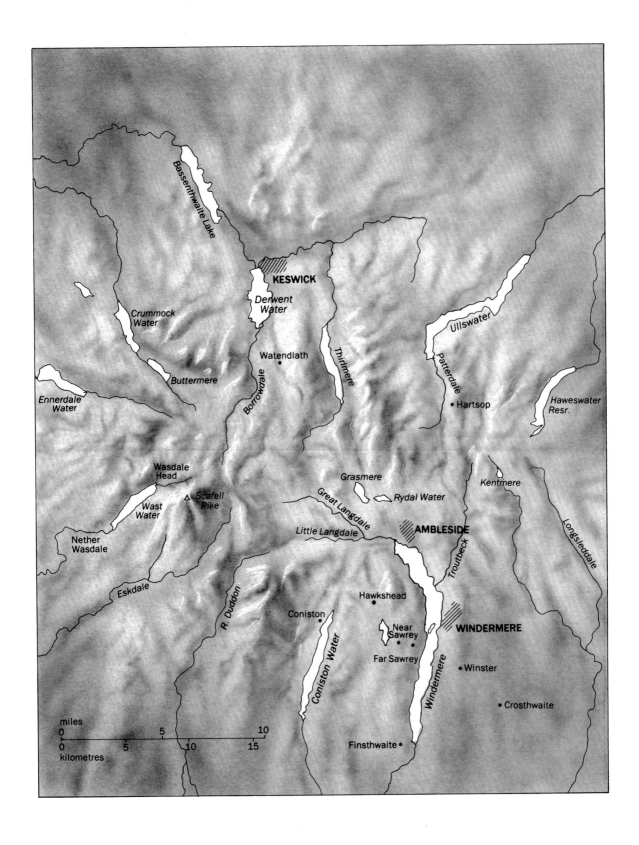

Bassenthwaite Lake

KESWICK

Derwent Water

Crummock Water

Watendlath

Thirlmere

Ullswater

Patterdale

Buttermere

Borrowdale

Hartsop

Haweswater Resr.

Ennerdale Water

Wasdale Head

Scafell Pike

Grasmere

Rydal Water

Kentmere

Wast Water

Great Langdale

Nether Wasdale

Little Langdale

AMBLESIDE

Troutbeck

Longsleddale

Eskdale

R. Duddon

Hawkshead

Coniston

Near Sawrey

WINDERMERE

Far Sawrey

Windermere

Winster

Coniston Water

Crosthwaite

miles

0   5   10

0   5   10   15

kilometres

Finsthwaite

1

A Cabinet of Beauties

In Cumberland and Westmorland there is a cabinet
of beauties – each thing being beautiful in itself,
and the very passage of one lake, mountain or
valley, to another, is itself a beautiful thing again.
S. T. Coleridge

Few places as small as the Lake District have made such a lasting impression on people and on their perception of nature. Of those who have been inspired to write about it, many like Coleridge have seen it as a place of natural beauty, almost untainted by man. But ultimately its appeal, and its importance, lies much more in the way that the valleys and fells and lakes have provided the raw materials for a continuous and mostly peaceful settlement over the last thousand years; and in the way that that settlement – individual buildings, groups of buildings, small fields bounded by stone walls – has made a harmonious mosaic in the valleys against the backdrop of the wilder fells.

The patterns of settlement that have evolved are distinct and strikingly different from almost any other part of England. Thomas Gray saw Grasmere as 'a white village with a parish church rising in the midst of it: . . . Not a single red tile, no flaring gentleman's house, or garden walls, break in upon the repose of this little unsuspected paradise; but all is peace, rusticity, and happy poverty in its neatest, most becoming attire'. Gray's was a romanticized view of rural simplicity and tranquillity, shared to some extent by William Wordsworth, who in his poem 'Michael' idealized the rural life of what he called the Statesman Farmers, investing them with an aura of frugality, independence and virtue, in a golden age before the gradual disruption of rural life by tourists, carriage roads and the effects of the industrial revolution. The reality was more mundane and more complex: but there was a kernel of truth. The Lake District had evolved a discrete cultural identity, not as static or as self-contained as the early nineteenth-century writers would have us believe, but nevertheless engendering a certain pride and independence and, in the first half of the eighteenth century at least, producing a degree of prosperity not matched by many small-scale farmers elsewhere in the country.

The landscape pattern that evolved was the product, as it was elsewhere, of the interaction between man and his environment, a

opposite
The Lake District

meld of economic, environmental and cultural factors. Inevitably in any area some themes are more dominant than others. Three themes emerge as crucial to the way the Lake District landscape developed: its frontier position, near the oft-disputed border with Scotland; its physical remoteness with valleys cut off from each other and the rest of the country by high fells; and a landholding pattern binding uplands and lowlands together, which was strikingly different from that of the lowland areas of the midlands and south of England. These three motifs cannot be separated entirely, as they influence one another, nor are they the only forces at work.

The Lake District can be considered almost as an island of mountains set down in a plain, or a series of plains. To the north are the flat lands of the Solway and the Eden valleys, to the west the hinterland of the Cumberland coast, in the south Low Furness and the valleys of the Kent and Lune, and only in parts of the east does higher ground merge into the Pennine fells. Within the encircling lowlands, the mountains are transected by numerous flat, narrow valleys, most pointing towards the centre of the area like the spokes of a wheel and each one separated from its neighbours by fells at least 1,000 feet high. The high ground is only some thirty miles across and twenty miles from north to south, and 'from a point between Great Gavel [Gable] and Scawfell, a shepherd would not require more than one hour to descend into any one of the eight principal vales by which he would be surrounded'. This compactness gave, according to Wordsworth, a rightness of scale to the scenery; it also means that the valleys are comparatively numerous and small in scale and, in England, only in parts of Devon and Cornwall is the landscape as fragmented.

The height of the mountains (in the central massif from Scafell to Helvellyn there are numerous peaks over 2,500 feet), combined with the latitude and the westerly orientation, makes the Lake District one of the coldest and wettest parts of England. The rainfall in parts is as much as 110 inches per year and only on the periphery does it fall as low as sixty inches. The warm seasons are short, spring coming at least a month later than in the Home Counties. The configuration of the valleys limited the amount of land that could be put under the plough, and the climate further limited what could be grown: barley and oats were the only cereals that would thrive. Arable cultivation was thus always a marginal and subsistence occupation, not one producing large surpluses that could be traded out of the area.

Crops were grown (and could only be grown) on the flat valley floors, the valley sides being either grazed or exploited as woodland, while the fell-tops were only suitable for grazing. Gradually during the course of the mediaeval period the fells and woodlands came to be used communally. Indeed the sharing of these resources and the organization of the valley-bottom fields came to be the forces which held the scattered valley communities together.

After the Norman conquest, Cumbria, like other parts of England,

Hartsop village and
Brotherswater, Patterdale.

was apportioned amongst great feudal landholders. But the central
Lake District was an area without baronial seats, for although each
barony was made up of pieces of lowland country as well as wedges
of the high fell country, the seats and power centres of these estates
were all in the lowlands. The Kendal barony, with its seat in Kendal,
stretched into the Lake District as far as Great Langdale and Grasmere; the barony of Westmorland, based at Appleby, controlled
Patterdale and Martindale. The way these baronies were organized
varied considerably between the lowland and upland sections. In the
lowlands the communities near the baronial seats functioned much
as they did elsewhere in lowland England, tenants being bound by
various dues and services to the nearby overlord. In the uplands of
the Lake District, however, a different system prevailed. Technically

13

above
Painting by an unknown artist.
'Westmorland cottages as a class
have long been celebrated for
their picturesque forms and very
justly so: in no part of the world
are cottages to be found more
strikingly interesting to the eye
by their general outlines, by the
sheltered porches of their
entrances, by their distribution
of the parts.' Thomas de
Quincey wrote these words in
1806 about the time that this
scene was painted.

these areas were under the direct control of the lord and were private
forest or 'free chase'; in practice, colonization was allowed on the
valley-bottom land (some of which was granted to monastic houses),
the lord keeping only a direct interest in the daleheads, many of which
in the thirteenth and fourteenth centuries were developed first of all
as vaccaries (cattle ranches) and secondly as sheep granges. By the
end of the thirteenth century the pressure of population was such
that the lords had allowed settlement over most of their valley-bottom
lands, and most valleys had been completely colonized.

  These small farms were dotted across the flat lands in the valley
bottoms. The farmers were called tenants at will, holding their lands
'at the will of the lord, according to the custom of the Manor'. The

below

**The Painter's House,
Clappersgate, by Julius Caesar
Ibbotson.**
'The heavy slated roofs are often
shagged and richly covered with
ferns, lichen, houseleek and a
plant called golden moss.'
Notice the squat chimney with
slab covering, 'a contrivance
which readily suggests itself for
counteracting the effects of
sudden gusts of wind sweeping
down the mountain slopes.' This
house still survives, although
much altered, and is now
known as Willy Hill.

newly settled plots were often called 'places', a word which survives
to this day in numerous farm names such as Middlefell Place, Great
Langdale, or 'grounds', such as Waterson Ground and Atkinson
Ground, near Hawkshead (the prefix being the name of the family
who enclosed the land from the waste).

The custom of most manors allowed tenants to devise* and also
sell land in return for fairly small payments of money and services.
A fine was payable at a change of tenancy or on the death of the lord,
together with a small rent each year for arable fields and meadows
and the right to graze on the open fell. In return, tenants had to
provide not only labour but also to accept a communal obligation to
share grazing and turbary (peat-cutting) rights on the open fells and
pannage (the right to graze swine) in the woods. The most compelling
obligation, at least for manors in the north of the area, was to serve
the lord in any border uprising. The attitude of one lesser lord to this

* That is, at death, hand over their land to their next of kin.

type of tenure was neatly recalled in 1675 when it was said that some hundred years previously

> Sir Lancelot Threlkeld . . . had three brave houses, one for pleasure: Crosbie in Westmorland wher he had perks [parks] full of dear [deer]: another Yanweth [Yanwath] for profit and warmth to live in winter ny pearth [near Penrith] and the third this Threlkeld well stored with tenants and men to go along with him to warrs.

The tenants thus had a great deal of freedom and security compared to their compatriots in the lowlands, paying small amounts of rent for 'land, pasture and panage' and in return having to give arms in time of war but none of the labour obligations of many lowland tenancies. They were copyholders of inheritance and were almost as secure as freeholders. What bound the tenants together was not the services and dues, as in the lowland barony, but rather their communal use of the 'wastes' or open fell-lands surrounding every valley.

By the late sixteenth century the influence of the lords had become limited and much of the land was in the firm grip of the customary tenants with their entrenched rights. And with the union of the crowns

below
Lane Cottage, Troutbeck,
photographed by William Bell in the 1880's.

above

The Browne 'arms'.
It appears that none of the
yeoman or statesman families
could justify armorial bearings
by showing grants from the
College of Arms. Nevertheless,
several families displayed coats
of arms on furniture or
elsewhere, and few outsiders
dared deny them the privilege.
This drawing, dated 1703,
shows the arms of the Browne
family of Townend, Troutbeck.
The Brownes' double-headed
eagle is quartered with the three
lion-paws of the Forrest family.
The Browne arms can be seen
on chairs and cupboards at
Townend, Troutbeck.

of England and Scotland in 1603, the need for defence of the borders against troops and cattle-raiders had largely gone. Through three reigns, for a century and a half from the 1580s, many groups of tenant farmers campaigned successfully to hold on to their customary tenant rights. These rights were eventually confirmed by the Crown at different dates for different estates, some after a series of prolonged legal battles, and despite the fact that the basic underpinning of the system had gradually been removed. After the status of the upland farmers had won this legal recognition, it became virtually impossible for lords to force leases on their tenants, as happened in many lowland areas elsewhere in the country.

The beginning of the eighteenth century saw the pattern of small-scale farming confirmed, and the way the landscape had been worked since mediaeval times continued to be the basis of farming life throughout the next 150 years. In contrast to the other northern border county, Northumberland, where the union of the crowns had led to a strengthening of the power of manorial lords and the reshaping of large parts of the landscape in the late eighteenth and early nineteenth centuries, change in the Lake District was gradual and piecemeal. Buildings and landscape altered slowly from one state to the next, leaving the landscape as a partially reconstructed document of the intervening years.

Over the last six or seven centuries the number of farms in the valleys has fluctuated considerably. From a mere handful in the twelfth century, the numbers increased in the thirteenth century, decreased in the following century and a half, and increased dramatically again up to around 1600 when the number of farmers working the land was probably at an all-time high. The next 150 years were a period of consolidation, some of the small farms being amalgamated, the larger and wealthier ones prospering. These were the years that have been christened the Age of the Statesman, when farmers, secure in their ways, began to rebuild their houses with a certain confidence and independence. These are the years that have made the most lasting imprint on the landscape. What we see now is largely a modification of the farming systems and buildings which then prevailed.

This farming landscape was divided into three main parts: the enclosed cultivated land in the valley bottoms, the patches of woodland on the lower slopes of the fells, and the grazed open fell-land above. Each of these three elements generated a need for building: shelter for the farmers, cows, sheep and pigs, storage for the grain from the arable fields and hay from the meadows, storage for bark and charcoal from the woodlands, and for peat and bracken from the open fells.

How these needs developed and the distinctive ways in which they were met will be looked at in detail in the subsequent chapters.

2

Domestic Interiors

As we have seen in chapter 1, the years 1600-1750 were a period of relative prosperity for Lake District yeoman farmers. Secure in their holdings and touched only lightly by the agricultural upheavals in the south of England, they consolidated their position and turned their attention to building and rebuilding their farmhouses and farm buildings. For a century and a half these middle-class yeoman farmers, as they have been called, made their distinctive and confident imprint on the Lake District landscape.

Of all the houses now owned by the National Trust in the Lake District, some three-quarters appear to date back to this period. The precise dating of this building or rebuilding is difficult; even more problematic is the question of what preceded this apparent spate of reconstruction. Much clearer is what happened after 1750 when some houses were either rebuilt or remodelled to reflect a changed perception of space and privacy, a national development which brought the planning of Lake District houses into line with what was happening elsewhere.

The next chapter will look in detail at the variations in building traditions between valleys, at the evidence for pre-seventeenth-century buildings, and at the way buildings were modified in the late eighteenth and nineteenth centuries. This chapter will highlight the typical features of a pre-1750 Lake District farmhouse, both the building itself and the furnishings and fittings that turned it into a working home.

The main elements of the farmhouse were a firehouse, buttery and parlour on the ground floor, to which was sometimes added a downhouse and, on the first floor, lofts for storage and for sleeping, and occasionally sleeping chambers.

FIREHOUSE

'The most publique room of the house called the firehouse' was how William Jackson described the main downstairs room of his farmhouse, High Wallowbarrow Farm in the Duddon valley, when he wrote his will in 1692. The firehouse or houseplace, or sometimes simply 'the house', was the setting for the main daytime domestic activities and also acted as a central circulation space. Typically, the main door opened into it so that the family had to pass through it to get to the sleeping quarters, the buttery and the parlour; often it was the only heated room in the house.

Chimney Recesses

The word firehouse admirably evokes the atmosphere of this main room; a wide, deep, open chimney recess stretched across one gable-end wall. Although the room sizes varied, from a mere ten feet by twelve feet in some Langdale houses, such as Low Hallgarth, to as much as thirty feet by twenty feet at Ashness Farm in Borrowdale, the depth of the chimney recess remained remarkably consistent, most being between four and six feet deep. In the smaller houses, therefore, the chimney took up almost as much as a third of the length of the room. Whatever the size of the room, the fireplace dominated household life, providing warmth, a place to cook, and a place to sit in the long winter evenings.

Spanning the firehouse, immediately in front of the fire, was a large firebeam whose function was to carry the funnel-shaped chimney-hood which drew smoke into a stone chimney projecting above the ridge of the roof. Two-thirds of the way along this firebeam, a vertical partition normally divided the space behind the beam to form a narrow passage. The partition was usually called a 'heck', the passage a 'mell'. The passage led to the main outside door and also into a downhouse or back kitchen if the house had one. As will be discussed later in this chapter, these arrangements varied considerably from house to house and area to area. For instance, some small houses had the staircases tucked between the heck and the outside wall and had the main entrance door in the long window wall of the house.

Hecks were either masonry structures, built of freestone and plastered on both sides, or they were of oak muntin-and-plank panelling. Many stone hecks survive; fewer panelled ones. Notable examples of stone hecks are at Park End Farm, Sizergh, Glencoyne Farm,

Fireplace at Glencoyne Farm, Ullswater, c.1900.
By 1900, open-hearth fires were rare survivals and this one was probably photographed as a curiosity. Smoke from the fire would have been drawn up into a wide chimney-hood resting on the fire-beam just visible at the top of the picture. The hearth was lit by a small window to the right. The little cupboards, recessed into the back wall of the chimney, are called spice cupboards. A fire-crane fixed to one side of the hearth supported a variety of 'reckons' or strap-hangers for hanging kettles and pots over the fire.

Ullswater, and Caffle House, Watendlath, while panelled hecks can be found at Green End Cottage, Colthouse, and High Arnside Farm, Coniston.

Within the chimney recess on the opposite side to the heck, a small fire-window lit the hearth, while on the back wall a rectangular recess with a panelled oak door provided a dry keeping-place for salt and spices. The doors of these 'spice cupboards', as they were commonly known, were often embellished with initials and decorative motifs. Such fire recesses or chimney-corners were usually deep enough to accommodate a seat of some sort – either a high-backed box-settle set against the heck, or sometimes, as at Low Park-a-Moor Farm, Coniston, more simply a fixed wooden bench. An inventory of 1731 for Townend, Troutbeck, mentions 'a high back settle or screen', and another for Seatoller Farm, Borrowdale, in 1748 also mentions 'two skreens'. It seems that these settles sometimes acted like screens on cold winter evenings when they were moved across the front of the fire from the corner of the heck, thus shutting off the fire from the rest of the room and creating a 'little parlour', 'a place of peculiar warmth and comfort'. Occasionally it seems that the chimney-corner was even further enclosed, with a curtain drawn along the firebeam making a room within a room. As late as the 1930s the farmer and his wife at Low House Farm, Troutbeck, sat by the fire in the evenings shielded from draughts by such a curtain.

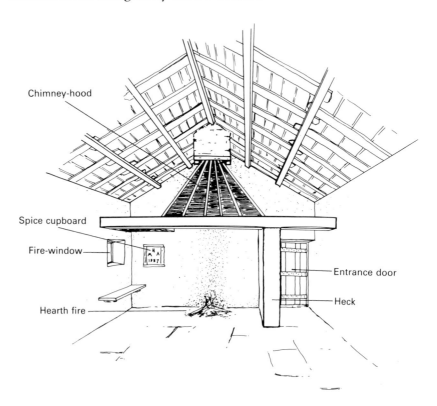

Chimney-hood

Spice cupboard

Fire-window

Entrance door

Heck

Hearth fire

right
Sketch showing the arrangement of a chimney-hood, hearth and heck.

above

Spice-cupboard door, High Arnside Farm, Coniston.
These small doors, covering recesses into the back wall of the main fire, were commonly ornamented with dates and initials as well as decorative motifs. On this cupboard the initials are of Henry and Elizabeth Robinson, who married in 1685, so this carving quite possibly commemorated the rebuilding of their house in 1697.

Chimney-Hoods

Above the firebeam the massive chimney-hood was carried on two transverse beams, from six to eight feet apart, morticed into the bressumer beam. Surviving hoods are built either of stone or of lath and plaster on a timber framework. The Revd Mr Hodgson, writing in 1822, described wickerwork hoods smeared with clay or cow-dung. Only one is known to survive, at Cropple How Farm, Muncaster, where what is now an outbuilding contains a complete hood of woven wattles plastered with a daub of clay, straw and dung. Even timber-and-plaster hoods are now extremely rare; the best surviving one is at High Birk Howe Farm, Little Langdale. It tapers steeply from some twelve feet across at the base to three feet at the top where it fits into an oval stone stack, supported on a cross-beam resting on two timber corbels. The laths in the hood are attached to the underside of the timber framework and the whole is plastered smooth on the inside. Evidence of plaster hoods has been found in a large number of houses, indicating that they were once quite widespread. In all these cases the timber hoods appear to have fitted into stone chimneys corbelled out from a stone gable wall.

Many more stone hoods than timber ones survive, no doubt partly because of the obvious difficulty of removing them. Where surviving hoods can be examined in detail (some are now boxed in), they are found to use a corbelling technique, each course receding from the one below. In all cases the stone used is rubble with mortared joints, parged on the inside with a mixture of lime, sand and cow-dung. At Park End Farm, Sizergh, the stone courses form pronounced steps on the outside face, while at Fell Foot Farm, Little Langdale, and Holeslack Farm, Helsington, the hoods taper gradually.

It is by no means clear whether stone hoods generally superseded timber-and-lath hoods, and too few of either survive to justify any attempt at analysis. However, there is documentary evidence for a progression from timber to stone in at least one case, albeit in a somewhat grander farmhouse than most of those under consideration. At Rydal Hall on 5 July 1673, Sir Daniel Fleming paid three wallers for 'getting of stones and walling ye Brewhouse stone (formerly wood) chimney'. As the building in question seems to have been built in the sixteenth century against an earlier largish barn and was clearly not in any way a 'humble' building, the example suggests that timber-and-lath construction for chimneys was not always a poor man's option.

Peat

In the fires which these chimney-hoods were serving, the traditional fuel was peat. This was burnt on a low, flat, stone-flag hearth raised only slightly above floor-level, the ash gradually forming at the base of the fire into a biscuit-like block which absorbed heat and then gave it out into the room. Peat fires had the capacity to lie almost dormant for hours, giving out only a little heat and little or no light or flame. They could then be poked or blown on 'by means of a long tube' and made to glow with extra fuel. John Briggs, writing of his visit to an inn in Kentmere in 1821 or 1822, tells how the maid revived the fire on the arrival of the visitors:

> She first collected all the red fragments of the former fire and placed them in a neat heap. Then she surrounded this heap of fire with a circle of half peats, set on end; and again with two rows of whole peats set on end. The hollow in the middle was then filled with small fragments of peats, so as to rise highest in the middle. In about five minutes the fire began to burn brightly . . .

Peat fires were usually left dormant overnight. This was achieved by raking out the fire last thing and covering the glowing embers with ash or flat peat. Next morning the fire was revived by putting dry sticks on the still-glowing embers. Such an arrangement meant that the fire rarely or never went out completely so long as the house was lived in or cooking was needed. Indeed in 1864 Dr Gibson wrote about two remote farms, High Park-a-Moor and Lawson Park, high up on the fells above the east shore of Coniston Water, where the fires were reported to have been maintained for centuries. One was probably the same as the farm 'near Coniston' written about by the vicar of Torver in 1893 and where it was said the fire had been

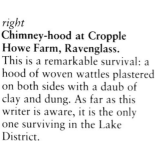

right
Chimney-hood at Cropple Howe Farm, Ravenglass.
This is a remarkable survival: a hood of woven wattles plastered on both sides with a daub of clay and dung. As far as this writer is aware, it is the only one surviving in the Lake District.

far right
Timber and plaster chimney-hood, High Birk Howe Farm, Little Langdale.
This surviving hood is constructed with laths nailed on to roughly-shaped timber uprights. The inside is plastered smooth.

maintained for three generations. In a nearby farm a man claimed he had 'his grandfather's fire', and when this was accidentally left to go out, glowing embers from the fire of a neighbouring woodcutter, originally lit from his, were brought to revive it. Other farms had a 'keeping spot' – a small recess at the base of the back wall of the fire, where hot embers from the evening's fire could be put, covered, and left to stay warm enough to provide the 'leaven' for the next day's fire. The abandoned farmhouse at Dale Head in Martindale has one of these recesses still visible.

Cooking

Cooking was done by suspending iron pots and pans over the fire from a chain fixed to a 'rannel-baulk', a beam which rolled back and forth on two further beams which crossed the chimney from front to back at the level of the first floor. Pans could be moved up and down by raising or lowering crooks or S-shaped hooks from link to link on the chain. Like open chimney-hoods, rannel-baulks are not rare survivals. Both are still in place in the abandoned farmhouse at How Green in Hartsop; and an open hearth (although now raised on a small grate) beneath an open stone chimney-hood still provides warmth for visitors to Caffle House at Watendlath.

A more adaptable arrangement for suspending cooking-pans was the provision of a rotating pot-crane – an L-shaped bracket, fixed to one side of the fire, from which were hung ratten-crooks or adjustable hangers for pots and pans. Most of these were made of iron, and examples of blacksmith-made fire-cranes are still in place at Fold Head Farm, Watendlath, and Townend, Troutbeck. At Park End Farm, Brigsteer, is the only example so far recorded of a wooden crane. Made of oak, it is pivoted between the floor and a beam spanning the edge of the chimney-hood, and has been fitted with a handled lever for raising and lowering a chain from which the cooking-pots were hung.

Oatcakes

The staple food cooked over these open hearths was oatcake. Despite being much maligned (by Dr Johnson and others since), oatcake freshly made is both delicious and nutritious. Known locally as 'clapbread', it was usually made from oats grown, threshed and milled locally and stored in oak meal-chests in house lofts. The fine oatmeal was mixed with water and sometimes a little lard or mutton fat, formed into thin flat cakes, and cooked on a girdle (a flat iron pan) which either hung from a ratten-crook or sat upon a trivet over the fire. A detailed account survives of how this unleavened oat bread was made in the seventeenth century, written by that indomitable traveller Celia Fiennes. Fortunately she found more interest in writing about the domestic routine of making clapbread than in putting down her reactions to the scenery when she travelled through the Lake District in 1695.

> They mix their flour with water so soft as to rowle it in their hands into a ball, and then they have a board made round and something hollow in the middle riseing by degrees all round to the edge a little higher, but so little as one would take it to be only a board warp'd, this is to cast out the cake thinn and so they clap it round and drive it to the edge in a due proportion till drove as thinn as a paper, and still they clap it and drive it round, and then they have a plaite of iron same size with their clap board and so shove off the cake on it and so set it on coales and bake it; when enough on one side they slide it off and put the other side; if their iron plaite is smooth they take care their coales or embers are not too hot but just to make it looke yellow, it will bake and be as crisp and pleasant to eate as any thing you can imagine . . .

After baking on the girdle the oatcakes were slid off on to a lightly inscribed board. Several of these survive. They are made of a thin piece of fruitwood or sycamore, square in shape, between twelve and fifteen inches long and with a short handle. They are sometimes, but not always, incised with a diaper pattern, presumably to stop the oatcake sticking. These boards may be the 'backboards' which occasionally occur in inventories. For example the possessions of Edward Taylor of Plum Green, Finsthwaite, listed in 1599, included 'girdle, brandreth, cresset, backboard'.

Andrew Pringle, writing a century after Celia Fiennes' visit, help-

Cooking oatcake on a girdle, Townend, Troutbeck.
The Young National Trust Theatre visited Townend in 1985 and, as part of their routine, schoolchildren were invited to act the role of Mrs Browne for a day and to make oatcakes and cook them over the open fire.

fully quantifies the process of oatcake-baking. He reported that the cakes (the term he actually uses) were usually twenty inches in diameter, that fifteen cakes could be made from sixteen pounds of meal, and that enough oatcakes could be made in one day to feed a family of four for a month. A somewhat more exaggerated claim for the speed of baking as well as for the keeping properties of clapbread was made by J. H. Martindale in 1895 when he wrote that enough bread was baked in a day to last a year!

The oatcakes seem generally to have been stored in oak cupboards built into one wall of the firehouse. Laying-up in such cupboards 'within the influence of the fire, has the quality of preserving its sweetness for several months'. Quite how the clapbread was dried for storing is unclear. In the Yorkshire Dales, where the making of oatcakes persisted much longer than in the Lake District, the process is remembered. After baking, the cakes were hung over oat 'flakes', narrow rails suspended from the floor joists in front of the fire. But the mixture used was more liquid than for clapbread and also contained a little leaven; moreover it was usually thrown or poured on to the girdle rather than being rolled and placed, and so emerged after cooking rather more like a pancake than a biscuit. Oat-flakes are unknown in the central Lake District. The weight of the oatcakes described by Pringle, and the fact that he stresses there was no leaven, clearly suggest something more substantial than the Yorkshire oatcakes (or indeed the Derbyshire or Staffordshire oatcakes which are slightly leavened mixtures of oat and wheat flour and are still made today). Clapbread seems to have been something more akin to Scottish oat 'biscuits' or Norwegian *haverbrod* or *flatbrod*, and possibly needed no more drying than occurred during cooling near the fire on a backboard. It has been suggested that rolled (rather than thrown) oatcakes (as remembered in those parts of north-west England nearest to Cumberland and Westmorland) may have been the precursors of the lightly leavened pancake type, and that clapbread was thus formerly much more widespread in the north of England.

Celia Fiennes described how clapbread was cooked on a 'plaite of iron'. This was often called a girdle or griddle and was a circular flat plate, between two and four feet in diameter, which either had a hoop handle with a hook to suspend it over the fire from the ratten-crook, or was simply placed upon a brandreth, an iron trivet sitting on the hearth. Such implements appear very frequently in inventories. Benjamin Satterthwaite of Colthouse, who died in 1711, possessed 'girdle, brandreth and all iron gear'. In late eighteenth- and early nineteenth-century farmhouses iron plates were sometimes built in above a masonry firebox, thus providing a large, evenly heated plate for cooking oatcakes. They were usually set up to one side of the main flue and linked into it, or occasionally – in a newly built downhouse or back kitchen – connected to a separate flue, as at Townend, Troutbeck. The fuel which provided short, sharp fires for these plates was kindling-sticks or dried bracken. A stove with plates of this kind was put into the newly built Croft Foot at Colthouse as late as 1852.

These built-in stoves were sometimes called backstones, a name suggesting that originally a sheet of stone was used rather than a metal plate for cooking the clapbread. Yorkshire inventories and diaries of the seventeenth and eighteenth centuries record the use of such stones, a type of mudstone quarried especially for the purpose. In the Lake District too, the names Bakestone Barrow Wood at Holme Fell, above Tilberthwaite, and Bakestone Moss and Low and High Bakestones, all on Scardale Fell near Kirkstone Pass, may well indicate areas where stone was formerly gained for making backstones.

Wheat Bread

When Celia Fiennes made her visit, she wrote that oatcakes were the only bread produced in the area. Certainly the cold, wet uplands of the central Lakes are too inhospitable a place for growing wheat, and are much better suited to oats; but around the periphery near Keswick, Ravenglass and Kendal, wheat can be grown and indeed was grown in increasing quantities after the 1750s. On the other hand, prices quoted for oats and wheat in Cumberland markets show clearly that until the mid-nineteenth century wheat was not affordable by all, its selling price averaging three times that of oats. Rather it seems to have been purchased for special occasions: at Christmas for cakes and puddings – in December 1791 George Browne of Townend noted in his account book the purchase of white flour for Christmas puddings and cakes – and at funerals for wheat bread (called arvel bread) traditionally handed out to bidden guests.

Wheat flour was almost always used for making leavened bread, which needs to be cooked in a sealed container rather than on an open griddle. Over a hearth fire, the wheat bread was cooked in a covered pan which had a base looking rather like a deep-sided frying-pan, and a tall domed lid with a wide rim. The pan was heated up either by hanging it over the fire or by standing it on a brandreth. The dough was then put in and covered, and hot embers from the fire beneath were piled up on the edges of the lid. The resulting bread was called 'pan-bread'.

Ovens

During the course of the eighteenth century, as wheat bread came to be more regularly baked, some farms and cottages had their large, wide hearth fires adapted for cooking wheat bread more easily by the insertion of beehive-shaped ovens into the back wall of the fire. Usually near the top of the wall on the side of the fire away from the windows, these ovens either fitted into the thickness of the wall, as at Harrowhead Farm, Wasdale, or were built to project behind it – as at

Pan-bread cooking at Rook Howe Meeting House, Rusland, 1901.
Even at this date wheat bread was rarely cooked in a pan. This photograph was taken when some bread was made to show 'the mysterys of baking in a pan . . . to those who have never witnessed the process'.

Cragg Farm, Buttermere, Chapman House, Finsthwaite, and Beckside Cottage, Colthouse. Either way, their small wooden doors were flush with the wall surface. They were lined within by clay bricks or red sandstone; they had no flue. Ovens such as these, varying in size and in degree of elaboration around the door openings, appear all over the country and were not specific to this area. Surviving Lake District examples are usually plain and small in size. The way they were used was described admirably in 1800:

> Lay a quantity of shavings or light dry fuel in the centre of the oven and some small branches of faggot wood upon them; over these place as many of the larger branches as will make a tolerably large fire, and set light to it. From one to two hours will be required to heat the brick oven thoroughly. When the fire is burnt out and the red pulsing ceases, scrape out the charcoal, letting it drop down through the slot at the oven door. Then take a large clean mop, dip it in hot water, and mop over every part of the inside of the oven, clearing out the last of the dust, and leaving a little steam within the oven. Leave the oven closed for some little time, to even the heat, before you open it and fill it. Once the bread is packed in, do not open the oven door till two hours have elapsed.

Benjamin Browne of Townend, Troutbeck, recorded in his account book the building of just such an oven at Townend in 1727: 'Allowed for a new oven 40 new bricks 2/- Carriage for Kendal 1/3 Lime 1/3 Wallers 5 day 2/6 Their meat 1/8 60 III bricks of James Longmire 6d [Total] 9/2 And I gave more-10d In all 10/-'.

Interestingly, fourteen years earlier he had put down that he had sold an iron oven to George Birkett of Fold for fourteen shillings. It is not clear what this apparatus was, but its size – recorded meticulously by Benjamin Browne in his account book: '20″ long, 14″ broad & 6½″ deep' – suggests either a sort of box which hung over the open fire or stood on legs within it (perhaps similar to the pot ovens recorded in Wales and Ireland, which were heated below by the hearth fire and above from coals heaped on to the lid), or what is now called a Dutch oven, an upright box open towards the fire and within which meat was hung for roasting. However heated, it had clearly baked satisfactorily, for Benjamin Browne's grandmother recorded in her commonplace book recipes for such delights as spinach tart. A similar iron oven is recorded in the inventory of Fletcher Fleming of Fellfoot Farm, Little Langdale, in 1716.

The disposition of recorded ovens in the central Lake District is patchy. They appear quite frequently in the eastern valleys (Ullswater, Martindale, Longsleddale, Kentmere) and in the western valleys (Buttermere and Wasdale); less frequently in Borrowdale and Windermere; and rarely in Langdale, Coniston, Hawkshead, and Troutbeck. It is tempting to see this distribution determined by proximity to wheat-growing areas; but the pattern could equally well reflect the degree of modernization, with ovens removed or masked by later iron ranges or fireplaces. Townend is just such an example, as Benjamin Browne's beehive oven is no longer visible.

There may also have been an element of personal choice – perhaps pan-bread was preferred to oven bread, or wheat flour eschewed altogether in certain households. But what should be made clear is the relatively short time which elapsed between the ready availability of wheat in the upland areas and the ready availability of coal, which was to have a profound effect on hearths and cooking techniques. Just as in the lowlands, where canal transport had the briefest of heydays before steam power and railways stole its thunder, so in the upland areas of the Lake District, many housewives had only recently taken to wheat bread and beehive ovens when the black iron range loomed on the horizon.

Coal

Open hearths persisted only as long as peat and wood were the common fuels. Once coal became widely available and cheap enough for the ordinary householder to afford (in the Lake District largely as a result of the development of the west coast ports of Whitehaven and Maryport), fires were adapted to burn it. Coal needs a greater quantity of air to keep up the combustion and narrower flues to produce strong draughts to direct the burnt gases up the chimney. Both these can be provided by metal grates raised up off the hearth and set below and within shaped flues. Such fires were fitted to new houses from the 1750s onwards but were hardly in general use for another fifty to seventy years. An item in the parish accounts for Hawkshead on 30 July 1793 is for the fitting of a 'fashionable

right
A farmhouse fireplace drawn by T. L. Aspland (1807–90).
Here the large open fireplace has had a smaller chimney inserted and a raised grate fitted to burn coal.

No 508. A LAKELAND FARM-KITCHEN (ABRAHAMS' SERIES)

Firehouse at Brotherilkeld Farm, Eskdale, c.1900.
As well as a raised grate, an oven and a hot-water boiler have also been fitted within the chimney set in the old open fireplace. Notice the heck partition, the firebeam and the large spice cupboard.

grate with freestone hob-slabs' for the church vestry, the adjective 'fashionable' suggesting that grates had a certain novelty in the area.

Large open-hearth fires with wide hoods were adapted for coal burning by the addition of two freestone hobs with a grate suspended between them. These hobs were constructed in three main ways: on to the back wall of the hearth, with a channel for the smoke to travel up into a reduced opening in the chimney-hood (as at Park End, Brigsteer); or within stone surrounds beneath the firebeam, with the smoke channelled back into the existing hood (as at Townend, Troutbeck); or (and much more commonly) within a stone chimney-breast formed within the depth of the hood, and either fed into the hood or carried up through the first floor and roof-space to replace the hood (as at Ashness Farm, Borrowdale).

Such fire surrounds provided opportunity for display. In earlier examples of infilling, lintels consisting of stone slabs were set above walling jambs. In later examples, all three surrounds – lintels and jambs – were of sawn stone. From the 1820s, examples of surrounds with canted lintels appear in the more prosperous houses, sometimes embellished with fan-shaped keystone motifs and surmounted by projecting shelves, as at Orrest Head Farm, Windermere, and Green End House, Colthouse.

So throughout the nineteenth century hearth fires gradually gave way to grates and ranges. In 1855 Harriet Martineau bemoaned the by then commonplace disappearance of 'chimney corners', although she was practical enough to realize that 'it is rather a drawback to the romance hanging about those wide old chimneys, to know that the good man had to sit with some special covering over his head

and shoulders to protect him from the soot the rain brought down!' – hallan drop as it was locally known. Just less than fifty years later, a correspondent of the *North Lonsdale Magazine* was reporting, in an article entitled 'Survivals in Hawkshead', that only one hearth fire survived in Hawkshead proper, at Brown Cow Cottage. 'Here the kitchen fire is daily made on the hearth and the pots and kettles hang on a crook above it.' Although a second was apparently still in existence at Gallowbarrow and a third at Crag Farm Cottage, these were clearly unusual survivals and worthy of note. Open fires probably persisted longest in the remoter farmhouses, simply because of the problems of transporting coal along the tracks to reach them. In 1861 a visitor to Cockley Beck Farm, near the head of the River Duddon in a remote valley between Wrynose and Hardknott passes, remarked on the hearth fire to the farmer and was told that 'brushwood and turf [peat] was all they had to burn. Coals were too far off, and would cost too much for carriage.' Or, as the farmer himself put it, 'we're verra nee oot o' t'warld'.

At first the change from peat and wood to coal meant little more than a change towards greater convenience and efficiency, from a fuel that had to be harvested, dried and transported, and which burnt slowly with low heat and little flame, to one that was bought ready for burning and burnt brightly and with greater heat. Initially the change had little impact on the cooking routine. Oatcakes were still cooked on an open griddle, the occasional trout roasted on a lark-spit, and meat boiled in a large cauldron. What revolutionized cooking and significantly changed the appearance of the firehouse was the development of the cast-iron cooking range, with ovens heated by

opposite above
**Part of the firehouse at Hill
Top, Near Sawrey, c.1900.**
This old photograph shows
several spherical objects hanging
from a shelf-support below the
ceiling beam; they may be wang
cheeses.

opposite below
**View inside chimney-hood,
Cropple How Farm,
Ravenglass.**

hot air circulating around them, and hot-water boilers built in next to the fire.

Good examples of ranges still survive at Yew Tree Cottage, Stonethwaite, Brighouse Farm near Ulpha, Townend, Troutbeck, and Low Loanthwaite, Hawkshead.

The new ranges gained rapidly in favour and considerably expanded cooking possibilities. Ovens, which were formerly the prerogative of the few, became commonplace and oven-baked bread gained in favour over pan-bread. At the same time there was a marked decline in the consumption of oats and the making of clapbread; wheat prices had fallen dramatically in the slump of the 1820s, making wheat flour accessible to all but the poorest farmer, and they stayed comparatively low throughout the nineteenth century. Fewer and fewer oats were grown in the central Lakes for local consumption, and the corn mills gradually fell into disuse and disrepair. By 1900 clapbread had almost ceased to be made at home (although it was produced in one Kendal bakery until as late as the 1950s), and even pan-bread was remembered with affection and nostalgia by a few elderly people as the bread of their childhood and youth, and was seen as something to be fancied when 'out of sorts' and made only for invalids or on special occasions.

Food

Just what were the general eating habits of the yeoman farming families living in these houses? The evidence is patchy and scarce, and sometimes contradictory. An anonymous writer stated in 1766 that in Cumbria there were some 10,000 petty landowners who 'very seldom taste meat or wheatbread'. What he said was probably true; what he implies is less plausible (bearing in mind that wheat bread was still relatively scarce at that date), that the farmers generally had an unsatisfactory diet. Oatcakes, cheese, butter, milk and ale, with occasional meat – salted pork, mutton fresh or smoked, poultry or fish – seem to have been the staple diet. But as will be explained, this was not necessarily an inadequate or insufficient regime, and was a great deal better than country people had in the south of England.

Two inventories of Troutbeck families, made on the deaths of the heads of the households, tell something of what food was stored in the winter months. James Longmire, who died in 1665, had his larder stocked with 'beefe, bacon, butter and chiese', while Benjamin Browne had 'butter, cheese and flesh to the value of £5' stored in his larder at the time of his death in December 1747. A similar picture emerges from the will of Robert Fletcher of Low Burnthwaite, Wasdale Head, who died in 1699 and left the following food to his son: 'oatmeal, dried flesh, a great cheese, half of all the suet, two geese, a salt suet loaf' (what the last item refers to is not clear). Baily and Culley reported in 1797 that 'a labourer lives as well now as the farmer did

40 or 50 years ago', and gave typical meals: breakfast was 'very ancient food pottage, with the help of cheese and bread'; dinner was 'butcher-meat and potatoes and pudding', while supper consisted of 'potatoes and pottage or bread and cheese'. If they were correct, the menus they gave were presumably typical of what a farmer had been eating regularly before about 1750. The bread referred to was said to be either of oats or of a mixture of oats and barley, and was presumably oatcake. The 'ancient pottage' was sometimes also called 'hasty pudding' and was either oats or barley cooked in water – what would now be called porridge. Meals were washed down with milk or ale.

As has been mentioned earlier, wheat flour and wheat bread were not consumed generally until the mid-nineteenth century. Throughout the eighteenth century wheat bread tended to be reserved for special occasions, such as funerals, where bidden guests were given small loaves called arvel bread to '"take and eat" at home, in religious remembrance of their deceased neighbours'. Wheat flour was used on Good Fridays for 'fig-sue', a 'mess made of ale, boiled with fine wheaten bread and figs, sweetened with sugar' – in other words figgy pudding, also eaten at Christmas.

Meat

'Butcher meat' – whether beef, pork or mutton – was generally boiled or roasted, but the prime cuts were often set aside for smoking within the capacious chimney-hoods. A well-filled chimney was considered a valuable asset; at the end of the eighteenth century smoked and cured meat could command a price double that of fresh meat. Although by that time smoking was not necessary as a means of preserving food for winter use, smoked meat was clearly valued and appreciated for its flavour. Hams, sides of beef and legs of mutton were all cured by smoking. The pieces of meat were first dry-salted on the larder slabs and then hung up in muslin bags to be smoked. Occasionally they were air-dried rather than smoked, as at Townend, Troutbeck, where a drying-chamber was formed in the downhouse within the space between an inserted stone chimney-breast and a stud wall rising above the old firebeam. Smoked meat ceased to be produced in farmhouses after the massive hooded chimney recesses were filled in; probably by 1900 all but a few farms had ceased smoking. High Birk Howe, Little Langdale, may have been one of the last; Mrs Hodgson, who was living there in 1934, remembered bacon being hung in bags to smoke when she was a child at around the turn of the century. Now smoked mutton, known as Macon, is once again being produced locally, although the smoking is not done in a farmhouse chimney. Nevertheless the combination of wood-smoke and local Herdwick mutton produces a delicious result, and would certainly have justified the high price-tag of 200 years ago.

Cheese

'Skimmed milk cheese is the principal kind made here and chiefly consumed at home,' wrote Bailey and Culley in 1797. Perhaps surprisingly, considering that cheese seems to have been a staple of the farmer's diet, very little evidence for cheesemaking survives in farmhouses. Unlike in the Yorkshire Dales (where large stone cheese-presses were commonly found in porches and dairies, and still survive in considerable numbers), presses are now extremely rare in the Lake District. Where they are found, or where remains are found, is mostly in houses on the periphery of the upland areas such as Low Fold Farm at Crook, Low Longmire Farm, Bouth, and Ashes Farm at Staveley. True cheese-shelves (i.e. shelves hanging from the ceiling and away from walls to keep cheeses free from vermin) are rare too, although many larders have bracket shelves. Even so, a few pieces of evidence suggest that presses at least were once more widespread. A curious watercolour drawing by Robert Hills (1769–1844) shows an outdoor cheese-press, apparently in Great Langdale, consisting of a large weight suspended from a tree and pulling down a wooden lever over a cheese-mould. This was obviously not unique: Wordsworth, writing of the typical accoutrements of a Lake District home, described 'a cheese press, often supported by some tree next the door'. In 1916 two trees in Hall Bank, Rydal, were still remembered to have presses attached. That none of these has survived is probably not remarkable, considering their makeshift construction; whether they were in general use is open to question.

Descriptions of the types of cheese made give some clues as to the process of manufacture and suggest that presses may not have been essential equipment for all kinds of cheese. An article of 1821 on North Country cheeses described two varieties on sale in Lancaster market: Lancaster cheese and Country cheese. Lancaster cheese was clearly what would now be called Lancashire cheese, a full milk

Drawing of a cheese-press by Robert Hills (1769–1844). This may have been in Great Langdale, as it was drawn on the same sheet of paper as a sketch of Pavy Ark, one of the Langdale Pikes. None of these cheese-presses is known to survive, but their existence is confirmed by several written descriptions.

above
Interior of a single-storey detached downhouse, Brotherilkeld Farm, Eskdale. To the left of the fireplace is a heated copper or wash-boiler. On the right of the fireplace can be seen a small door for a beehive-shaped bread oven, which projected beyond the gable-wall of the small building.

cheese, moulded and pressed and with a light, crumbly texture. The Country cheese, on the other hand, apparently came from the upland areas of the central Lakes and was made from skimmed milk; it was hard and leathery, and was often called 'wang' cheese, from the word for a leather thong or shoelace. Wang cheese was variously described as 'hard as iron', 'harder than buck-thorn', and 'flint cheese', and stories were told of the cheeses 'striking fire' when cut with an axe or when one rolled accidentally from a cart. By that date Lancashire cheeses were being made at some farms in the Lake District, for sale as well as for home consumption: Borwick Ground Farm, Hawkshead, was selling 10–12lb. cheeses in 1818 (and the cheese-press weight still exists at the farm); many other farms, however, were still producing small wang cheeses.

These skimmed-milk wang cheeses could have been made without presses or keeping-shelves in rather the same way as Italian *provolone* cheese is made to this day, and one slender piece of evidence seems to support this theory. *Provolone* is kneaded rather than pressed. The separated curd is kneaded in hot water or whey, shaped into spheres, cylinders or pear shapes within muslin bags, soaked in brine, and finally air-dried by hanging from hooks or staves. Skimmed-milk cheese made by this method hardens quickly without the need for a press. Wang cheeses could have been made in precisely the same way. Wang cheeses were also made in Wharfedale, Yorkshire; and there is evidence to suggest that what were called brine cheeses were once made in that dale too, a fact which may support the general idea that wang cheeses were kneaded and salted rather than being pressed. Only one piece of visual evidence has so far come to light for the Lake District and that is a photograph of the kitchen of Beatrix Potter's home, Hill Top, Near Sawrey, taken in the early 1900s. It shows pear-shaped cheeses hanging from supports beneath one of the main ceiling beams: could these be wang cheeses? (*see* p.30)

Beer

After meat, bread and cheese, the fourth and final main element of a farming family's diet was beer or ale.

Ale was drunk almost universally and was often prepared at home with locally grown barley (bigg), the second most important crop on the farm and produced mainly for brewing. The barley was first harvested then malted, a process which involved steeping the grain, letting it sprout, spreading it, turning it several times a day for fourteen days or more, and then drying it in a kiln with a gentle fire of straw. After this the grain was threshed, winnowed, ground, and finally fermented with yeast to produce ale or beer. Beer is simply ale with the addition of hops, and it seems that both were brewed in some households: on 11 April 1755 George Browne of Staveley wrote, 'Tim'd my ale & table beer, Bottled my old ale.' Similarly,

Hugh James writing from Levens Hall in the seventeenth century mentions brewing strong ale, small ale and small beer. It is difficult to say when hops became used as a matter of course in Lake District brewing. They were produced commercially in Kent from the eighteenth century onwards and may have been available in markets in the north from that source. But wild hops now grow profusely in several old gardens, suggesting that small quantities were once grown locally for brewing.

Malting is a time-consuming and skilled process. Was it done by the yeoman farmer or his wife or was malt bought in? Evidence is very sparse and provides no conclusive answer. Special malt-houses, such as are found in Devon and other parts of the country (three- or four-storey buildings used for steeping and sprouting the grain), do not exist in this area. Furthermore, in his account book between 1775 and 1791, George Browne of Townend records buying malt in various quantities (sometimes in bushels, between a half and nine, and sometimes in measures – up to forty) on six separate occasions, and it is known that the Browne family owned a malt-kiln in Troutbeck village, now converted into Kiln Cottage. There is no indication of who had the right to use this kiln, but presumably it was a commercial enterprise. No other malt-kilns have yet appeared, although kilns are known which may have been primarily for corn but could have been used for drying malt, such as the one that still exists at Hartsop village.

However gained, the malted and crushed barley was almost certainly converted to beer and ale in the farmhouses. The interesting question is which part of the farmhouse was used for brewing. It is suggested tentatively that firehouses were used mainly for cooking, and that in houses that had a second fire-room this was used mainly for brewing.

'Downhouse' was the name given to this second fire-room, which was usually positioned at one end of the house adjacent to the firehouse, with the fire either back-to-back with the firehouse fire or,

right
Detached downhouse, Brotherilkeld Farm, Eskdale.
This small building is sited parallel to the farmhouse with its door almost opposite the main door to the house. The interior is shown on page 34. Notice the bread oven projecting from the gable wall.

above
Drawing of the firehouse at Low Fold Farm, Grasmere, by A. MacDonald, 1913.
This view is taken from next to the fireplace. Notice the oak-panelled partition at the far end of the room with two doors leading through it. The left-hand door led to the staircase and larder, the right-hand door to the parlour.

above right
Interior of the firehouse at Turn How Farm, Grasmere, c.1932.
Here the two doors lead on the left to the parlour and on the right to the buttery. The staircase is in a projection at the back of the house.

more often, in the gable end of the building. Occasionally, as in some houses around Hawkshead, the downhouse was in a one-storey wing at the back of the house, and even more rarely in a small detached building parallel to the long wall of the house. Detached downhouses have been surveyed at Crag House Farm, Irton, Brotherilkeld Farm, Eskdale, and Brunt How Farm, Netherwasdale. The Revd Mr Hodgson, writing in the early 1800s, said of the downhouse: 'here the baking, brewing, washing and such like, of the wealthier classes of yeomanry was performed. Others used it as a receptacle for elding, the provincial name for firing whether wood or turf.'

Inventories do not use the word downhouse and instead mention kitchens and occasionally brewhouses. A kitchen (in addition to a firehouse) is mentioned in 1744 at Cragg Farm, Colthouse, while at Tock How, Hawkshead, in 1750 a detached kitchen is listed, and at Ghyll Farm, Wasdale, an out-kitchen appears in an inventory of 1883. At Townend, Troutbeck, in 1731 both 'kitcheng' and miln loft (possibly above the kitchen) appear. As we have already seen, not many ovens survive and the majority of those that do were found to be in the firehouse fireplace and not in the kitchen or downhouse. This suggests that baking was done in the main room of the house and not in the downhouse. Most downhouses have been altered or modernized, so that little evidence remains of their original function other than the form and size of the fireplaces. In many examples such as Caffle House, Watendlath, Stonethwaite Farm, Borrowdale, Rectory Farm, Windermere, and Low Park-a-Moor, Coniston, the chimneys in downhouses are similar in virtually every way to those in the respective firehouses; the only major difference is the lack of a fire-window (though even that is present at Rectory Farm, Windermere, and Town Head, Grasmere).

So the available evidence is not conclusive for the use of downhouses primarily as brewhouses. In Lancashire, however, where inventories are more detailed, it has been suggested that heated kitchens were in reality brewhouses and that all the cooking was carried out in the housebody or firehouse. A similar pattern has also emerged in Wiltshire, where a considerable number of kitchens had evidence of brewing.

Cupboards

If the fireplace dominated family life at one end of the firehouse, visually the room was often dominated at the other end by exuberantly decorated cupboards built into the partition or screen separating the firehouse from the parlour and buttery beyond. This firehouse partition was most commonly constructed of muntin-and-plank oak panelling or occasionally plank-and-stud work; through it two doors, equally spaced, led into the rooms beyond, and between these two doors the large press cupboards were usually set.

The plainness of the outside of the houses hardly prepares visitors for what lies within, a wealth of oak joinery: stairs, doors, floors and walls, but above all the sometimes full-height cupboards set up rather like family altars facing the fire, the centre of family life. The cupboards are the glory of Lake District farmhouses. Today they are often known locally as court cupboards, a name that has possibly been brought in by antique-dealers; seventeenth-century inventories simply employ the single word cupboard. These cupboards had a practical use, being the store-place for clapbread, which was often made in sufficient quantities to last the family for a month or two. Doubtless they were also the repositories for other family valuables, such as pewter and silver and the smuggled spirits brought in from the west coast ports in increasing quantities during the eighteenth century. (So much so that rum butter is now considered to be a local delicacy and was customarily fed to mothers after childbirth.)

In form, most cupboards were basically similar: two storeys high, with double doors below and a recessed superstructure consisting of smaller double doors with a narrow shelf in front. Occasionally the lower cupboard had drawers above, and sometimes the top of the piece was fitted with a projecting frieze carrying turned drop-finials or turned pillars at either end linking the frieze to the lower storey. The front and two sides of the cupboards were normally of panel construction, with a framework of rails and stiles enclosing thin oak panels. Usually at least one of the stiles had a chamfered edge. The back and internal shelf-boards were usually thick planks nailed to the superstructure. Oak was used throughout, even sometimes for door hinges – small pegs project above and below the doors which had lightly convex sides fitting into adjoining concave stiles.

Where these cupboards varied was in the extent and elaboration of their carved enrichments. Sometimes this was limited to the frieze rail, often it extended to one or more of the panels in the upper half, and occasionally it spread further to cover all the front of the upper

below
Cupboard at Lane Head Farm, Patterdale, dated 1660.
The centre panel of this cupboard is unusual in having a design of stylized fruit and leaves. The other motifs – lozenges, lunettes, arcading and feathered scrolls – are more commonplace.

storey and part of the lower panels and rails as well. What is significant is the way that some of the recurrent motifs reflect a clear stylistic dialect and are not merely retarded versions of metropolitan fashions.

These motifs can be divided into four dominant iconographical groups: floral motifs; interlace and feather patterns; scrolls with zoomorphic detailing; and lozenges and other geometrical motifs. These categories cannot, however, be considered watertight as scrolls merge into interlace motifs in places – nor exhaustive, as lunettes and gadrooning, for example, appear on some cupboards and fit into none of these categories.

Floral patterns are the least common of the four types. These take the form of rosettes or just occasionally stylized plants, but they are nearly always accompanied by examples of other categories. The centre panel of the cupboard at Lane Head, Patterdale, was embellished with stylized fruit and leaves.

The lozenge, with feather and rosette patterns within, and sometimes with scroll ends to the corners, is the one dominant motif that is found not only in the central Lakes but also in Yorkshire where the pattern is widely used on the panels of wainscot chairs and chests.

The two groups which are most specific to the area and whose origins perhaps predate the earliest known cupboards are the interlaced patterns and scrolls with hints of serpents or dragons. They occur widely and were mostly used to fill panels, whilst serpents and scrolls ran along friezes, rails and stiles. 'Serpent' is the description given to a scroll one end of which resembles the tip of a serpent's tail tightly coiled, and the other end its head, with eyes and twin fangs.

One further important aspect of cupboard embellishment should be mentioned here. Most cupboards were dated and initialled, both features usually appearing in the centre of the frieze or occasionally in one of the other panels. The form taken by these letters and numbers is remarkably consistent, and the ends of both are often adorned with 'fangs' or twin scrolls, linking them closely to the linear motifs.

It was suggested as early as 1902, by H. S. Cowper, that the origins of both scrolls and interlaced patterns should be sought in surviving Celtic or Nordic traditions in the Lake District. Cowper tentatively proposed that such continuity could be credible in an isolated and self-contained area like the Lake District where Nordic traditions persisted in agriculture, buildings and language. The idea was put forward again in a catalogue for an exhibition of Lake District furniture at Temple Newsam in 1973, where the similarities between two early carved stones and seventeenth- and early eighteenth-century wood-carving motifs were highlighted. The two stones were a twelfth-century stone lintel at St Bees Priory with tight interlace decoration either side of a scroll dragon, and a Viking-period hogs-back tomb at Penrith showing a serpent within interlaced decoration. The catalogue merely noted the similarity to later motifs. If these early carvings themselves are looked at more closely, however, the motifs on both are found to have been borrowed from even earlier sources. First of all, Viking carving in Cumbria (of which the hogsback tomb is one example) not only depicts Scandinavian myth and ornament, but also shows strong links both with pre-Viking Anglian sculptural traditions and with Celtic traditions from the Irish Sea province. Secondly, the fourteenth-century monastic carving at St Bees looks backwards to Viking traditions of the tenth and eleventh centuries. The link between them and, as it turns out, with the carvings on cupboards, is the repertory of Viking motifs. Despite strong Anglian elements, Viking sculpture in Cumbria did produce distinctive motifs not found in Viking sculpture in Cheshire and North Wales, for example. These were certain zoomorphic, knot-work and figural motifs – just the sorts of things that are prevalent on seventeenth- and eighteenth-century built-in cupboards. Unwittingly or not, seventeenth-century Cumbrian wood-carvers used motifs

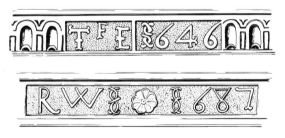

Initials and dates from three cupboards.

similar to those of their Viking predecessors. Perhaps theirs was a revival, rather than a survival, of a strong local Anglian-Viking-monastic tradition. Wherever the motifs came from, Cumbrian wood-carvers made them very much their own, producing an inward-looking but vigorous school of decoration within a discrete geographical area.

This is not to say that all Cumbrian carving was homogeneous, or that it did not vary over time. Beatrix Potter, who was a keen patron of local auctions in the early 1900s, turned her astute eye to furniture designs as well as to animals and plants and kept a record of what she saw as the distinctive features of Coniston cupboards. Three cupboards similar in form and decoration, two in Colthouse, one in Coniston and all apparently the work of a single carver or school of carving, show well the features described by Beatrix Potter and could perhaps have been made in Coniston. All three are dated to within four years of each other and while not identical, they have the same basic shape, with no projecting cornice and two doors either side of a fixed decorative panel in the upper storey, and similar decoration. Where they differ is in the lower storey, with one of the Colthouse cupboards having a horizontal division and an extra decorative panel.

Examination of the motifs found to date on other cupboards suggests several distinct schools of carving or sources of inspiration, and confirms Beatrix Potter's idea of a Coniston base for one of the groups. Coniston/Hawkshead, Kendal/Staveley, Ravenstonedale and Keswick could well have been centres of production. This judgement is based purely on stylistic analysis of similar cupboards, an analysis which is imperfect for various reasons: several cupboards do not fit into obvious groups; motifs and patterns change over time as well as within areas; and relatively few cupboards have survived *in situ* in the more westerly valleys such as Wasdale.

So far all attempts to marry styles with individual carvers have failed. In fact only one joiner/carver has been identified, and then not positively. The initials *N. T. Fect. A. D. 1673* carved on the frieze of the cupboard built into High Oxenfell Farm, Coniston, are the only known example of a maker signing his work. (*Fect.* is presumably a contraction of the Latin *fecit*, 'he made'.) The initials could possibly be those of Nicholas Turner, a joiner who lived and worked in Coniston at the time the cupboard was made.

The majority of cupboards, as has been noted, are dated and initialled. The initials are usually three in number, the first being the first letter of the husband's Christian name; the second (usually slightly higher than the other two) is the first letter of his surname; and the final letter is the wife's Christian-name initial. In all cases where the three initials have been identified, the date given is either the date of the marriage of the partners or a year or two afterwards. For example, at Robinson Place Farm, Great Langdale, the initials are those of Thomas and Agnes Fearon and the date 1693; at Low Hallgarth, Little Langdale, the initials are of those of John and Margaret Holme who married in 1682. The cupboards may have been made to commemorate marriages, but they may also have been built into houses, newly altered, into which the recently married couples moved. In the Penrith area the cupboards are still called 'brideswains' from the tradition that they were carried on the wain or waggon in the marriage procession, and this lends support to the first suggestion. On the other hand, for the few cupboards which survive with only two initials (and whose owners have been identified) the date appears to commemorate the rebuilding or alteration of a house. Townend Cottage, Colthouse, was rebuilt by Edward and Benjamin Satterthwaite, father and son, in 1703. The cupboard built in at the time bears the initials of the son: *B. S. 1703*. At that date, Benjamin was not yet married – he married a year later and, as things turned out, never lived in the house at all.

The earliest date so far recorded on a built-in cupboard is 1628, on cupboards at both Common Farm, Windermere, and High Wray Farm. The latest date is 1735 at Jackdaw Cottage, Easedale, although it is clear that this date does not signify the end of cupboard-building. After that date cupboards were quite plain and embellished with neither patterns nor dates and initials. The 1730s seem to have seen the end of the tradition of richly carved cupboards that had flourished in the Lake District for at least a hundred years.

Tables and Chairs

Some farmers had other pieces of oak furniture in the firehouse such as tables, benches, stools and occasionally wainscot chairs, though cupboards certainly seem to have been the most widespread items. When the Royal Commission for Historical Monuments carried out its survey of Westmorland buildings in 1933, it noted, as important pieces, fourteen chairs (in both churches and houses), twenty-three chests and fifty spice cupboards, but these were overwhelmingly outnumbered by the cupboards, two hundred and fifty of which are mentioned. The high number of surviving cupboards may reflect their importance as status symbols or may perhaps be a consequence of the fact that they were fixed into the fabric of the farmhouse and were therefore less likely to be sold than portable chairs and chests. Nevertheless many were sold, as shown by advertisements in the *Connoisseur* magazine earlier this century. As early as the 1850s Harriet Martineau complained of London dealers plundering the Lake District; and at the turn of the century Beatrix Potter was

below

Furniture in the firehouse at Townend, Troutbeck.
The table and forms were almost certainly made for the room in the seventeenth century. In an inventory of 1731 they are listed as 'One Long Table, two Buffett Forms before it'. The moulding running along the rails of all these pieces is also found on the oak panelling of the walls.

right
Part of the downhouse, Townend, Troutbeck.
At the end of the nineteenth century, the last George Browne 'improved' much of the plain oak furniture at Townend by adding carved decoration. He also added new furniture, joining up older pieces to achieve a 'built-in' look. The forms of his carved decoration were reworkings of traditional motifs.

distressed to see oak cupboards 'riven out of ancestral cottages' and subjected to what she saw as the humiliation of the sale rooms.

William Satterthwaite of Beckside, Colthouse, who died in 1717, not only had cupboards, tables and stools, but also chairs and an old clock in his firehouse. An inventory of 1731 for Townend, Troutbeck, shows that the 'house' not only had 'one long table, two buffett forms before it' but also 'four chairs and one skreen or long settle'. The table, forms and two of the chairs are still in the same room at Townend. Few old tables now survive in farmhouses but those that do (such as at Glencoyne Farm, Ullswater, Barker Knott Farm, Windermere, and Causeway Farm, Windermere) are on a massive

above

Wainscot chair, Townend, Troutbeck.
This chair was made in 1742 and must be one of the last wainscot chairs to be made. The crested top rail, with its scroll pattern terminating each end in serpents, is characteristic of Lake District decoration.

scale, thick oak-plank tops supported on either square or turned legs, usually six in number, which are braced by robust stretchers. Some have elaboration along the front rail and nearly all are too big to have been assembled outside the building; which suggests, as with cupboards, that the joiners made component parts and then assembled them on site to suit the owner and the house. The traditional position of these long tables appears to have been under the main window of the firehouse at right angles to the fireplace. Forms or benches were then lined up against the table on the side nearest the fire, and when not in use were turned on their sides and tucked under the table with their legs resting on the table stretchers.

Many inventories give the impression (although there are no surviving examples) that some table-tops were not fixed to the frames which supported them. In 1762 Thomas Addison sold Penny Hill Farm, Eskdale, and all its furniture except 'a table frame'. Similarly in 1749 an inventory of Isaac Singleton of Buckbarrow Farm, Netherwasdale, lists a 'table and frame in the firehouse'. Presumably these frames were trestle-like supports for a plank top, harking back to the mediaeval prototype of a board (as in board and lodging) supported on collapsible supports, an arrangement which could be dismantled and stored against a wall of the room.

Nowadays most of these old plank-top tables glow from polish rubbed in with care over many decades. Quite probably many, if not most, were scrubbed clean when first made, as the one in the downhouse at Townend, Troutbeck, still is. A few inventories provide evidence of table coverings. Leonard Rawlinson of Low Longmire Farm, Bouth, who died in 1589, is listed as having a 'table cloth' but tantalizingly no more details are given; while Benjamin Browne of Townend purchased a damask table-cloth on 4 March 1740 for the high price of ten shillings.

Chairs in houses came in many different styles. The most elaborate were wainscot chairs, elbow- or arm-chairs made in oak with panel backs, plank seats and turned front legs. Both the back panels and top rails were usually intricately carved, with scrolls running along the top rails and elaborate, tight interlace motifs fitting into the centre panel; both of these features picked up elements used on cupboards. Wainscot chairs were also made elsewhere, notably in Lancashire and Yorkshire, but the Lake District chairs are distinctive in several ways, particularly in their treatment of the top rail. This was often crested – the rail swelling slightly in the centre – with at either end a scroll decoration terminating in pronounced coiled serpents. The form of this top rail seems to have allowed carvers much freer rein than did cupboards. As a result, what was only hinted at on some cupboards becomes fully developed on chairs: almost three-dimensional serpents emerge, in distinct contrast to the somewhat mechanical spirals found on chairs from neighbouring regions. At Townend, Troutbeck, the Brownes were still making such wainscot chairs (or having them

made) in the 1740s – one of the chairs is dated and initialled *D. B. B. 1742*, i.e. only twelve years before Thomas Chippendale published in London his famous pattern-book *The Director*. This highlights the remarkable persistence of this type of chair in the Lake District through almost one hundred and twenty years from 1623, the earliest dated example so far recorded.

Most houses probably had no more than one such wainscot chair. 'One large elbow chair' is mentioned in an inventory of Fletcher Fleming of Fellfoot, Little Langdale, in 1716. In the same house, as well as forms, were 'twelve matted chairs' – perhaps a description of chairs with rush seats serving everyday needs. When all the goods and chattels of William Hawkrigg of Underhelm Farm, Grasmere, were sold after his death in 1710, the sale particulars recorded eleven 'throwen' chairs which fetched between ½d. and 9d. each. These would have had legs and stretchers turned or 'throwen' on a lathe, probably rush seats, and again would have been cheaper and more for everyday use than wainscot chairs. Chairs of this type were made in Eskdale Green until the early years of this century in a small workshop near the post office, the last turner being called Brockbank. Several examples made there are still in the area.

The accounts of Benjamin Browne of Townend reveal a little more of the cost of this furniture. On 16 December 1737 he paid one pound four and sixpence for six chairs and one elbow-chair. In November three years later he paid William Brownrigg two shillings for covering three chairs with leather, giving one and sixpence for 'A skin for 1 of them' and sixpence for 'Brass nails; hair for stopping'. At the end of the same year, on 27 December, two shillings was paid 'To Brownrigg for makeing a chair which I sit in at fire. I found wood.'

Floors

In 1812 it was said that some floors were 'coarsely paved with pebbles' and some were of 'loam'. Only two houses so far examined have yielded evidence of floors such as these. A cobbled floor was discovered beneath a wooden one in Harry Place Farm in Great Langdale, while at Low House Farm, Troutbeck, at the foot of the stairs, there still exists a fascinating mosaic floor made from small pieces of slate laid on edge in a pattern of divided squares. Stone flag floors came to replace cobbles and earth, and by the mid-nineteenth century they had become almost universal. These flags came in various sizes, thicknesses and colours depending on the area or quarry from which they were riven. At Millbrow Farm, Skelwith Bridge, the floor has been used to record political feelings – this inscription was cut into the stone flags, perhaps at the time of the John Wilkes agitation in the 1760s:

Civil and Religious Liberty all over the world – The Liberty of the Press, if we have it not Tis like the air we breath; We die. Limited monarchy for ever. (By Longmire)

Whether matting was in common use to cover floors is not known. But at Townend, Troutbeck, there does exist a carpet, woven in the village by William Birkett in 1768. It is a double cloth of Herdwick wool, in its natural colour and also dyed black and red, woven in a pattern of repeated squares. This is a remarkable survival.

Windows

Two or three windows provided light for the firehouse, one within the chimney recess and one or sometimes two larger ones further along the same outside wall. Very few houses had windows on both sides of this main room. Until the early eighteenth century, windows had chamfered and pegged oak frames, with one or two mullions and one or two diamond-shaped wooden bars within the spaces. Some houses, such as Hoathwaite Farm, Coniston, had taller windows with transoms. For glazing, small rectangular or diamond-shaped pieces of glass would be fitted into the opening with ties around the wooden bars. Very few early glazed windows survive and the attic windows at Hoathwaite Farm and one or two at Townend, Troutbeck, are rare and interesting examples. However, in his meticulous drawings of houses in Ambleside and the surrounding areas in the early nineteenth century, William Green records dozens of examples of leaded lights, suggesting that many survived at least until the 1820s.

Not all windows were glazed; some were merely shuttered with internal plank shutters mounted on hinges, while others show no evidence of glazing or any fittings for shutters. Examples of this last category are a small oak fire-window with central mullion recently opened up at High Park Cottage, Coniston, and two surviving windows – one on the stairs and one in the attic space – at Hoathwaite Cottage. Whether some sort of cloth was stretched over these openings is unclear. Window cloths do appear in inventories but are probably winnowing-cloths rather than something to stretch over windows, for they tend to be listed along with sacks and pokes. On the other hand, in parts of Scandinavia cloths oiled to make them windproof and slightly translucent are stretched tightly over frames to be fitted into window recesses. It is hard to imagine some openings in Lake District farmhouses being left entirely uncovered – the heat of the fire would barely compensate for the draught from the windows – but until more evidence turns up that is the tentative conclusion that must be drawn.

Rushlights at Townend,
Troutbeck.

Rushlights

By day, light came in through these windows; by night the firehouse
would have been lit either by candles or, more commonly, by rushlights. Candlesticks, candle-boxes and lanterns are only occasionally
mentioned in inventories. Candles were probably often home-made
and, at least from the early nineteenth century, formed in tin moulds
such as the one that still exists at Hill Top, Near Sawrey. They were
made either from tallow or from more expensive beeswax. Beeswax
candles were extremely expensive to buy. On 6 January 1733 Benjamin Browne of Troutbeck paid two shillings for 'A wax candle 1 lb.
weight'. Much more common were rushlights, made from rushes
(*Conjuncus conglomeratus* or *C. effusus*) locally called 'sieves', which
were gathered in marshy places, peeled, dried and dipped in mutton
fat. This was autumn work, the rushes being picked when plump and
in the second year of their growth. The skin was peeled with the
exception of one or two strips which were left on for strength. The
pith was then dried and passed through, but not soaked in, mutton
fat before being laid to harden on a framework of sticks. In 1861
Cockley Beck Farm in the Duddon valley was still lit entirely by
rushlights and the farmer told a visitor at that time how it took him
about two days to make enough rushlights to last the entire year.

Unlike candles, rushes burn best when held at an angle of 45
degrees; if upright they burn only slowly, and if horizontal too fast.
Rushlight-holders were usually of iron and took the form of a
V-shaped piece of metal, or nip, to hold the rush, fixed either into a
wooden base or on to a hook to enable it to be hung from the ceiling.
Some holders combined fittings for tallow candles with fittings for
rushlights. A few had considerable elaboration, with shaped tripod
feet and arrangements for adjusting the level of the light, while others
were basic – such as the 'iron clip, something like a pair of curling
tongs, hung from the ceiling by a string' at Cockley Beck Farm in the
1860s. The variations were enormous and no standard type of pincer,
as they were called, seems to have been prevalent in the Lake District.

Merry Neets

Such then were all the main elements of the firehouse: the fire and
cooking utensils, cupboards, tables, forms or chairs, occasionally
clocks and dressers, possibly table-cloths and always rush nips or
pincers. The firehouse was the common room of the family, the heart
of the house around which family life revolved. Here people cooked
and ate and carried out most of the daytime domestic activities. Just
occasionally the room goes by a name other than house, firehouse or
house place, but one which still emphasizes the central role it played
in family life. The 1752 inventory of Joseph Hawkrigg of Grove Farm,
Windermere, calls it the 'Bodystead of the House'. The firehouse was
the public room into which visitors would be invited, perhaps when

bidden to funerals or weddings or perhaps to celebrate a birth. It could also be the scene of Merry Neets, gatherings to celebrate the harvest or just to make merry. Benjamin Browne's account books record several payments to fiddlers for 'Merry nights'. The spirit of these was memorably captured by Hugh Walpole, writing in the 1930s and drawing on his knowledge of Borrowdale farms, in his novel *Rogue Herries*:

> In Peel's house the hallan opened straight into the downhouse. This was in his case the great common room of the family, the place of tonight's Christmas feast ... the floor tonight was cleared for the dancing, but at the opposite end trestle tables were arranged for the feasting ... in other parts of the room were big standard holders for rushlights. All these tonight were brilliantly lit and blew in great gusts in the wind ... Many were already dancing. It was a scene of brilliant colour with the blazing fire, the red berries of the holly glowing in every corner, old Johnny Shoestring in bright blue breeches and with silver buckles to his shoes perched on a high stool fiddling for his life, the brass gleaming, faces shining, the stamp of the shoon, the screaming of the fiddle, the clap clap of the hands as the turns were made in the dance — and beyond the heat and the light the dark form of the valley lying in breathless stillness, its face stroked by the fall of lingering reluctant snow.

BUTTERY

Two further rooms opened off the firehouse through doors set into the timber screen opposite the fire. These were the buttery and the parlour. Usually the parlour was slightly the larger room, taking up two-thirds of the space beyond the screen. Both rooms were lit by windows. The orientation of the house determined the side on which the buttery was placed, the parlour usually being on the warm side and the buttery on the cooler north or east side. This, of course, was only an ideal arrangement and many variations existed which will be discussed in the next chapter.

Buttery was the word used in most inventories, although according to James Clarke, writing in 1787, buttery was then a fairly modern term which had replaced 'the old name of Ambry'. In modern parlance the room was a larder or pantry where both food and eating utensils were stored. It was usually furnished with slate benches or sconces, supported on plastered stone piers, above which were wall-mounted wooden shelves. The slate benches would have been used for salting pork and storing milk, butter, meat and cheese, while the wooden shelves housed pewter and wooden vessels and occasionally brass and copper pans. Inventories give some details of the types of utensils found in these butteries. Pewter is commonly mentioned and comes as doublers (large dishes), flagons, tankards, and also just plain plates and dishes. When William Hawkrigg's possessions were auctioned at Underhelm Farm, Grasmere, in 1710 he had eleven doublers, while

opposite
Detail of cupboard at Greenend Cottage, Hawkshead.

right
**Chimney, How Green Farm,
Hartsop.**

below
**Hogg house, Caudale Beck
Farm, Patterdale.**

left
Re-roofing barn, Wall End
Farm, Great Langdale.

below
Wrostler slates, barn, High Birk
Howe Farm, Little Langdale.

bottom
Stairs in farmhouse, High Birk
Howe Farm, Little Langdale.

the inventory of the possessions of George Taylor of Plum Green, Finsthwaite, made in 1758, lists nine pewter dishes, five pewter plates, one pewter bottle, and twelve pewter spoons, a great rarity. Earthenware is hardly ever specified in inventories other than as dishes. Wooden 'trenchers and piggins' complete the eating and serving vessels found in this room. According to the Revd Mr Hodgson, writing in 1822,

> the richer sort of people had a service of pewter; but amongst the middling and poorer classes, the dinner was eaten off *trenchers* [flat wooden plates]. Hasty pudding and liquids were served up in small wooden vessels called *piggins*, made in the manner of half barrels and having one stave longer than the rest for a handle.

Other pieces of equipment occasionally mentioned are flesh forks and skewers, wooden cans, tin pots, chafing dishes, pestles and mortars, and dairying equipment such as 'cheese-rums and fatts' (frames within which cheese was pressed) and brass or copper pans which were probably for separating curds from whey in cheesemaking. ('The great brass pot' was willed in 1670 by John Walker of Fell Foot Farm in Little Langdale.)

PARLOUR

The name parlour, which was given to the room adjoining the buttery, today conjures up the idea of a small sitting-room; and that is just what this room became in many houses during the nineteenth century when a second flue and fireplace were added to it. But in the seventeenth and eighteenth centuries the parlour was unheated and used as the best bedroom, chamber or bower, where the master and mistress of the house slept. A bed, bedding, a chest for clothes, and sometimes a chair were the basic accoutrement of this room, their elaboration depending on the wealth of the owners. Inventories occasionally mention bedsteads, more commonly pairs of 'bedstocks' and more rarely 'truckles'. Bedstocks would have been wooden bed-ends between which was fixed a frame to support the mattress. Inventories do not distinguish between simple low plank or panel ends and the more elaborate beds with posts to support hangings and wooden testers (panel canopies between the head and foot of the bed). Also inventories presumably only mention movable beds, although these do seem to have been more prevalent than any of fixed type. Unlike in the Yorkshire Dales and parts of Scotland, box-beds (cupboards into which beds were fitted) were never common, it seems. One documented example survives at Hill Top, Near Sawrey (albeit without its bed), and a cupboard at Hoathwaite Farm could possibly have been used for sleeping, but these are the exceptions.

Evidence is scarce for the wide range of beds that probably once existed. Three pairs of bedstocks were sold at William Hawkrigg's

opposite top
Byre, Troutbeck Park Farm, Troutbeck.

opposite below
Bank barn, Troutbeck Park Farm, Troutbeck.

above
Tester bed, Townend, Troutbeck.
This is one of two elaborate beds at Townend. Both carry the initials of George and Ellinor Browne; this one is dated 1672, the other 1686. Some of the carved panels seem to be the work of the last George Browne at the end of the nineteenth century.

sale of Underhelm Farm in 1710; they only fetched between sixpence ha'penny and one shilling and twopence and must have been fairly plain articles. By contrast beds still at Townend, Troutbeck, and two others which survived until recently, one at North Fold Farm, Troutbeck, and the other at Causeway Farm, Windermere, were heavy, elaborate pieces. The bed at North Fold Farm was built in and had a panelled back and tester and carved footposts; two of the Townend beds are similar in form but free-standing, and have end-panels carved with patterns and motifs similar to those found on cupboards and chairs. Tester beds such as these would have been hung around with curtains for warmth. Benjamin Browne's accounts for the year 1732 show just how much he spent on bed hangings, an amount that suggests that such items were a luxury beyond the means of most farmers. On 17 January 1733 he bought 'a whole piece of stuff for my bed curtains £1.12.0 Lace for them – 7½ yds 7/6 Buccheram – 7 yds 6/- Curtain rings – 8½ doz 2/6 Curtain poles – my iron 3/-'. On the 9th of the following month he wrote, 'a silk rug £1.8.0 My bed whole charge in all £4.3.11 Incl. 4/8 to Taylor'. Presumably the rug was a bed-cover. The sums do not quite add up – threepence is missing somewhere!

The mattresses of the Townend beds originally rested on rope supports threaded through holes in the ends and sides, an arrangement no more elaborate than would have been found on a basic truckle bed – a rectangular frame threaded up with rope and with no raised ends. Benjamin Browne apparently slept on a chaff mattress, for on 14 April 1731 he records 'tickin chaff bed for self 4/6'. Whether he covered this with a feather mattress for comfort is not clear. Perhaps surprisingly, William Hawkrigg had a feather bed which was sold at his sale for the princely sum of eighteen shillings and threepence, as much as one of the heifers fetched at the same sale.

Blankets made from blanketing or kersey cloth, and sheets of linen or harden cloth (a fabric made from the 'hards' or coarse parts of flax or hemp), both woven locally, together with coverlets and bolsters (all widely listed in inventories), would have completed the soft furnishings of the bed. In 1628 Agnes Taylor of Penny Bridge bequeathed to her brother Miles, along with a pair of harden sheets, the 'worse coverlet of the two on my bed'.

The other main item of furniture in the parlour would have been a chest for storing clothes. From the end of the seventeenth century chests with drawers, as opposed to chests with hinged lids, gradually became more and more common and eventually superseded the simpler box-chests for clothes storage. But in the Lake District box-chests continued to be made throughout the eighteenth century. Surviving ones are normally in oak and of panelled or wainscot construction (i.e. a framework of rails and stiles filled in with thin wooden panels), rather than of plank construction as were meal chests. This is neatly confirmed in the will of George Cowperthwaite of Tarn Foot, Loughrigg, dated 1702, in which bequests were made first of all to his son Stanley of 'as much wood at Dale End as will be a convenient wainscot chest', and secondly to his granddaughter Isobel Tyson of 'enough wood for a wainscot chest for her clothes'.

Only in comparatively grand houses did the parlour furnishings extend beyond this basic complement of bed, bedding and chests. And when householders became wealthy enough to buy chests with drawers, looking-glasses, warming-pans and so on, so they tended to enlarge their houses beyond the confines of the yeoman farmer's plan already outlined and to add wings with chambers for sleeping at first-floor level; a move which the simpler houses were to follow as the eighteenth century wore on, with parlours gradually turning into heated sitting-rooms and attics being upgraded into bedrooms. The time-scale for this change is very extended. By the 1670s grand houses such as Townend, Troutbeck, and Fellfoot, Little Langdale, had several chambers at first-floor level; in the mid-1700s inventories of smaller houses commonly list firehouse, parlour, buttery and kitchen on the ground floor and a succession of lofts on the first floor, even though by that date many new houses were being built in the western valleys with heated sitting-rooms and first-floor bedrooms. At least one house was still using a downstairs bedroom as late as the 1850s, for Beatrix Potter describes how a resident of Sawrey was born in the box-bed in the parlour at Hill Top. Rather like open fires and hand-threshing, downstairs bedrooms hung on and may have survived in a few remote places until the early 1900s.

LOFTS

Until the main bedroom moved upstairs, the first floors of houses were lofts open to the roof and were used for storage and as sleeping accommodation for children of the family and for servants. Access was from stairs which usually opened off the firehouse. The exact position and construction of these stairs varied considerably, as we shall see in the next chapter. However, three main types predominate. The first is a spiral staircase on the opposite side to the main windows. It could be constructed either of stone or less frequently of blocks of oak, as at Holeslack, Sizergh, and Townend, Troutbeck. This type of staircase often formed a semi-cylindrical projection at the back of the house, the main roof being brought down over it. Spiral staircases were also fitted tightly into the recess between the heck and the back wall. This kind was nearly always of stone. The third type is a dog-leg staircase of oak treads with turned or splat balusters, usually sited in a projecting wing at the back of the house and quite often apparently superseding a stone spiral staircase. Sets of balusters on these staircases are wonderful flights of fancy, no two balusters being quite the same and hardly any of pattern-book design. The dates of most seem to span the era of cupboard-making; by the 1780s softwoods and

above
**Fold Head Farm, Watendlath,
c.1900.**
In a few houses the stairs were
not shut off from the firehouse,
as can be seen here. Notice the
legs of cured mutton or ham
hanging from the firehouse
ceiling. This farm was
traditionally called Watendlath
Farm.

formality had taken over, and plain, almost severe pine staircases were beginning to appear.

The lofts to which these led were generally unceiled, the undersides of the slates being 'tiered' or plastered with a mixture of lime, sand and hair, both to stop the slates twisting and to seal the loft-space from the weather. A modicum of warmth was provided by the chimney-hood which projected into the roof-space, providing just enough warmth to make the lofts ideal places for storing grain, both malted barley and oatmeal.

Chapter 5 explains how oats to meet the family's needs were grown, threshed, winnowed, dried and finally ground at the local mill. The resulting oatmeal was then brought back to the farm for storage in one of the lofts above the living-quarters. Granaries outside the house were quite rare. Malted barley would similarly be returned to the lofts for storage. Both were kept in arks, large oak chests of plank construction with hinged lids, and side planks which projected below the baseboards to form feet. A good selection of these chests survives in farmhouses; many are mentioned in inventories, where they are usually referred to as chests, arks or meal-arks. A few are dated, notably the pair in the kitchen loft at Townend, Troutbeck, which bear the date 1666 and the initials *GEB* and were up-ended in the early nineteenth century to form wardrobes when the grain-loft was converted into bedrooms. Some of these plank chests may be considerably older, but their dating is problematical. They occur in many parts of the country, in churches as well as in houses, and differ little region by region or over time; some may be as early as the sixteenth century, others as late as the mid-eighteenth. That some meal-arks in the Lake District date back to the earlier end of this time-span is perhaps borne out by an inventory of the belongings of Clement Taylor of Finsthwaite, dated 1742, in which are mentioned 'ancient chests and arks' – though it depends, of course, on how long it takes a chest to become 'ancient'!

Lofts were often divided to reflect the arrangement of the house at ground-floor level, and the space thus formed would be named after the rooms beneath. Kitchen loft, house loft, parlour loft and buttery loft are listed in an inventory of Grove Farm, Applethwaite, in 1732. In other houses the rooms were named after their use, such as miln-loft, apple-loft, corn-loft, or after their position – middle loft, far loft and so on. The lofts were partitioned from one another by screens which filled the spaces within the trusses or cruck timbers. Occasionally the area at the head of the stairs was walled off to form a corridor giving access to the rooms either side. These screens were usually made either from oak muntin-and-plank panelling or of oak studs filled in with lath and plaster. These studs were sometimes sawn timbers grooved on either side to accept laths, or in other cases roughly shaped uprights against which the laths were nailed. At Hoathwaite Cottage, Coniston, the partitions are of a much more primitive construction, with a daub of clay and straw plastered over a framework of small upright poles. According to one nineteenth-century writer, some lofts remained altogether unencumbered with formal partitions. Rather, 'a rope was stretched across this nocturnal receptacle of the family upon which coats, gowns and other articles of apparel, both male and female hung promiscuously.' It is difficult to judge how widespread this arrangement was; there is no doubt that inventories commonly indicate loft divisions.

Where muntin-and-plank partitions were used, the edges of the thicker planks were sometimes moulded, the degree of elaboration varying from room to room and seeming to suggest relative import-ance. At Robin Ghyll, Great Langdale, the room above the parlour had every leading edge moulded, which may indicate that it was the most favoured room and used for sleeping. The second-best room was evidently opposite the stairs with two walls of moulded plank-work, while the remaining room containing the firehood was un-embellished and presumably used as a meal-loft. Similar degrees of elaboration are found at Fellfoot, Little Langdale, and Robinson Place, Great Langdale; in both cases only the room above the parlour is panelled, giving it a higher status than the rest of the loft and probably confirming it as a sleeping area.

Above the partitions the lofts were often unceiled and open to the rafters and the underside of the slates. Despite tiering (a lime-and-hair plaster applied to the underside of the slates) or mossing (stuffing the spaces between the slates with moss), many small cracks remained; these were certainly large enough for those sleeping below to find snow squeezing through – and on occasions something larger. Thomas Mandall of Tarn Foot, Loughrigg, awoke one night to find a 'Jenny Hullet' (barn owl) perched on his bed hooting at him and 'forthwith he got his bedroom ceiled'. Mr Roberts, who was born at Oak Cottage, Rosthwaite, and lived there until his death in 1984, remembered how, when he was a boy, his mother used to stretch muslin across the top of the loft partitions to catch dust and to stop snow falling on him while he was sleeping. In fact the lofts at Oak Cottage were only boarded out when the family started taking bed-and-breakfast guests in the 1930s. At High Birk Howe, Little Langdale, the loft remained open until as late as 1948. In most houses, however, by the 1900s lofts had been upgraded to become bedrooms with plastered or boarded ceilings and many were fitted with fireplaces.

From the middle of the eighteenth century, the move towards greater privacy – embodied in separate sitting-rooms, indirect en-trances and upstairs bedrooms – ran parallel with a decline in self-sufficiency in grain and beer, so that the demands engendered by the former could to a large degree be satisfied within space freed by the latter. By 1900 many yeomen's farmhouses had metamorphosed into polite dwellings with remarkably little change to their structure, as the next chapter will show.

3

House Plans

THE PREVIOUS chapter looked at what might be called the archetypal layout of a Lake District house for the years 1600–1750 and analysed the various elements within it. But the arrangement of these elements was by no means static; it varied over time and also from valley to valley across the area. Some features of the plan assumed more prominence or importance in one valley and less in another; others were modified to reflect changing degrees of prosperity. The variations are not substantial, but sufficiently significant to enable us to identify dominant local characteristics and to suggest tentatively how these might have emerged. These variations concern both the disposition of the rooms and the construction of the buildings.

Houses are made up of a series of bays – a bay being the space between adjacent roof supports or between a support and an end wall. Obviously the more bays, the greater the length, although the width of individual bays also affects the equation. The main part of nearly all surviving houses built before about 1750 was of two, two and a half or three bays with a first floor. Despite this overall consistency the actual size and layout varied, but the variations appear to show a progression from a basic rectangular shape one room deep, through plans with outshuts and later with two-storey wings, and

right
Low Fold, Ambleside, c.1900. Very few single-storey houses survive. Low Fold is one of the best preserved. The layout is similar to that of a two-storey house: the stairs lead up to a low loft lit only by small roof-lights. The house has been altered little since this photograph was taken, although the area has become urbanized.

finally to houses two rooms deep. These variations can, to a certain extent, be linked to individual valleys. They also probably formed a progression for the most prosperous houses only. Smaller, less important buildings seem to have lagged behind. If that is so, it cannot be said that at any date a certain type of plan was the current fashion. Gradual and uneven rates of change seem much more likely.

The houses themselves are almost never dated. Unlike north-east Lancashire or west Yorkshire, where almost every house of some substance built in the seventeenth century had a date-stone (usually over the main door and frequently with initials, too), Lake District houses remain largely mute about their origins. The type of stone used probably had a lot to do with this discretion; slate cannot be carved as easily as sandstone. For these reasons it is difficult to be precise about the date of many of the houses under consideration. The exceptions are where the house contains a fixed, dated and initialled cupboard and where the initials can be traced to known owners of the house, though, as noted earlier, the date can sometimes be of a wedding rather than a rebuilding.

The next few pages will look at the variety of plans found and their distribution, valley by valley. This is not to say that one can make out a watertight case for valley styles or that changes were necessarily progressive; it is also quite possible that personal preference played a large part in planning.

As we have seen, most houses had a basic complement of rooms on the ground floor – firehouse, buttery and parlour. The firehouse was the core of the house and it is the position of this in relation to the other components which gives us the variety of plans.

THREE-BAY HOUSES WITH GABLE ENTRANCE AND INTERNAL STAIRCASES

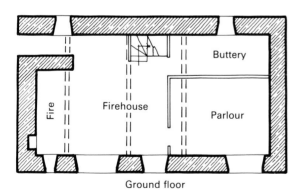

Ground floor

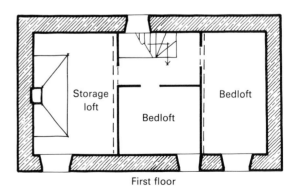

First floor

above
Robin Ghyll, Great Langdale.

This is the simplest type of plan found, with rooms and staircase fitted into a simple rectangle. The wooden staircase was commonly built at the back of the firehouse. The entrance is generally in the gable wall next to the fireplace, leading through the mell into the firehouse. In this arrangement the parlour and buttery were at the end of the house away from the fire, the parlour being on the 'front' or window side. On the first floor the space was divided crosswise into three rooms, with the central staircase often leading into the centre room. This plan is found in a few houses in Langdale but in a much greater number around Hawkshead. Slight variations of the position of the staircase are found: in Holehouse near Hawkshead the staircase takes up half the buttery space; in Low House Farm, Troutbeck, the staircase takes up the whole of the buttery space, the buttery being beneath ground-level below the parlour.

In many cases the buildings have had later alterations and there are few firmly datable features to suggest when they were first built. Nevertheless, from the available evidence the date-range seems considerable. At the early end of the scale are the cruck buildings possibly dating from the late sixteenth and early seventeenth centuries (all of which originally seem to have had internal staircases). Millbeck, Great Langdale, has the date 1734 on a spice cupboard in the firehouse. Robin Ghyll, Great Langdale – perhaps the most complete example of this plan type so far studied – has a wealth of muntin-and-plank oak panelling decorated with a moulding that suggests a late seventeenth/early eighteenth-century date.

Three-Bay Houses with Gable Entrances and External Outshut Staircases

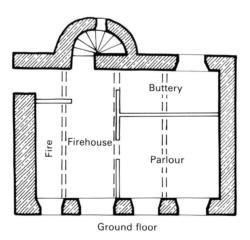

Low Millerground Farm,
Windermere.

Ground floor

These houses are similar to the preceding category except that the staircase projects into an outshut roofed over by an extension of the main roof, at one side of the central bay. This plan is found patchily across the whole area but is most prominent around Coniston and

right
Low Millerground Farm, Windermere.
The small semicircular projection houses a spiral staircase at the back of the house. Beyond it is the main door leading into one side of the firehouse fire. At the far end of the building is a barn. Upon the apex of its roof a bell once hung which was tolled to announce ferries crossing Windermere.

below right
Millbeck Farm, Great Langdale.
Here the staircase projection is rectangular in form and houses a dog-leg staircase. Notice how the back of this house is mostly unrendered, in contrast to the front shown on page 66. The rear first-floor windows are comparatively recent additions.

less frequent in Langdale and Hawkshead. It is, of course, possible to convert an internal staircase house to one of this pattern; such a conversion often leaves little or no trace and so is not easily identifiable. The variety of staircase types within this plan is considerable and suggests that in many houses alterations have taken place. They range from small semicircular stone spiral staircases (High Birk Howe, Little Langdale, and Millerground, Windermere), through almost elliptical spirals (Glencoyne Farm, Ullswater, and Fold Head Farm,

Watendlath) to substantial wooden spirals and wooden dog-leg stair-cases (Holeslack Farm, Sizergh, and Far End, Coniston, which has an elaborate turned baluster staircase, suggesting a date of about 1720).

THREE-BAY HOUSES WITH GABLE ENTRANCE AND STAIRS AND BUTTERY OUTSHUTS

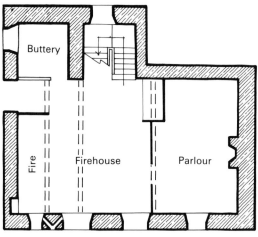

Buttery

Fire   Firehouse   Parlour

Wall End Farm, Great Langdale.   Ground floor

Inscription on spice cupboard.

F
T A
1692

This shows a further elaboration of the basic plan with the outshut widened to cover both stairs and buttery. With the buttery in the outshut, the area beyond the screen can be used entirely for the parlour and is therefore undivided; only one door leads through the screen, the press cupboard being displaced to one side. Like most plans this is found sporadically throughout the area, but it appears to be predominant in the Langdale valleys and has so far not been identified at all in Coniston, for example. The form of the stairs varies, a few being stone spirals, others having a dog-leg shape. The latter type may well be a replacement for the former in some houses. In some cases part of the outshut may have been an addition to one of the earlier plan types. In Wallend Farm, Great Langdale, however, the screen panelling shows no sign of a second door through to an earlier buttery, so presumably the house was built with a partial outshut. It contains a very plain press cupboard dated 1725 and a wooden stair with fairly crudely moulded rails. Robinson Place, Great Langdale, has a carved spice cupboard with the initials and date *T. F. A.* [for Thomas and Agnes Fearon] *1692* and also the date *1693* on a plaster panel. Fellfoot Farm, Little Langdale, has no dates but a wealth of internal detail including a fine plaster overmantel in the main, first-floor, chamber, and various fielded panel walls downstairs, all suggesting a date of about 1710 (which ties in with the known

right
Thrang Farm, Little Langdale.
The outshut at the rear of this
house covers a staircase and a
larder and runs the full length of
the house. Notice how it has
two chimneys, one for the
firehouse and a second for the
parlour.

family history, as Fletcher Fleming rebuilt the house at this time).
This last house is also much loftier than most Lake District farmhouses. High Birk Howe, Little Langdale, has a timber firehood and
fine studded oak doors which suggest a much earlier date. The upstairs
organization of all these houses is similar to the two previous plans,
with three rooms arranged around the central stairs.

THREE-BAY HOUSES WITH GABLE ENTRANCE AND STAIRS AND BUTTERY IN A REAR WING

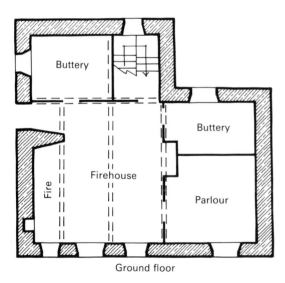

Ground floor

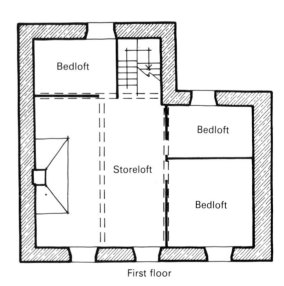

First floor

above
High Arnside Farm, Coniston.

The layout of the main part of this plan is similar to the ground-floor
arrangement in the outshut house just described. The simple rear
outshut has, however, been supplanted by a two-storey wing, giving
extra accommodation on the first floor. This plan occurs in a signifi-

above

Low Yewdale Farm, Coniston. Here the rear extension has developed into a full wing housing a staircase and larder on the ground floor and an additional bedloft on the first floor. At the front of the house on the ground floor, the two windows to the left of the door light the firehouse, the one nearest the gable being the fire-window. The window to the right of the door lights the unheated parlour.

cant number of houses in and around Hawkshead and Coniston. In only two cases does the wing appear to be original; in all other houses the wing shows signs of being an addition or at least a rebuilding. In several, such as Hill Top Farm, Near Sawrey, a large first-floor landing suggests that the houses originally had internal staircases and therefore internal butteries. Evidence that some of the parlours were formerly divided tends to confirm this, or at least suggests that the butteries were moved from within the house to an outshut at some point. At High Arnside Farm, Coniston, the wing appears to be original for here the rear wall of the firehouse is of oak muntin-and-plank panelled construction, in contrast to houses where the wing is an addition and a solid wall is found in this position.

High Arnside is an almost perfectly preserved example of this type of house-plan: all the elaborate internal joinery (floors, panelling, doors, stairs and cupboards) survives intact, and there is a date of 1697 on the spice cupboard. Low Tock How, Hawkshead, also appears to have an original wing, although the internal layout has been much altered, the house being divided into two in the 1950s. It contains one remarkable feature – a fragment of a wall-painting which originally covered much of one upstairs room. This decoration was revealed in 1966 during alterations and half a square yard remains exposed. The design, attributed on stylistic grounds to the period 1680–1730, is of free-flowing flowers and foliage executed in yellow, red and a dark blue-black. (Wall-paintings on plaster have so far been recorded at only one other house in the area, namely Wood Farm, Troutbeck.)

The first-floor layout of High Arnside, like that of most of the other houses of this plan found in the Coniston area, differs from the three-room layout so far described for truss-roofed houses. This type has a large room at the head of the stairs, incorporating the firehood; the remainder of the space is divided lengthwise to form a front and back room above the parlour. The back room is lit by a window at the rear of the house. This is one of the few occasions where houses were lit at the back at first-floor level until double-pile houses were introduced after the middle of the eighteenth century.

Many of these buttery outshuts and wings have had chimneys added at a later date, turning them into kitchens/downhouses or wash-houses. A few may have been built originally with chimneys. Staveley Park, Staveley, could be an instance, although the house had a wing large enough to be divided at ground-floor level into one heated and one unheated room, and so still contained a buttery.

Two- and Three-Bay Houses, Non-Gable Entry

right
Low Tilberthwaite Farm, Coniston.

below
Stepps End Farm, Watendlath, formerly known as Above Becks Farm.
This early-eighteenth-century house has a layout similar to the one in the next illustration. Its massive porch with slate benches shelters a studded oak front door.

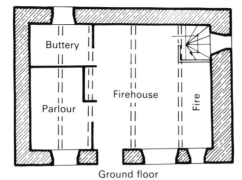

Ground floor

The dominant characteristic here is the position of the stairs next to the fireplace, which makes a gable entrance impossible. The staircase is always tucked in between the heck and the gable wall. The main entrance is in the centre of the front or window wall and leads straight into the firehouse. A second important characteristic of such houses is their small size; even three-bay examples are almost always smaller than three-bay houses with a gable entry. These plans are most commonly found in Coniston and Langdale; very few survive in Hawkshead or Borrowdale, for example. In some cases the house is so small that it was clearly impracticable to subdivide the upper end beyond the screen. Four houses in Coniston have such an undivided space, presumably used as a parlour rather than a buttery (although this is not clear from what remains). Even though some of these houses are tiny their interiors are by no means unembellished. Low Hallgarth, Little Langdale, has a large, impressively decorated cupboard dated 1682 and set into the screen partition in the firehouse; presumably it is contemporary with the building of the house. Many have muntin-and-plank partitions similar in form and detailing to those of much grander houses.

right
Low Hallgarth Farm, Little Langdale.
The staircase in this small house is tucked in next to the fireplace. The main door always seems to have been on the front or window side, rather than in the gable-end. Inside, a fitted cupboard is dated 1682. The barn to the right is of full-cruck construction and predates the house.

HOUSES WITH DOWNHOUSES

The provision of a downhouse was not the norm; only the more prosperous farmhouses seem to have had a separate kitchen/brewhouse. The downhouse was occasionally in a separate building, in which case it usually took the form of one room open to the rafters with a fireplace on one of the gable walls, the whole building being built parallel to the farmhouse. Much more commonly the downhouse was part of the main farmhouse range. In the majority of buildings so far studied, the downhouse shows signs of having been added on, usually at the firehouse end or at the back of the building. These two positions will be looked at separately.

Downhouses at Firehouse End of House

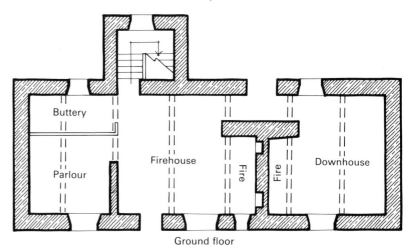

Caffle House, Watendlath.

Ground floor

The downhouse in this position could be either one or two storeys in height. If the latter, the upper storey was not always connected to the main house, sometimes having separate access from the outside. Single-storey downhouses are now very rare. Hill Top, Near Sawrey, had one before Beatrix Potter altered the house in the early 1900s; a good example still exists at High Skelghyll Farm, Ambleside. In some houses, particularly in Borrowdale, the downhouse fire and the firehouse fire were arranged back to back, with the main entrance opposite the side wall of the two fires and opening into a small lobby which gave access to both firehouse and downhouse. This plan looks superficially similar to the classic lobby-entrance plan found extensively in seventeenth-century houses in the south of England. Closer inspection shows that the Lake District examples (and indeed northern examples in general) differ from the southern norm in two important respects. First, the main door is next to the stairs at the 'back' of the house, rather than being on the same face as the main windows. Secondly, the room behind the firehouse is not a parlour

above
Hill Top Farm, Near Sawrey, c.1900
The lean-to on the left was a one-storey downhouse. This was rebuilt as a two-storey wing in 1905, when Beatrix Potter bought the farm.

above right
Wallend Farm, Great Langdale.
The door on the left leads to a downhouse, the firehouse is in the centre and the parlour on the right. The slit to the left of the centre window is a spyhole, covered in the daytime by shutters but open at night when the shutters are closed over the main windows, thus giving visibility to the road outside.

right
Simpson House, Low Hartsop.
The main door gives access into the downhouse, at the right of the building, and from there to the firehouse through a door to one side of the main fire. The outshut houses the stairs and larder. Notice the crow-stepped gable.

but a downhouse. In the south of England a desire for privacy seems to have been one of the main motives for the lobby-entrance plan, the lobby providing an independent access to the parlour. In the Lake District on the other hand, until the mid-eighteenth century, the parlour remained at the upper end of the house – a sort of inner sanctum to which only family members were admitted, having first crossed the public housebody.

Downhouse in a Rear Wing

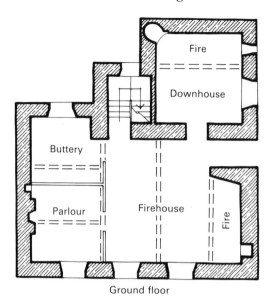

Fire

Downhouse

Buttery

Parlour

Firehouse

Fire

Ground floor

right
Townhead Farm, Grasmere.

below
Townhead Farm, Grasmere.
The gable entrance leads into
the firehouse. The wing on the
right houses a downhouse with
bedloft above. The arrangement
of the downhouse fire is unusual
in having a fire-window. Usually
only the main firehouse fire was
lit in this way.

It is sometimes difficult to distinguish between a buttery in a back
wing to which a fireplace has been added at a later date, and one in
which the fireplace is original. The size and build of the chimneys
gives a guide. At Staveley Park, Staveley, the chimney in the rear wing
appears to be original. It also seems to have been built at the same
time as the fireplace in the chamber over the firehouse; this has a
dated overmantel of 1682, which thus gives a probable date for the
downhouse wing. Town Head Farm, Grasmere, has a downhouse
with what appears to be an original firebeam, suggesting that the
chimney is contemporary with the wing.

STATESMAN'S PLAN

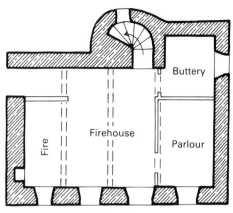

Buttery

Byre

Fire

Firehouse

Parlour

Ground floor

A typical statesman's plan for Lake District houses has often been described: a three-bay house with a firehouse in the centre, a buttery and parlour at the upper end, and at the lower end a downhouse separated from the firehouse by a cross-passage. James Clarke, writing in 1787, was perhaps responsible for coining the description and giving the name 'hallan' to the cross-passage, off which opened both the downhouse and the firehouse. Other writers have taken up his suggestion. Unfortunately only a small number of houses measured have plans that fit this stereotype exactly. Henhow, Martindale, (a farmhouse long since abandoned), Causeway Farm, Windermere, and Glencoyne Farm, Ullswater, are three good examples. Several other houses have a modified version of the plan with the downhouse undivided from the hallan and with doors in opposing walls. Instances are Thrang Crag and the abandoned farm at Dale Head, both in Martindale. These arrangements are possible only if the downhouse chimney does not back on to the firehouse chimney. The one broad generalization that can be made is that the plan exists more commonly in the east of the region. In the central and western valleys, where

above right
Beckstones Farm, Patterdale.

right
Glencoyne Farm, Ullswater.
This farm is one of the few with a through-passage across the house with a door at each end. The firehouse with its small fire-window is to the left of the porch and the former downhouse to the right. Notice the circular chimneys and crow-stepped gables – the latter apparently added since the early nineteenth century.

downhouses exist at all, they tend to have chimneys back to back with the firehouse chimney, making a cross-passage impossible.

LONGHOUSES

It is sometimes suggested that cross- or hearth-passage houses, found in several regions of England, developed independently from two sources. One source is thought to be the mediaeval 'gentry houses', which had service rooms at the lower end separated from the hall by a screen and cross-passage. The second source is said to be the longhouse, which housed both people and animals under one roof and was divided by a 'through-passage' giving access on one side to the byre and on the other to the hall.

Mediaeval hall houses such as Yanwath Hall may possibly have influenced the much later cross-passage houses in the central Lakes. It is equally possible that they may have been reflecting a local longhouse tradition. Elsewhere where examples of longhouses have survived, such as Northumberland and parts of Ireland, the variety of plans shows that longhouses embraced a wide social range. Some are merely small one-room houses with a central hearth and no division between men and animals; others are substantially built in stone with a wide through-passage and dividing walls between byre and house.

In only a few of the houses so far studied in the Lake District is a longhouse plan discernible. One example is Wall End, Deepdale, where the byre is still extant. A second is Beckstones Farm, Patterdale, where the present downhouse fire is in a wall across what was formerly a byre. The reconstructed plan is shown on page 65. Elsewhere a number of houses do have small byres attached to one end, with

right
Millbeck Farm, Great Langdale.
Here a small byre and loft (both now converted to domestic use) are set apart from the main house by lack of render. In this case they are at the firehouse end of the house backing on to the main chimney, and a barn is attached to the parlour end.

above
High Birk Howe Farm, Little Langdale.
A few houses have a small byre, with loft above, attached to one end of the house. In this case the byre is differentiated from the main house in the way the outside walls are treated. They are whitewashed directly on to the stone rather than on to a render as is the rest of the front. The byre is at the parlour end of the house.

above right
Townend Cottage, Colthouse.
This house was built in 1703. The front door appears to be in its original position. The stairs rise up next to the fireplace. The windows have been enlarged and altered. A barn, built later than the house, is attached to the parlour end.

lofts over, but their entrances are quite separate from that of the main house. Interestingly, these byres are often found at the upper or parlour end of the house, rather than at the lower end behind the firehouse fire. Examples of this layout are at High Birk Howe, Little Langdale, and Birks Farmhouse, Underbarrow. Other houses have much larger barns attached, with underhousing for cattle below and grain and hay storage lofts above, but again many of these barns are attached to the parlour end of the building. Such an arrangement is particularly common in the Hawkshead area (as at Town End Cottage, Colthouse) and in Borrowdale (as at Stepps End, Watendlath). Most appear from building joints to be of a later date than the house. In one instance – at Oak Cottage, Rosthwaite – the barn appears to have been a rebuilding and extension of an earlier downhouse rather than a barn subsequently converted into a downhouse.

A few farmhouses, such as Cropple How, Muncaster, have a cross-passage between house and barn without direct entrance to either. At How Green Farm, Hartsop, a passage (but not a through-passage) separates house and barn but gives access to the house alone. Houses with barns attached are by no means the norm, and indeed the arrangement is very rare in the case of the earliest single-storey threshing-barns.

The source of these cross-passage houses must remain uncertain until archaeological work reveals more about the fifteenth- and sixteenth-century houses in this area.

THREE-BAY HOUSES WITH STAIRS, BUTTERY AND DOWNHOUSE WITHIN THE MAIN ROOF

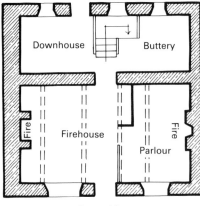

Ground floor

The plans so far considered have indicated a gradual evolution in the layout of houses, with service rooms and stairs being moved from within the main block first into outshuts and then later into two-storey wings. The next logical step was to incorporate these extra rooms beneath the main roof, producing a so-called 'double-pile house' with a ridge central to the whole building rather than just to the firehouse. This type of building still often had a gable entrance, and at the front a firehouse with firehood and a parlour; at the rear the space was taken up by stairs in the centre, with a buttery to one side behind the parlour, and a downhouse to the other side behind the firehouse.

above right
Ghyll Farm, Netherwasdale.

right
Yew Tree Farm, Coniston.
This farmhouse was built in two distinct phases and is now L-shaped in plan. The older rear wing (not visible in the photograph) is of cruck construction. The later wing was added in 1743. In the new wing, both the door and the staircase are off-centre with, on the ground floor, a firehouse on the left and a parlour on the right. There is no firebeam. The firehouse was built with a stone chimney-breast and a raised fire.

This double-pile plan was adopted as the norm in very few valleys; it occurs sporadically over the whole area and predominates only in the most westerly valleys such as Wasdale. In many cases, such as Ghyll Farm, Wasdale, it seems the plan was achieved in three phases. First a stair and buttery outshut was built, then it was raised to first-floor height, and lastly it was extended across the width of the building, the roof being heightened and widened to cover the extension. The roof of the new wider house was adapted to take account of its greater depth: two rows of purlins were no longer sufficient, so three were used on each side. To help carry this extra weight of slate, king-post trusses began to be used rather than the simple collar-brace type.

The downstairs layout of these houses was largely repeated on the first floor, the stairs giving access to four rooms, one in each corner.

DOUBLE-PILE HOUSES WITH CENTRAL DOORWAYS

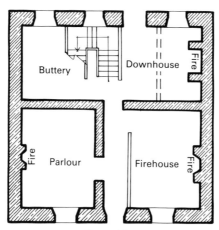

Ground floor

right
High Snab Farm, Newlands.

The second type of double-pile house took much longer to develop and was a more radical departure from previous layouts. All the plans so far discussed had the firehouse as the centre of the house; the main door opened into the firehouse which acted as a central circulation space for family life. Elsewhere in the country, from the mid-seventeenth century, gentry houses of double depth were being built, with a central front door leading into a passage off which opened the parlour and the firehouse, the latter having a stone chimney-stack rather than a chimney-hood. Very few early examples exist in this area. As the eighteenth century wore on, however, the advantages of this plan began to be accepted by some yeoman farmers. The new plan was far more centralized, giving easy access to all rooms; but more important, it also provided much greater privacy. No longer did rooms open off one another either on the ground floor or on the first floor. The parlour and stairs could be gained from the hall, the service rooms from a rear lobby next to the stairs; and the position of the stairs meant the bedrooms could all be reached from a small central landing. The central doorway allowed the front of the house to be symmetrically arranged, with a window either side of the door and three at first-floor level. This symmetry, like some other aspects of the plan, did not appear in the earliest double-pile houses; it was achieved during the course of the eighteenth century almost as a logical development of what lay within.

In the western valleys especially, existing houses were adapted or even rebuilt to reflect some or all aspects of this new planning. This change was far more fundamental than anything that had gone before; it was a move away from the distinctive local plan towards an emerging national fashion. Not everyone approved. In all generations it is the self-assigned prerogative of travellers and outsiders to criticize new amenities and fashions and applaud the quaintness of traditional life. The eighteenth-century travellers and 'offcomers' to the Lake District were no exception. De Quincey bemoaned the disappearance of the ancient architecture of Hartsop; and the Revd William Ford wrote of Haweswater:

> all is rural beauty and silvan sweetness . . . I only regret that the ancient cottage with its accompaniements is superceded by the modern house with its five windows in front. I should have preferred . . . the ancient cottage with its antiquated windows, its lowely roof fringed with moss, and its chimneys smoking through the trees, as the abode of quiet and the home of solitude. The change here so eloquently lamented has, unfortunately, so often been the case in numerous instances, which the stranger will have been obliged to notice.

The reality was less of a wholesale change than Ford was suggesting. Many valleys did not enjoy increased affluence in the late eighteenth and early nineteenth centuries, so that the older houses were left relatively untouched. Only the offcomers built new boxes. In the western valleys, however, the flourishing ports of Whitehaven and Maryport brought a prosperity which was not experienced elsewhere to the same degree. With the new-found wealth many farmhouses were rebuilt on the double-pile plan. In a few cases the building was completely resited at some distance from the old house, which was left to crumble away as at Bengarth, Wasdale. Other houses were altered by extending the roof to cover outshuts and by inserting new front doors and symmetrically arranged windows. The prosperity was relatively short-lived; by the 1850s, Wasdale was experiencing the same economic problems as other valleys and very few major alterations or rebuildings date from this time. Compared with its fellows, Wasdale thus has a notably different feel; it reflects the tastes and fashions of the late eighteenth and early nineteenth centuries and now accommodates a collection of early double-pile houses with

below

Harrowhead Farm, Wasdale. This is now a 'double-pile' building, two rooms deep. Like several others in Wasdale, it almost certainly developed from an earlier seventeenth-century house one room deep. The front door is now roughly in the centre of the house and opens into a passage. On one side is the firehouse, on the other the parlour. At the back are the downhouse and larder, with a dog-leg staircase rising centrally between them.

above
above
Heelis office, Hawkshead.
Ferdinando Taylor, a local
architect, was possibly
responsible for redesigning the
front of this building in the
1840s. But behind the
somewhat elaborate facade, the
plan of the seventeenth-century
house can still be discerned. The
door opens into what was the
firehouse. A stone stack has
been built within the space of
the firehood.

remarkably complete interiors. Harrowhead, Wasdale, is typical. Its
central doorway is surrounded by a dressed sandstone porch, with
two upright slabs for the sides below an arched stone lintel. The
central passageway has some oak panelling (on only one wall, suggesting that the other wall is an addition), but here the muntin-and-plank
type found in earlier houses gives way to fielded panels beneath a
dentillated frieze. Both the ground and first floors have four rooms,
each occupying a corner of the building. The firehouse is small (only
twelve foot in length) and, like all the other rooms, almost square in
plan. It has a compact stone chimney-stack projecting only two feet
into the room instead of the earlier arrangement of a firebeam
supporting a wide hood.

In much of the rest of the central Lakes, comprehensive remodelling
and rebuilding such as happened in Wasdale did not take place.
Nevertheless in a few areas and a century later, phases of prosperity,
similar to those which must have produced the significant differences
in plan between one valley and the next in the seventeenth century,
brought about smaller-scale amendments to the three-unit firehouse/
parlour/buttery plan. In the Hawkshead and Sawrey area, a certain
prosperity in the late eighteenth century and the first half of the
nineteenth (based largely on the Furness coppice woodlands to the

south and west of the town rather than on sheep-farming), led to an upgrading of houses so that they appeared at least from the front to be fashionable double-piled houses with symmetrical façades. Low Greengate, Near Sawrey, now has a central front door (beneath a delightful blind fanlight framed by an open pediment supported on fluted pilasters) and five shuttered sash windows arranged symmetrically around it. Inside the house, the old seventeenth-century plan remains but with the original front door blocked and a central passageway from the new front door inserted across one end of the firehouse; the fire-window has been blanked off and the old hearth fire replaced by a hob grate. Very similar alterations took place at Greenend Cottage, Colthouse, but there the owners chose not to go through the major upheaval of realigning windows; so existing openings were merely adapted to take sashes, the fire-window was blocked, and a new centrally placed panelled front door was added, protected by a trellis porch. This achieved a semblance of symmetry.

More extensive alterations were carried out at the Heelis solicitor's office in Hawkshead (now the Beatrix Potter Gallery), where the façade was completely remodelled in the mid-nineteenth century, leaving it with a deep projecting cornice, a Venetian window, several sashes, and a small bay at ground-floor level. Interestingly, the interior was touched much less; the seventeenth-century layout is still discernible and much seventeenth-century joinery and plank-and-plaster walling have been retained. The remodelling of this building could be the work of Ferdinando Taylor (who despite his name was from a local family) who lived for part of his life at Blackbeck Cottage, Hawkshead, and also kept the Red Lion Hotel. He was a plasterer by training but also a self-taught architect, and H. S. Cowper records that he had a taste for architecture and designed several houses in the valley. At about the same time as the Heelis office was altered he remodelled his own residence, turning a narrow seventeenth-century gable-entry house into a petite villa which had gables, bays and ornamental bargeboards, and bore some of the hallmarks of the new Heelis office façade.

But essays such as Ferdinando Taylor's were unusual. Most alterations done at this time in Hawkshead and in other valleys were the work of unlettered local joiners and builders, and were confined to rearranging windows and providing a central passage to give a polite façade and a private parlour separate from the houseplace.

4

Animals

SHEEP

TODAY THE most common breed of sheep in the central Lakes is the Herdwick. Indeed it is unique to this area and is thus often regarded as an indigenous breed. The term 'Herdwick' originally referred not to the sheep but to the land upon which the sheep grazed. In 1537 the Cistercian abbey of Furness was said to have a number of 'Herdwykes' or separate holdings in the lands of upper Eskdale. By the eighteenth century the name had become firmly attached to the animal itself and the earliest illustration, of 1787, shows an animal with a coarse brown-grey fleece and white face, just like those now grazing the Lakeland fells.

There are several legends about the origins of Herdwick sheep: one suggests that forty animals swam ashore from a Scandinavian vessel shipwrecked on the west coast, perhaps in the tenth century. But in fact there is very little reliable information for breeds anywhere in the country before the eighteenth century, by which time much of the west – Wales, south-west England, Cumbria and Lancashire – had white- or tan-faced sheep with coarse wool and hornless ewes. Within that group, as well as the Herdwick, were variations such as the Cheviot and Welsh Mountain breeds. The most distinctive difference between the Herdwick and other British hill breeds is the possession of heterotype hairs which are coarse in summer but grow to fine wool in winter. This feature is found elsewhere only on some Scandinavian breeds such as the primitive Goth sheep. Perhaps there is some truth in the shipwreck theory after all.

The crucial reason for the persistence of the Herdwick breed in the cold, wet uplands of the Lake District is its legendary hardiness. The earliest description of Herdwick sheep, written in 1787, mentions their stamina and their ability to stand exposure to the coldest winter weather much better than other breeds. They thrive on relatively poor pastures and can be left on the fells all winter, surviving in snow-drifts for as long as fourteen days by drinking melted snow and living off their own fat, or even sometimes by eating each other's wool.

In the eighteenth century it was said that most farmers had either pure or half-bred Herdwicks. What they were crossed with at that date is not at all clear – possibly a 'Black-faced Heath breed', apparently common in east Westmorland in the eighteenth and nineteenth centuries and from which developed the Rough Fell and Swaledale sheep. By the nineteenth century several local farmers were experimenting with breeds new to the area, producing Herdwick and other crosses. In the 1870s George Browne of Townend, Troutbeck, responding to the demands of the Yorkshire woollen trade for fine, lustrous wool for ladies' dresses, built up a celebrated flock of Leicester–Cheviot crosses with long, fine fleeces. He commissioned the local artist W. Taylor Longmire to paint these and his other sheep against backdrops of the Troutbeck valley. The paintings still hang in Townend. Today very few farms run pure Herdwick flocks; many have mixed flocks, Herdwicks running with Swaledales (known locally as Swaddles or Swardles) and Herdwick–Swaledale crosses. Dalesbred and Rough Fell sheep are also now commonly kept.

Herdwicks, like many mountain sheep both in Britain and in other parts of Europe, have the ability to identify with the particular piece of fell on which they were weaned and will always return to their own heaf if they stray. Such sheep are said to be 'heafed' or 'hefted'. Building up a totally heafed flock obviously takes several generations; such a flock cannot be readily moved to another fell or even to another part of the same fell, for the sheep will use their homing instinct to try and get back to their original heaf.

Herdwick sheep, Taw House Farm, Eskdale.
At birth the fleece of Herdwick sheep is dark grey, turning a lighter grey at maturity.

Numerous stories are told of sheep returning from many miles away to where they were originally weaned. Even Little Bo-Peep knew about heafing: 'Leave them alone and they'll come home bringing their tails behind them.' Sheep flocks firmly tied to one farm or one area of fell were thus often passed on as fixtures to new tenants or owners when a farm changed hands. Even today on many farms the land and sheep are let together; a stated stocking of sheep, known as the 'landlord's flock', goes with the farm and the outgoing tenant agrees to pass on to the incoming tenant an equivalent number of sheep to that which he himself took over.

SHEEP PRODUCTS

Of all domesticated animals, sheep probably provide the greatest range of products for their owner: wool and milk while they are alive and meat, fat (tallow), skin for parchment and apparel, and bone and horn after their deaths.

Wool

The relative value of all these products has changed over the centuries, but the most pronounced fluctuations have been in the value of wool and meat. It has been estimated that in mediaeval times a fleece accounted for about half the value of a sheep; by the eighteenth century this proportion had been reduced to less than a third, an average price for wool being one shilling and threepence and for meat three shillings. Today the fleece is worth no more than 10 per cent of the value of the sheep; indeed, so low is the price that many farmers get for the coarse Herdwick fleeces that they claim it is hardly worth their while to go to the trouble of shearing the sheep. This dramatic drop in price is largely explained by the improvements in breeding and fodder that have taken place elsewhere in the country since the Middle Ages, leaving the Lake District – for reasons that will have become apparent – as one of the last resorts of sheep with short, coarse wool.

There is evidence to suggest that in the twelfth century much of England's output was coarse wool from sheep similar to Herdwicks, only one out of approximately a hundred producing fine wool. By the fifteenth century, with the introduction of Merino sheep from Spain into some parts of the country and improvements in fodder and pastures, as well as in breeding, the pattern had become more variable. Much of the centre of England, from Hereford in the west and Hampshire in the south up to Yorkshire in the north, produced fine wool, the coarse wool being left to the uplands of the Lake District, Wales and the south-west. Even so, surviving price lists from abbey account books in the fourteenth and fifteenth centuries show that some coarse wool continued to command relatively high prices.

In Cumbria ten to eleven marks per sack was given for wool as against the highest price of fourteen marks for fine Hereford wool and the lowest of less than six marks for wool from Devon and Cornwall. Interestingly, 8 per cent of the annual production of 2,400 lb. of wool from the Fountains Abbey estates was 'grisia' wool, a grey-brown wool that may have come from the abbey lands in Borrowdale.

By the end of the sixteenth century, with the demise of the monastic wool trade, much of the wool production of the central Lakes was finding its way to Kendal market to be woven, undyed, into a coarse grey material known as Kendal cloth. By this time such cloth was firmly associated with the poor, the grey-brown wool no longer commanding a high price.

> A man about fifty years of age
> of Kendal very coarse his coat was made
> upon his gyrdle hung rustye blade
> This was a husband man, a simple hinde

wrote one anonymous writer in 1577; 'Your meane yet necessarie commodities' was how the Reverend Ralph Tyrer, vicar of Kendal in the early seventeenth century, saw the foundation of his town's wealth. Immortalized by John Peel in his 'coat so grey', Kendal cloth, both the undyed grey variety and Kendal green, continued to be made until the mid-nineteenth century. Pack-horse trains carried wool from Borrowdale and other Lakeland valleys into Kendal until as late as the 1870s.

SHEEP HUSBANDRY

Monastic practice

In mediaeval times peasant colonies were largely confined to the valley bottoms, while the valley heads and higher reaches of the fells were exploited by the landholders, both lay and monastic. Initially the latter areas were used as cattle ranches, known as vaccaries, and later as vast sheep-granges. The Cistercians were the outstanding sheep-farmers, not only in the north-west, where their principal houses were Furness Abbey and Holme Cultram, but also in Yorkshire and the east Midlands. Their largest house, Fountains Abbey in Yorkshire, did, however, have its most westerly holdings bordering the Furness Abbey lands at the south end of Derwentwater.

So well organized was the monastic wool trade that Holme Cultram had one monk assigned exclusively to it. He was known as the monk *de Lanificio* (i.e. of wool-working). Most of the wool produced by the monastery was sold to itinerant Italian merchants for export. The records of one Italian buyer, Pergolitti, in about 1315, list his transactions with Furness Abbey and show that it exported some seventy-six sacks of wool. It has been estimated that this would have been the produce of 20,000 sheep, a sack weighing 364 lb.

Little detail can be gleaned from documentary sources about how the monasteries organized their land or how they interacted with local farmers in the Lake District. It is improbable that they took over uncolonized spaces, and much more likely that they took over existing colonies of small-scale farms. We do know, however, that monasteries not only sold their own wool but also traded in the wool of local farmers which was sold with their own in a system known as *collecta*. Entries in the Fountains Abbey lease book relating to Borrowdale also reveal that small farms and hamlets whose names are still recognizable today, such as Staynthwaite (Stonethwaite), were given on long leases of between twenty and thirty-five years to local tenants, and it appears that these tenants herded the flocks within their care. These small farms would have been co-ordinated by monastic granges where the affairs of an area were managed and the accounts kept. Hawkshead, for example, became a grange for Furness Abbey, overseeing the land between Coniston Lake and Windermere; and the hamlet of Grange-in-Borrowdale was established by Furness Abbey, perhaps in the thirteenth or fourteenth century, to control its holdings in Borrowdale.

Thorough investigation and partial excavation of one of the Fountains Abbey granges at Malham in Yorkshire, has yielded valuable information on how its sheep-rearing activities were organized. What happened at Malham can probably be taken as standard for all granges on the estate. Malham seems to have been the centre of a collection of small farms each of which provided a base for several hundred sheep. There were small meadows where hay was grown and enclosed pastures for grazing various groups of sheep; in one such field, lambs were apparently fed cows' milk in order to save the more highly prized ewes' milk, which was made into cheese. Written records mention two large sheep houses; one has been excavated. It consisted of a large rectangular building with internal dimensions of approximately 48 feet × 13 feet, built against an enclosure wall, and a yard with an open lean-to of the same length. Massive boulders laid on edge provided the base of the walls and supported posts at three-foot intervals. These posts were probably clad with timber boards, for in 1290 the building was repaired using 1,000 boards; the cost included 23 pence for drinks for the men who carted the timbers. The roof was probably either thatched or clad by wooden shingles. Down the centre of the main buildings ran a paved gangway, which suggests that there were standings for animals on either side.

Precisely how these sheep houses were managed is unclear. Sheep housing seems to have been built all over Europe in the Middle Ages and sheep-wintering sheds are illustrated in books such as the fifteenth-century *Très Riches Heures du duc de Berry*, which shows a long thatched building with half-height wattle walls. Similar buildings, sometimes curved like a horseshoe, with full-height matting walls and thatched roofs, are still erected today in Bulgaria for the winter housing of sheep. Mediaeval examples seem to have been used like their modern counterparts, the animals being brought down in the winter months to pastures surrounding the houses into which they were put at night and perhaps also during the day in severe weather. Shepherds would have fed the animals with hay. Clearly the two sheep houses at Malham cannot have housed all the flocks from the surrounding farms. We cannot be certain which sheep were put under cover and which remained outdoors on the surrounding fields or even on the fells. Probably the yearlings and the milking ewes were kept inside. If the pattern at Malham was at all typical of monastic arrangements in general, then sheep housing of some sort was probably widespread across the Lake District in the Middle Ages; but remains of such buildings have yet to be identified.

In many parts of Europe sheep housing was abandoned at the end of the mediaeval period. The Lake District was one of the few areas of England (another being north-east Yorkshire) in which the practice continued until as late as the eighteenth century. Elsewhere the practice is known only from documentary evidence, but in the Lake District many sheep-wintering buildings survived to be studied.

Tenant Farms

By the 1550s most land in the Lake District was in the hands of small farmers. Their farmsteads were surrounded by arable fields grouped loosely across the valley bottoms, each farm having grazing rights on the higher fells. The pattern that largely subsists today had been established.

Farmers kept both sheep and cattle, some small farmers having no more sheep than cattle. Thomas Dixon of Scale Farm, Netherwasdale, who died in 1670, had only seven sheep on his tiny twelve-acre farm; at the other end of the spectrum, Glencoyne Farm, Ullswater, was recorded in 1785 as having 687 sheep (plus another fifteen which were found when the flock was counted to be taken over by the incoming tenant). The average size of flocks in the eighteenth century was probably about one hundred, like that at Blea Tarn Farm, Little Langdale, which had 117 sheep in 1698 and almost the same number, 120, when it was next sold in 1773.

Fell Grazing

In theory the unimproved land of the fells over which the farms had grazing rights was common to all farmers in the valley; in practice it was often divided, not by physical boundaries but by a code of practice regulated by the manor courts. The lower, more sheltered, pastures were kept for cattle while grazing on the higher fells was reserved for sheep, with each farm or small group of farms having a named heaf. In Eskdale on the western flanks of Scafell there were three sheep heafs: Hardrigg for the flocks of Spout House and Borrowdale Place farms, Broad Tongue for Hows, Gill Bank, and Paddockwray farms, and Quagrigg for the Boot farms. Similarly on the fell-land above Wasdale Head, seven blocks of land were each named as separate heafs in 1664: Green How, Lingmell, Coves (between Great Gable and Scafell Pikes), Kirk Fell, Betwixtbecks (the flanks of Pillar), Capplecragg (the flanks of Red Pike) and Yewbarrow.

For such an arrangement to work, flocks have to be regulated – otherwise if one farmer overstocks, his animals will begin to stray on to other heafs. Surviving records of manorial courts between the mid-sixteenth and mid-seventeenth centuries show how much regulation was needed to keep sheep in the right places. However careful the control, some sheep inevitably strayed on to other farms' heafs. Returning these strays was formalized into social gatherings called meets. These took place every year around September just at the time when sheep were being brought down off the fells. Farmers would gather primarily to exchange strays but also to enjoy horse-racing, wrestling and suchlike country diversions. Until 1835 farmers from Hartsop, Troutbeck, Mardale and Kentmere met on the summit of High Street. Today farmers' meets are still held, but on lower ground and in more convivial surroundings.

Even though grazing is far less complicated today than in the sixteenth and seventeenth centuries, with very few cattle being grazed on the fells, disputes are frequent and the mechanism for solving them through the manorial courts is no longer available. Consequently, pressure for enclosing heafs is especially strong on freehold fells (which are no longer commons) in areas where, for botanic or conservation reasons, flocks have to be reduced in numbers. It would be sad indeed if wire fences began to criss-cross the open fells, and if a system of mutual co-operation which has persisted since at least early mediaeval times were to break down not in the face of commercial expansion, but to meet the needs of conservation.

From as early as the sixteenth century in some valleys, and more generally in the seventeenth century, the lower cattle-grazing area of the fells began to be enclosed and tied to specific farms. The creation of these 'intakes' sometimes blocked the tracks from farms to their sheep heafs on the higher fells and led to the building of drift ways or outgangs, walled tracks leading from the farm through the new intakes and out on to the open fells. In some valleys each farm had an outgang and their survival can sometimes help identify the site of an old farmstead. Ash Busk in Great Langdale was amalgamated with Stool End in the eighteenth century and although the farmhouse no longer stands, a few pollarded ash trees delineate the site from which an outgang leads to the open fell. These outgangs were jealously guarded and were certainly not considered public rights of way. In

· 1654 a dispute over who had rights over an outgang between Rossett and Middlefell Place Farms in Great Langdale got as far as the manorial courts.

Winter Housing

In 1797 it was noted that

> Almost all the sheep ... except the wedders after the first year are brought from the mountains on the approach of winter and kept in the inclosed ground until the month of April ... The wedders remain until they are four and a half years old and are then sold. After lambing ewes are sent back to wastes where the flock pastures indiscriminately without an attendant.

Farmers divided their flocks into four groups: rams (tups) for breeding, wethers (wedders), castrated males kept for their wool and meat, ewes for breeding, together with their lambs, and gimmers and hoggs (young ewes and yearling sheep respectively). Only wethers were grazed on the fells all year round; in the winter months the ewes and the younger sheep were brought down to lower pastures where they were fed and sheltered in a way not dissimilar to the monastic practice.

The small buildings used for sheltering these animals are known as hogg houses. A significant number survive, especially in the eastern valleys. They were typically sited against a wall in one of the higher hayfields near the fell boundary. Most have a loft and are built on sloping ground with two entrances, one to the loft at the higher level and one to the underhousing beneath. In some of the more exposed sites, such as the most southerly one at Hartsop Hall Farm on the lower slopes of Kirkstone Pass, the hogg houses are given their own small enclosure within which there is a shelter belt of trees.

On the western slopes of the Troutbeck valley above Townend Farm, one fairly sizeable hogg house was built alongside a track used by sheep for getting from the higher to the lower pastures. The building is sited at the narrowest part of the track, and alongside the hogg house a covered stone tunnel was erected, running for some twenty yards. This is known as a sheep creep and allows sheep to escape if snow is blown across the track and blocks their way down. The tunnel was restored in 1985 and is still used for the purpose for which it was originally designed.

The lofts of the hogg houses were used for fodder, usually hay from the surrounding fields, and this was fed to the animals sheltering below. Typically, the lower spaces of these buildings were undivided and were floored with beaten earth possibly covered with bracken for bedding. In all buildings so far examined, the walls were built dry with no mortar between the courses. A most picturesque hogg house is to be found on the island in Grasmere; mentioned by Thomas Machell in 1692, it is built around an outcrop of rock and sheltered by Scots pines, the whole island forming a small, safe winter pasture for sheep.

At some stage, as yet undetermined, these small buildings began to fall out of use and the practice of keeping sheep indoors during the winter months was abandoned. In 1797 it was said that in 'Eskdale and Miterdale they formerly kept their hoggs in the house all winter on hay, and drove them to water once a day; but all this practice is now laid aside and they winter them upon the inclosed grounds'. This change seems to have been linked to the advent of the idea of moving sheep, except those overwintered on the fells, to a lower-lying area away from their home farm where either the weather was slightly less harsh or there was simply more valley-bottom land available than in the valley-head farms. This sort of transhumance apparently gained ground in the late eighteenth century and is still in use today.

The distances travelled were sometimes fairly small; in the 1920s sheep from Brotherilkeld Farm, Eskdale, went to Cunsey; from parts of Little Langdale they were sent to Cartmel Fell and the Winster valley, while in the 1950s Mr Grizedale of Baysbrown Farm, Langdale, sent his hoggs and shearlings to Coniston which is only eight or ten miles away. More common now is the transfer of sheep in October to the wide grassy meadows of the Duddon estuary or around Morecambe Bay, whence they are brought back in early April. Some sheep are sent even further to Lincolnshire and Leicestershire to graze on the remains of the sugar-beet harvest.

Winter Fodder

Although hay was the principal fodder it was by no means the only crop fed to sheep during the winter months. Hollies grow widely in the lower valleys, especially in the central and western areas. The dozens of isolated hollies in Eskdale are a notable feature of that valley and holly clippings were commonly given to sheep. Writing in 1774, Thomas West suggested one good reason for this practice: 'At the shepherd's call the flocks surround the holly bush, and receive croppings at his hand, which they greedily nibble up and bleat for more. . . . The mutton thus fed has a remarkably fine flavour.' West thought he was witnessing the tail-end of a mediaeval custom; it persisted longer than he anticipated, for as late as 1957–8 Harry Greenhow, farming Harry Place in Langdale, was still cutting holly for his sheep in the winter months.

Ash-leaves were also highly prized as fodder. The ash-trees were grown in hedges or alongside walls and were pollarded at about eight to twelve feet from the ground every twelve years or so. The cutting was usually done in early autumn, the thin, straight branches complete with their leaves being fed to sheep in the fields; by the spring both the leaves and the bark would have been cleanly stripped from the branches which could then be used for thatching or fence-posts or

Hogg house, Hartsop Hall Farm, Patterdale.
This small building and its enclosure were used for overwintering sheep. A first-floor loft, entered from the back, housed fodder. The sheep came into the ground floor of the building at night, but used the walled area for feeding and shelter in the daytime.

in swill-making. Pollarding ash-trees has the added advantage of increasing their lifespan; uncut ash-trees rarely live more than a hundred years as they are apt to lose limbs and split, whereas it has been suggested that pollarded ashes may live as long as 5–600 years. This point was not always appreciated; Henry Westray, writing in 1718 about Eskdale, Miterdale and Wasdale, said the trees were 'very much abused by cutting of the tops, there being not one in sixty with the top on'. 'Croppynge' of trees was recorded as early as the thirteenth century when sales of branches formed a regular part of the lordly income from the Derwent fells, while in the fifteenth century

holly and ash were specifically mentioned as being harvested around Kendal for 'croppynges' and 'shreddynges'. Records of Furness Abbey in the sixteenth century likewise show customary use of leaves for fodder. Some farmers merely gathered the leaves, storing them in kists and feeding them to sheep in winter. Some years ago a Langdale farmer's wife recalled: 'My husband's grandfather carried ash-leaves and hay mixed from Millbeck to a croft on the fellside; it was a place where they gathered sheep to sort them when they were at t'fell. Sometimes the leaves were carried on pony-back.'

Ash-trees continue to be pollarded in Borrowdale and Langdale, and at Harry Place Farm in Great Langdale their leaves are still fed to sheep during the winter months. The number of trees still standing, however, seems to be a fraction of what used to be scattered throughout the valley-bottom fields. William Green's etching of Great Langdale in 1819 shows a well-treed landscape, each field having substantial trees along its boundary; similarly the Ordnance Survey map of Borrowdale, drawn in 1862, depicts on the east side of Watendlath tarn small fields bordered by stone walls heavily interplanted with ash-trees. Today only a handful of these ash-trees remains. And Wordsworth's comment on the 'sylvan appearance . . . heightened by the number of ash-trees planted in rows along the quick fences and walls for the purpose of browsing . . .' would hardly be applicable in most valleys today.

Another native plant, ivy, was also occasionally used as fodder. A retired farmer from the Loughrigg area recalls feeding ivy to sheep grazing in the Skelwith woods when snow was on the ground in the 1940s, while in Borrowdale an elderly resident recalled some late winter visits to his parents' home in the 1920s by a local farmer who stripped ivy off the house walls and took it away as sheep fodder.

In early autumn sheep would almost certainly have been 'folded' – penned on arable fields where the crops had been harvested, and allowed to graze on the corn-stalks. Some valleys in the eighteenth century still had large open fields, in which the sheep would have been confined by hurdles. These hurdles seem not to have been woven wattles like their south of England counterparts, but rather a framework of alder or birch backed with bracken and broom. Just in time for the autumn grazing in September 1791, George Browne recorded: 'Sept 1st Carried a cart of broom from Ibbot Holme to Scale How for backing hurdles with . . . Sept 5th Cutting bracken for backing hurdles.'

After the ewes had lambed in spring, all the sheep that had overwintered in the lower pasture would be driven up to the higher fell-grazing to join the wethers and left to feed during the summer on grass and heather. Lambing generally took place between mid-April and mid-May, and by the end of it the weather would normally be getting warmer and the fells would be clothed in spring green. Some years the weather defied the farmers; the winters were severe and long, and spring hardly seemed to arrive before midsummer. These years brought devastation. The winter fodder was exhausted and the sheep housing insufficient to save the lambs. The closing years of the eighteenth century were notorious. Wharton's chronicle for 1799 records: 'No vegetation, nor blossom upon the fruit trees on 7th May 1799. The skins of upwards of 10,000 lambs which perished in the Spring were sold in this town [Kendal].'

Shepherding

Throughout the summer sheep grazed on the open fells. In mediaeval times, farmers followed the annual exodus of both sheep and cattle to the fells and camped for the summer in small houses known as scales or shielings. These buildings will be discussed under cattle husbandry. By the sixteenth century this system had been largely abandoned, and cattle were grazed on pastures enclosed on the lower slopes of the fells and only sheep were put to graze freely on the higher fells. Although farmers no longer decamped to the high pastures for the summer months, the sheep still needed regular visits either from the farmer or from a shepherd employed to stay up for the summer on the larger and more remote fells. Several of these shepherds' huts survive, testimony to an extraordinarily solitary way of life.

As late as the 1950s the hut on Wallacrag was lived in for three months of the year by a shepherd, Walter Scott, from Ashness Farm, Borrowdale. Woundale allotment is a remote pasture high up on Kirkstone Pass: there a small shepherd's hut was built in 1842, shortly after the allotment was enclosed. The building specification survives: 'The Building to be 12 foot square Inside of the Walls . . . the hight of the walls from the pavement to the under side of the joists to be 6 foot 10 inches [and] from the loft to [the] square height 5 foot 6 inches. A Chimney to be made . . . .' The building is now a ruin but enough remains for it to be identifiable. The chimney was on one side wall with the loft door in the gable. The hut is square in plan. Remains of similar almost square huts also exist on the fell above Raw Head in Great Langdale, one near a group of what appear to have been peat-houses and another one isolated within its own walled stock enclosures. The huts so far mentioned, although small (approximately ten feet square), could have provided a reasonable retreat for a few months for a single shepherd. Two other huts which survive, and a few similar ones now ruined, can have been no more than boltholes for emergencies, as some are barely large enough for a man to lie in. Their construction is quite different from that of any other surviving buildings. Built entirely of stone and incorporating natural rock outcrops, they merge into the landscape and only the doorway betrays human agency. The low stone walls, about three feet high, support a roof of stone slabs, covered by a loose layer of random stone arranged into a slightly barrel-vaulted shape. The door is tiny, only some two feet square, and the inside space barely high enough for a man to crawl in. One complete example remains on the north side of the Great Langdale valley; another, perhaps the most remote hut on the fells, is set precariously amongst crags north of Bowfell buttress, facing east across Mickleden. It is at a height of about 1,500 feet and is miraculously intact, unlike the hut at a similar height near the top of the central gulley on Gable Crag, whose form could be made out fifty years ago; all traces of it have now disappeared down the gulley.

Salving

In July sheep were brought down to the lower ground for washing and clipping and then returned again to the fells. In October they were again brought down to be 'salved'. Salve, a mixture of Stockholm tar and molten tallow or butter, was used to give protection against lice and scabs. It was also thought to make the fleece waterproof, to protect the sheep against the winter weather and to enable them to make more use of sparse food. 'Norway tar' is how George Browne referred to it in his diary. For a large flock vast quantities were needed. On 13 October 1782 George Browne wrote, 'Measuring tarr at Storeys 27 galls.' (Storey seems to have been some sort of agricultural merchant.) The tar was mixed with the butter in the proportion of approximately seventeen pounds of butter to one gallon of tar. Smearing with salve must have been one of the most laborious tasks of the farming year; the salve was applied to the fleece with the fingers, staple by staple, one sheep taking as much as fifty minutes or an hour to salve.

Salving dates back at least to mediaeval times: the Fountains Abbey

Salving-house, Armboth, c.1880.
These buildings no longer survive. Notice the small chimney at one end with a stove for warming the tar and butter. The wide openings give plenty of ventilation for the strong-smelling tar.

bursar's books for the years 1456–9 record that much tar was bought and mixed with grease as salve. The practice continued in some places until dipping became compulsory in 1906.

On some farms salving was undertaken in special buildings, salving sheds, built near the farmhouse and opening on to the yard. A well-preserved example is at Taw House, Eskdale. It is a one-storey building with one long side open between stone pillars which support the trusses and with a slightly raised cobbled floor. This open construction would give the salvers air and light – the former especially valuable in view of the pungent smell of the salve. When salving was discontinued, many sheds were probably altered or pulled down, and very few now survive.

Sheep-Washing

The great disadvantage of salve was that it stained the fleece which then had to be washed after shearing before it was sold. Mediaeval wool-buyers apparently complained of tar just as much as their later counterparts. Sheep-washing took place in small pools known locally as dubs, created by damming fast-flowing streams or rivers. Bends were favoured locations; on either side the banks were ramped to allow sheep to be driven into the wash on the deep side and out on to the shallow side; or as a ninety-seven-year-old man remembered a few years ago: 'We dammed t'beck, penned t'sheep up, then chucked 'em in.' As they swam across the dirt floated out. Many sheep-washes can still be identified, such as those at Stool End, Great Langdale, above Windsor Farm, Wasdale, and below Low Park-a-Moor Farm at Nibthwaite, Coniston. They were usually associated with a series of pens into which the sheep were driven before and after washing.

Sheep-washing was often a convivial time. Not only was alcohol consumed in the subsequent celebration (Benjamin Browne of Townend, Troutbeck, noted on 12 June 1721, 'Brandy for sheep wash at George Birketts ... 4d'), but also during the wash: the farmers who had to stand in the dub all day dunking and passing sheep from one side to the other were well fortified before they started and kept going during the day with draughts of whisky or brandy, on the principle that if the inside felt warm the cold water outside would be less noticed.

Although the practice of salving came to an end after the introduction of compulsory dipping earlier this century, some farmers continued to wash sheep in pursuit of two main benefits. First of all clean wool sold at a small premium over unwashed wool, and secondly it was thought that washing promoted the growth of new wool which helped to lift off the fleece. To this day carpet wool in Iran is washed only on the sheep's back and is not scoured again after clipping.

SHEEP-DOGS

A farmer's dog is now so much his constant help as well as his companion that it comes as a surprise to learn that highly trained farm dogs are a relatively recent part of sheep husbandry. The association between man and dog has a long history, possibly extending back to a period before the domestication of livestock, but only in the last 250 to 300 years have dogs developed from guard dogs into specialized gatherers of sheep. It is unlikely that one type of dog could fulfil the functions of both guard and gatherer, for a dog which was a match for a wolf (or for the 'martes' which Thomas Machell records as worrying lambs in Patterdale in the seventeenth century) would need to be large and strong and to have a loud bark; good gatherers on the other hand are small, quieter and more nimble. So until the extinction of wolves and other predators, farm dogs were almost certainly kept as guard dogs. Some years ago a farmer at

Thorn House, Hartsop.
There appear never to have been any special buildings for shearing sheep, an activity that was carried on in any convenient sheltered place. Sometimes shearing took place just within the main barn-doors, sometimes in a yard or, as here, beneath the shelter of a covered gallery.

Troutbeck Park Farm recalled these older breeds: 'the old fell type of dog, a barker', although as a farmer in Great Langdale remarked, it was preferable to have 'a dog that'd bark when you ask it to bark'. (Guard dogs with a good bark are still kept by farmers in northern Italy and have recently been introduced into America.)

Most sheep-dogs are now border collies, black and white and pedigree-bred. They were apparently introduced into Wales from the Lake District as late as the nineteenth century, though (as their name implies) they may have come originally from the Scottish borders.

Dogs are now kept wherever there is an odd space in farm buildings. When barns were used more fully, dogs would have had their own dog-hulls, small free-standing structures or adjuncts to larger buildings. At Yew Tree Farm, Coniston, part of the space beneath the 'spinning'-gallery, which projects at first-floor level from the long side of the main barn, has been filled in as a dog-hull. Now built of concrete blocks, it is shown in old photographs as formed of large upright slabs of stone called Brathay flags. On one side of the large seventeenth-century bank barn at Rydal there is a small lean-to dog-kennel which appears to be an addition, possibly of the eighteenth century, while at Townend, Troutbeck, two small dog-hulls have been formed beneath the ramp to the main bank barn. One or two houses have 'dolmen'-shaped constructions near the farmhouse and farm buildings which may have been dog-kennels – three vertical Brathay flags surmounted by a slightly sloping fourth stone. Greenend Cottage, Colthouse, has a good example of this construction, the three-foot-high stones covering an area approximately nine feet square.

Perhaps surprisingly, dogs have never yet been found in probate inventories. Rather like sheep, the old 'bearded' dogs, which apparently preceded the pedigree collies and were probably the now extinct breed of Cumberland sheep-dogs, became heafed to the land on which they worked and for this reason were perhaps considered to be part of the fixtures and fittings of the farm – rather like the heirloom furniture – and therefore not property to be willed or valued. Nevertheless they still seem to have been worth stealing. On 7 November 1779 George Browne wrote, 'Lost dogs out of kennel'; two days later he added in satisfaction, 'Nov 9th Robber and Thief taken.'

Some dogs must have made the transition from working dog to trusted friend and were thus allowed inside the farmhouse, for one or two houses have dog-gates on the stairs. Only found in somewhat grander houses, these gates are either at the foot or at the top of wooden staircases. Most of the simpler houses had full-sized doors shutting off the stairs at ground level, and these presumably obviated the need for dog-gates. Low Groves, Skelsmergh, Ashness Farm, Borrowdale, and Collinfield, Kendal, all have dog-gates.

CATTLE

An early eighteenth-century painting, rescued from a barn at Calder Bridge and hung for a while in the inn at Boot, shows a plough-team in Eskdale, two horses and two oxen leading a heavy wooden plough. The oxen have long horns and are piebald in colour. When William Kirkby of Blea Tarn Farm, Little Langdale, had his goods seized by his landlord for arrears of rent in 1785, these included, in the cow-house adjoining the house, 'One Blackish cow'd Schotch Cow, one light Branded Irish Cow, one dark Branded Cow, one Red spink'd Cow and one Black spink'd Cow'. (Cow'd means polled, while branded is brown and spink'd is spotted.) A painting of a house in Clappersgate in 1803 shows longhorn cows in a variety of colours in front of the buildings. Towards the end of the nineteenth century, Benjamin Browne of Townend, Troutbeck, had part of his herd of dairy shorthorn cows painted against the fields and fells of the Troutbeck valley.

Named cows are common. Some names seem to describe where the beast was bought, such as the 'Mockerkin why' mentioned in the will of Wm. Fearon of Robinson Place, Great Langdale, made in 1661. Other names perhaps suggest who sold the beast, such as the 'Eddie why' mentioned in the same will, or the 'black cow called Story' which John Walker of Underhelm Farm, Grasmere, left to his daughter Elizabeth in 1640.

Despite the economic importance of cows and their long association with man, very little is known about early types or breeds. In the Lake District, snippets of information such as those just mentioned have to be pieced together and compared with the little we know from elsewhere.

The picture that emerges is of small longhorn cattle, in a variety of colours, red, white and piebald, being kept to the near-exclusion of any other type until the middle of the seventeenth century. Then allusions to black cattle appear. These were mostly animals purchased from Scots drovers, and this trade gained ground in the eighteenth century as regular movements of large herds, or droves, began to be sent down from Scotland to the London markets. As many as 18,574 cattle passed through Carlisle on their way south in 1662 and at that date the trade was only just beginning. A few black cattle also seem to have been purchased from Wales; in Flintshire during the eighteenth century the breeding of cattle for the English market was of more importance than arable farming. Irish cows also appear in inventories, although more rarely.

During the course of the nineteenth century the shorthorn breed, which seems to have originated as a group of breeds in the north-east of England, was improved and introduced to the north-west, gradually taking over from the longhorn and black cattle. This century has seen yet more changes. Pied lowland cattle, which became naturalized in the early twentieth century as British Friesians, now account for the majority of herds, although a few farmers are showing an interest in Charollais and other European breeds.

CATTLE PRODUCTS

While alive, cattle had two main uses: to provide milk for butter and cheese, and to produce manure, without which continuous cultivation of the valley-bottom fields in the Lake District would have been impossible. After death, cattle carcasses produced meat, hides for tanning, fat for tallow, and horns for drinking vessels, lanterns and perhaps even small window-panes.

CATTLE HUSBANDRY

In some parts of the world pastoralists and agriculturalists are two different groups of people interacting to mutual advantage, the pastoralists' cattle being allowed on to the agriculturalists' land to graze the stubble and manure the arable fields. In the Lake District, the system of landholding was such that farms included both uplands and lowlands, farmers being both graziers and cultivators with fields in the valley bottom and grazing rights on the higher fells.

Vaccaries

In the early mediaeval period, the lords either reserved the heads of the valleys for their own use or granted them along with fell-land to monastic houses. These valley heads comprised fertile hay-meadows on the valley floor and good grazing on the higher fells above. On these reserve lands cattle as well as sheep were farmed, at least for a relatively short time in the late thirteenth and early fourteenth centuries when vaccaries, or intensive dairy farms, were established in several valleys. In England vaccaries seem to be a peculiarly northern phenomenon, for there is evidence of their existence not only in the Lake District, but also in Teesdale and Weardale in Northumbria, on land belonging to the abbeys of Rievaulx and Rosedale in Yorkshire, and in the Lancashire Forest of Bowland towards Skipton, but nowhere further south.

The earliest recorded vaccary in the Lake District was at Gatesgarth at the head of Buttermere, belonging to the lords of Cockermouth and first mentioned in 1267. By the 1280s it comprised a 'park', the high-fell grazing, enclosed meadows in the valley bottom, and a cowshed sixty-seven feet long for housing forty cows and their young in winter. What the cowshed was made of is not recorded and, unlike the sheep-houses on Malham Moor, its position has not been identified, although remains of the boundaries of the valley-bottom fields are still apparent. Other vaccaries are recorded during the succeeding decades: the abbots of Furness had one at Brotherilkeld,

Upper Eskdale, by 1292, the abbots of Fountains Abbey one at Stonethwaite, Borrowdale, by 1302, and by 1322 both Ennerdale and Wasdale Head had been developed, four vaccaries being established at Wasdale Head. The exact organization of these vaccaries is unknown, but there is a possible parallel with the lodges leased out by Fountains Abbey in Nidderdale in Yorkshire during the fifteenth century. There, in return for being allowed to farm the land and keep a specified number of cattle belonging to the monastery, the tenants delivered each year the profits of cheese, butter and calves to the abbot and exchanged nine of their oldest and most 'crochione' cows for nine heifers. In 1481 there were three bulls, eighty cows, twenty-four heifers and twelve stirks at Bouthwaite, Nidderdale; their keepers rendered 106 stone and eight pounds of cheese and fifty-three stone and four pounds of butter 'of good and lawful meit, houswyffely handelede' to the monk of the 'Cheishouse'. Presumably the abbots of Furness and Fountains expected similar returns from the vaccaries of Brotherilkeld and Stonethwaite. But the fulfilment of these expectations was short-lived: by the mid-fourteenth century a combination of events, some natural, some man-made, upset the stability and prosperity of the area and the vaccaries were abandoned, the land being divided into small tenements. In part this decline was common to a much wider area than the Lake District, for one of its causes was a general deterioration in the climate of western Europe. Perhaps linked to this was a series of devastating cattle plagues such as the rinderpest epidemic of 1319–21. Add to this the Black Death and unrest along the Scottish border brought about by the long-running hostility between the English and Scottish crowns, and it is not surprising that remote management of intensive cattle farms became uneconomic. By 1334 the four vaccaries at Wasdale Head, for example, had been let to tenants and by 1547 had been divided up into nineteen small farms.

These nineteen farms would have been organized in much the same way as the land not under lordly or monastic control: the tenants would have run mixed farms, with arable and hay fields in the valley and sheep- and cattle-grazing on the open fells. This mixture of upland and lowland within one system led to transhumance, the movement of stock from the lowlands to the uplands in the summer months – a ubiquitous practice in upland Britain during the Middle Ages.

Shielings

In 1610 Camden wrote of Cumberland, 'here everyway about in the wastes ... men ... from April into August lye out scattering and summering with their cattell in little cottages called scheales.' Camden was writing about northern Cumberland, near the Scottish borders, but he was describing a system that had once been prevalent over the whole of the Lake District: that of moving cattle and sheep with part of the farmer's family up to temporary houses on the high pastures for the summer months.

These shielings and summer grazings were sometimes quite near the permanent houses; in Great Langdale the farmhouses were only about a mile from the summer pastures. Others could be as far as eight miles away, such as the fells at Martindale which provided pasture rights for the men of Tirril and Sockbridge. Shielings seem to have taken the form of groups of cottages near a water supply, with walled or fenced cattle-pens into which the animals could be put for safety at night. Not all of the family can have stayed up on the higher pastures for the whole summer, as some would have been needed in the valleys to harvest the hay and attend to the crops. Similar transhumance is still practised in parts of mainland Europe to this day; in Corsica the younger men spend summer with the cattle in the upland scrub called the *maquis*, living in small one-storey cottages, burning dung for fuel, milking the cattle, and making cheese which is brought down to the lowlands with the cattle at the end of summer. The older men and the women and children remain in the valleys tending the farms. Closer to the Lake District, in Wales, vestiges of a similar arrangement persisted until the nineteenth century, with cattle- and sheep-farmers in Snowdonia moving up to the *hafod* or shieling on May Day and returning to their permanent dwellings in the lowlands on All Saints' Day.

In the Lake District, evidence for shielings comes both from place-names and from ruins on the ground. Shielings were also called 'scales', from the Scandinavian *scali*, and *saetr* and *erg*, both from the old Norse. The word 'scale' seems to have referred to the temporary houses (and to have been applied later to peat-storage houses or peatscales), and the words *saetr* and *erg* to the pastures surrounding the buildings. Analysis of place-names containing these words shows a progression in altitude from *erg* names on the periphery of the Lake District, through *saetr* names on the lower fells, to *skali* names deep in the heart of the central fells; this progression may reflect pressure on land in the centuries either side of the Norman Conquest, when colonization penetrated ever deeper into the central valleys and led to the conversion of some of the lower shielings into permanent homes. As early as the mid-fourteenth century Sadghyll (saetr-gil), a farm at the valley head in Longsleddale, had become a permanent farm, whereas a century earlier in 1246 it had been used only in the summer months as a shieling. At Wythop at the northern end of the Derwent fells, the summer pastures seem to have been improved and taken into permanent occupation between 1260 and 1307, while the Percy survey of 1578, which described large areas of the north-west Lake District in some detail, has only one mention of shielings: two 'scale steads in Husacre dale', i.e. near Uzzicar on the west side of Derwentwater. Hawkshead and Ambleside are examples of quite large settlements growing up on earlier *saetr* sites which are on comparatively low ground and were taken into permanent occupation at an early date.

The general picture that emerges is of many lower shieling sites becoming permanently colonized in the twelfth and thirteenth centuries and shielings being pushed up to the highest fells. How long the system of transhumance persisted, and how long the scales continued in use, is as yet unclear. By 1747 it was said that there were remains of 'some old shields where in former ages the people grazed their cattle in summer, a practice now quite disused'. The tentative conclusion from our present knowledge must be that although in a few places transhumance continued until the sixteenth century, this was only the last vestige of a tradition, going back to at least the eleventh century, that had begun to fade during the fourteenth and fifteenth centuries. In many areas the buildings doubtless survived and were put to different uses – few of which can have been as nefarious as that found for one shieling in the mountains in 1519, when a woman was accused in court at Loweswater of harbouring thieves there.

Remains of these scales litter the highest fells, but so far no extensive survey has been made. On Wallacrag six huts are linked by a well-defined path that leads down to the nearby farm, while on the Langdale Pikes, at around the 1,500-foot contour, a group of some twenty huts has been noted; one of these is fronted by what appears to be a well, and all are associated with large stone-walled enclosures and stand near the path and stream leading down from what is now Stickle Tarn. In other areas individual buildings have been noted, such as the one above Glencoyne Farm, Patterdale, and one at Scale Close, Borrowdale. Nearly all the surviving ruins are above the 1,000-foot contour, can be categorized as scales, and are presumably remains of the last phase of shieling-building, most of the lower-level examples being incorporated into permanent dwellings.

Such documentary evidence as exists (and it is admittedly very sparse), usually mentions groups of shielings rather than individual buildings. Analysis of those areas in the north of Britain where shieling sites are plentiful, such as the Upper Tyne valley and parts of Scotland, supports this picture of several buildings loosely grouped together; further confirmation comes from those parts of Europe where transhumance is still practised, such as Corsica, Turkey and parts of Spain, Switzerland and France. In these instances the number of buildings in a group can vary from as few as two or three to as many as twenty. In the Lake District the system of following cattle to their summer grazing-grounds persisted for at least five centuries, so it would be surprising if there were no variations in shieling settlement patterns. Perhaps the number of buildings depended, amongst other factors, on the amount of grazing to be had or on the availability of water.

The buildings that have been recorded display only a few points of similarity. All were built with drystone walls between two and three feet thick; where they are rectangular in shape and where doors can be identified, the latter are often in the gable-end rather than in the long walls, and the larger buildings have a dividing wall making two rooms within. None of the structures survives to a height that reveals anything of its windows or roof construction, and indeed some may have had turf walls above a stone base, like shieling huts recorded in Lewis, Ross-shire. None of the buildings so far examined offers even a hint of how it was used or laid out within. The classic description of Snowdonian *hafodtai* in the 1770s by the Flintshire traveller, Thomas Pennant, may capture something of the flavour of Lake District shielings: 'These houses consist of a long low room, with a hole one end, to let out smoke from the fire, which is made beneath. Their furniture is very simple: stones are the substitute of stools; and the beds are of hay arranged along the sides. . . .'

Cattle-Grazing

In mediaeval times a tenant's right to graze cattle on summer pastures was not necessarily a common right, but rather a right which had to be purchased on demesne land; in some valleys, the lord enjoyed an income from the use of pastures for summer grazing. At the end of each summer season, cattle would be collected in a pinfold, a large circular enclosure on the lower slopes of the fells, and not released until payment had been made. Such a pinfold had been constructed on Stockdale Moor by the seventeenth century, and a large, roughly circular compound on the Langdale Pikes, immediately below the scales mentioned earlier, may have fulfilled the same function.

By the sixteenth century, and possibly coincident with the general decline of transhumance, use of the open fells in some valleys had come to be apportioned by the manorial courts; cattle-grazing became confined to the lower slopes, with the higher fells being reserved for sheep. The fellside between Eskdale and Wasdale, for example, was divided into three zones. The lowest was pasture for milch-cows only, the slightly higher land around Burnmoor Tarn was reserved for bullocks, heifers, dry cows and horses, and sheep were confined to the highest fells. The lower cow-pastures seem to have been divided amongst farms, each farm having exclusive rights to a certain part of the lower fells. On Troutbeck Common a similar system obtained, one part being reserved for cattle, where 'no sheep are allowed to feed'. George Browne clearly had his own stint within that part of the common and took care to guard it, for on 29 July 1790 he wrote: 'Impounded Millers chestnut gelding for trespassing on my cow pasture and upon his promises liberated same.'

As early as the seventeenth century, the lower cow-pastures in some valleys were being enclosed by their occupiers. The large walled intakes behind Spout House and Wha House in Eskdale were instances of this development, as were the sheep intakes behind Raw Head Farm in Great Langdale, enclosed by 1691. Such enclosures were perhaps accepted to combat overgrazing, which appears to have been fairly widespread. The number of cattle on the fells was regulated in principle by simply not allowing a farmer to put on to the common more stock than he could winter in the valley with fodder off his own land. However, as was observed in 1797, 'this legislation is little attended to and the Commons are almost always overstocked to such an extent that many persons do not think it worthwhile to avail themselves of this right of commonage.' That may have been an exaggeration, but there is no doubt that the manorial courts spent much time trying to regulate cattle-grazing. In 1664 the local manor court ruled that on the Banks at Wasdale only cows actually in milk and one horse per farm were to be grazed. This may have been a response to an impassioned plea made five years earlier by the inhabitants of Wasdale Head that their cattle were not able to subsist 'without serving them with nettles and other weeds', presumably because of serious overgrazing.

Today, with the shrinkage of the arable area, many farmers do not stock cattle for milk or beef; those that do, keep them in the valley bottom throughout the year. In many valleys the walled intakes, stretching up the lower flanks of the fells, are unused or underused, being grazed only lightly by sheep. What were once considered to be the finest grazing areas are rapidly being taken over by bracken and becoming almost useless to the farmer. Cattle will trample the young bracken shoots to extinction, but sheep are not heavy enough to have any effect. Eighty years ago, it is said, from outside Fold Head Farm not a blade of bracken could be seen on the fells surrounding Watendlath. Now bracken has encroached right to the edge of what were once the arable fields.

Cattle Housing

Mention has already been made of the sixty-seven-foot-long cow-house built to house a herd of forty milch-cows and their followers at the Gatesgarth vaccary in 1283. This building is the earliest documented cow-house in the area. It is not clear exactly how it was used, but it may well have housed the cows in winter when they would have been stall-fed with hay. Cattle-houses turn up frequently in inventories from as early as the sixteenth century (some probably survive from that date), and they have continued to be built until the present day. The Lake District is one of the few areas of England where there seems to have been an unbroken tradition of indoor wintering, at least since the late Middle Ages.

It used to be commonly accepted that throughout mediaeval England most of a herd was slaughtered at the onset of winter, and that only a few cattle were kept to preserve the herd – the number left being that which could be fed on the available fodder. Recent research, however, has tended to discount the theory that wholesale slaughter was a feature of yeoman farmers' lives. Meat featured rarely in a farmer's diet until the mid-eighteenth century, and it is unlikely that butchers would have wanted all their meat in the autumn, or that vast quantities of salted meat were consumed during the winter. The Lake District was no exception to the rule: until the eighteenth century at least, cattle in this area were kept primarily for manure to fertilize the arable fields, secondly for milk, thirdly as draught animals, fourthly to pay fines or inheritance tax, and only last as a source of meat. Even more significantly, it was customary to allow a farmer only to put as many cattle on the open fells in summer as he could overwinter on his bottom land. In Eskdale in 1587 the manorial court ruled that 'no Tenant or Tenants shall take any cattle to Grassing . . . but such like as they winter', and in the fifteenth century in Windermere the number of cattle each holding could graze was similarly assessed and fixed. Such a system assumes a rough balance between summer and winter numbers, and would not have made sense if large numbers of animals were slaughtered each winter.

If one accepts that farmers did not slaughter most of their cattle in autumn, it follows that any arrangements for winter housing must have been for the whole herd.

In many parts of England a great debate raged during much of the eighteenth and nineteenth centuries over whether cattle should be wintered indoors or left out to pasture on the meadows and arable fields indiscriminately. Many advantages and disadvantages were listed for both systems, both from the standpoint of the animals and from that of the hay-meadows and arable fields. For the indoor point of view it was said that milk production increased, fields were less churned up and manure could be collected and used precisely where it was needed. In the Lake District this debate hardly began; there seem to have been few who dissented from the inside management view. Cattle have been wintered indoors since at least the sixteenth century, and possibly ever since prehistoric times; on many farms they are still wintered indoors today. Inventories taken in winter months frequently list dung-hills, accumulated while the cattle were kept indoors. On 25 April 1674, for instance, John Pearson of Buttermere had 'Seed and Ardey and dung hill' worth £2. (Ardey was the valuation of the seed and work expended on the coming season's crop.) One argument not voiced by the protagonists of in-wintering, but pertinent to the mixed buildings of the Lake District, is the central heating provided by the animals. Anyone who has walked into a full byre on a cold winter's day will remember the welcome warmth; this percolates through to the hay stored above and helps to keep it dry – a valuable benefit in the cold, wet uplands.

Cow-houses rarely exist on their own; they are nearly always part of a larger building. Specialized agricultural buildings were not a feature of the main Lake District farm complexes, and most farms had one general-purpose building for hay, corn, cattle and horses. The cattle were either housed at one end of single-storey buildings or on the ground floor of two-storey buildings, the grain and hay being stored above.

The one-storey buildings are often of cruck construction and appear to precede the two-storey 'bank barn' buildings which are such a distinctive feature of the Lake District landscape. The salient characteristics of bank barns are their mixed use and the way their siting and construction take advantage of a sloping site. The ground floor, entered from the lower side, was used for animals and sometimes also carts. The upper floor, with an entrance from the opposite, higher side by way of a bank or ramp, was used for storing grain and hay. These buildings exhibit many variations in both plan and layout and these are considered in the next chapter. For the moment we shall

Bank barn, Howe Farm, Troutbeck.
The ground-level doors open on to underhousing for cattle and stabling for horses.

just examine how the cattle were housed within them and also within the one-storey barns.

Byres

Most byres were built to accommodate between eight and twelve animals. Numbers of cattle mentioned in inventories suggest that variations in the size of herds were much less than with sheep. Herds of more than ten cows and fewer than two were exceptional. Even those elderly farmers who had retired and passed on their farms to their sons continued to keep a cow or two even when they had only a few sheep or sometimes none at all. On his death in 1620 John Middlefell, a farmer of Wallend, Great Langdale, had six cows, six young beasts and fourteen score and five (285) sheep, a sizeable flock, whereas when Reginald Wilson, a retired farmer on another farm at Wallend, died in 1665 he had only six sheep but also two cows and a horse.

The space within the byres was divided up into 'bouses' or stalls by vertical stone slabs set within a wooden framework called a boskin. The vertical post at the inside edge of each boskin was often carried up to meet the ceiling beams. In early barns these upright timbers were of oak and at their upper end were often curved towards the centre of the barn. They were known as 'celle-trees' – literally, crooked posts. One can only guess at the advantages of this shape. The stalls were usually arranged in pairs and the cattle tethered by a simple rope halter attached to an iron ring which was free to slide up and down a small vertical wooden rod fixed to one side of each boskin. The floors were generally cobbled, the lines of cobbles running across the stall to stop the cow slipping, and sloped down to a combined manure and feed passage, one step down from the floor of the stall. This passage also had a cobbled floor, with the cobbles laid the opposite way, and sloped towards a narrow central drainage channel. Separate feed passages were not common in Lake District barns before the middle of the nineteenth century.

Boskins were ordinarily laid out either in a double row running the length of the barn or in several pairs of rows running across the width of the barn. In small one-storey barns, a single row is sometimes found across one end. In bank barns, on the other hand, the most common arrangement is for the cattle housing to be aligned across the ground floor, with doors in the long side of the building opening on to the manure passages. However, there is evidence to suggest that the earliest barns had boskins arranged lengthwise. Both the old barn at Rydal Hall, possibly a sixteenth-century building, and Low Park barn, newly erected in 1659 around an earlier structure, had length-wise arrangements as did the main Rydal barn completed in 1670. (These variations are allied to the disposition of the barn – whether it is built along or down the slope – and this is discussed in the next

above

Cattle-stalls, Hole House barn, Troutbeck.
The wooden frames enclose slate panels. Notice the crotched stall-posts or 'celle-trees'. This shape is typical of many seventeenth- and early eighteenth-century stall-posts.

chapter.) In many ways the apparently earlier arrangement was the more logical. Many agricultural writers in the eighteenth and nineteenth centuries, although stressing the need for good ventilation in cow-houses, also stressed the need to avoid draughts, and suggested that cow-houses in model farms should be placed at right angles to threshing-barns and the prevailing winds. In bank barns the cow-houses are underneath the threshing-barn; and if the manure passages open on to the gable-ends, the doors are at right angles to the threshing-barn doors and so avoid draughts. In this lengthwise arrangement ventilation is also provided by small loop-lights in the long walls, whereas in the crosswise arrangement doors often provide the only means of allowing fresh air in and foul air out.

Field Barns

Some farms not only had a large barn near the farmstead but also one or two outlying field barns. Most surviving field barns resemble bank barns in having storage on the upper floor for hay, and occasionally for grain, from the surrounding fields while the ground floor was used for overwintering stock. Some of these field barns, such as the one at Crostenrigs built by Benjamin Browne in 1733, have very well-fitted stalls. The contract between Browne and four wallers for 'a Hoghouse to be Builded at Crostenrigs Yeat' for £18 10s. reads 'the House must be 12½ yards within . . . and 2 yards at least between Bouses selletree to ye Dorn' (the main beam supporting the first floor). The original fittings specified were 'setting flags betwixt all ye Bouses, and seting flags betwixt ye Cowhouse and Calf House; & alsoe be[t]wixt ye Calf House and Stable'. All survive. It is particularly interesting that Benjamin Browne uses the expression 'hogg house' to describe this building which was quite clearly intended to house cattle, calves and horses. One is tempted to imagine that he was rebuilding on the site of an earlier sheep-wintering structure. That this was not the case is shown by notes made by his grandfather in 1640: George Browne had twenty-two young cattle at Crostenrigs and there is mention of fetching water into the calf-house there. Perhaps 'hogg house' had come to mean nothing more than a building some distance away from the main farmhouse.

Many other field barns now show no evidence of cobbled floors or slated stalls. These were probably used as loose-boxes in which cattle for fattening were overwintered, untied, on deep litter – i.e. plenty of bedding material, usually bracken – and the manure was left to accumulate during the winter months. As early as the sixteenth century, bracken-gathering was regulated by parts of the wastes or common being set aside as 'bracken dalts' reserved for the use of certain farms. Bracken was used for thatching and potash-making, as well as for bedding; the bracken harvest was the third of the season, following on from hay and grain.

Painting of a plough-team, probably in Eskdale, early eighteenth century.
This painting was kept until about forty years ago at a farm in lower Eskdale and may well have been painted in that valley. It shows a plough-team of two yoked oxen and two following horses. The farmer is guiding the heavy wooden plough. One of the other men is driving the team while the third holds the ploughshare in place.

Oxen

Apart from cows and calves kept for milk, some of the larger farms also had oxen and bulls to house. Although ox is strictly a generic term for any cow or bull, it has come to mean a castrated bull kept for use as a draught animal. Oxen were used as plough-beasts either on their own or in a mixed team of oxen and horses. There is a remarkable painting showing a plough-team, probably in Eskdale, in the early eighteenth century, two single horses harnessed in front of two yoked oxen. The use of oxen declined in the eighteenth century and by 1797 it was reported that in Cumberland 'about seventy or eighty years since, teams of oxen or oxen yoked with horses, were very common; from that period, draft oxen gradually decreased; and for some years past we were informed that there has not been an ox team in the country'. At about the same time it was said of Westmorland that 'only one person in Westmorland uses ox teams'. When oxen were in general use, small farms almost certainly did not keep their own oxen; they hired them for ploughing and also to help with the harvest, perhaps harnessed to a cart. In Eskdale in 1613, the inventory of John Viccars included an 'ox appointed for the harvest'. Only in the larger farms, therefore, was there any need for ox housing.

The provision of an ox-house is recorded in Coniston, for on 6 March 1668, Sir Daniel Fleming of Rydal Hall wrote that he had been to Coniston Old Hall 'when I and my son Will went thither to sett out ye new great Barn, stable, Ox-house etc 4s. 0d.'. The barn was finished in the summer of 1668 and almost a quarter of the ground floor seems to have been taken up by the ox-house, which was located between the cow-house and the stable and separated from them by vertical stone walls. It was an undivided space approximately fifteen feet by twenty-three. Similarly at Rydal Hall barn, also built by Fleming in 1670, it seems the underhousing was originally all for oxen, an open space provided with a 'beef watering chist'. Only nine years later this was converted to cattle housing when payment was made to 'ye Grasmere wallers for flagging [making vertical slate divisions] and paving of ye ox house' on 22 November 1679. Identifying ox-houses in buildings for which there is no archival evidence is fraught with problems, for the space has no special characteristics. Many ox-houses must have been converted to stables when ox-power gave way to horse-power, or others could have had stalls added, as at Rydal Hall, to convert them to housing for dairy cattle.

Bulls

'Not many people kept bulls and folks used to take their cows to 'em. They walked their stock for miles.' This was written in the 1940s but could equally well have been set down at any time earlier: bulls, like oxen, were a prerogative of the gentry and the wealthier yeomen who hired them out to the smaller farmers. Clement Taylor of Finsthwaite, for example, sent his cows to Holker to be served in the eighteenth century. Bulls were often, in recent times at least, bought 'from away' to improve the stock and taking them home could be a hazardous task. A Borrowdale farmer, some forty years ago, 'bought a bull in Cockermouth, fetched it on t'train to Keswick, and walked it from Keswick to Seathwaite' (a distance of some eight miles) and, as he vaguely put it, 'what precautions you took depended on what age it was'.

Where bulls were housed is not at all clear: very little documentary evidence seems to be available and no bull-houses appear in inventories. At Townend Farm, Troutbeck, a single-storey building in one corner of a field above the farmhouse is known locally as the bull-pen. It has a wide door and may well have been used to house the bull. At Brimmer Head Farm, Easedale, a tiny building at the corner of a field right next to the farmhouse could likewise have been used as a bull-pen; it is too small to have been used for overwintering cattle or sheep. Elsewhere bull-pens were sometimes built on to the end of bank barns, an instance being the small one-storey extension at Low Longmire Farm, Booth. At Coniston Old Hall the field immediately adjoining Sir Daniel Fleming's barn and cow-house was known in the eighteenth century as the 'bull coppy', a name widely applied to small fields where the bull was kept, at least in the summer months. Similarly at Wallend Farm, Great Langdale, a field adjoining the cruck barn, and apparently a Tudor enclosure, was known as Bull Field. Whether these fields contained small buildings for bulls or were merely used as summer pasture is not known: no visible evidence remains.

Fodder for Cattle

As we have seen, provision of housing for all types of cattle was determined by the amount of fodder available to feed the animals during the winter months. The main fodder was straw, both from oats and barley (bigg), and hay. Hay was the preferred food, followed by straw, but with oat straw being favoured over barley straw. For as J. Mortimer wrote in *The Whole Art of Husbandry* in 1712, 'barley straw will quite dry up that milk that they have tho' it is good for dry cattle.' But cattle were not only fed on hay and straw; as with sheep, their diet was varied by the inclusion of leaves from various woodland trees. This was not arbitrary cutting to cover emergencies, but a systematic use of the woodland on farms, and one that was tightly controlled by manorial custom. Holly, ash and oak were harvested by 'croppynge' (pollarding the tops) and 'shreddynges' (removal of side branches). An early instance of this practice is documented in 1281 when the monks of Calder Abbey were granted leave to cut down the branches of trees in Copeland Forest to feed

Barn, Harrowhead Farm, Wasdale.
The large central archway was originally open and led into a cartshed. This was immediately beneath the threshing-floor. Cartsheds were usually without doors. The draught blew onto the underside of the threshing-floor through the open cartway and was considered to be beneficial for keeping the floor dry and mould-free.

their stock in winter and spring. The feeding of cattle with leaves from cut branches seems to have died out in the eighteenth century. Today cattle browse many woodlands; but whereas regeneration is possible in woodlands harvested annually by lopping and topping, nothing regenerates in those regularly browsed by cattle. This is not an entirely new problem: there is a seventeenth-century mention of cattle, grazing land at Troutbeck Park Farm, having to wear bells as the area was heavily wooded. Leaves for fodder seem to have been gradually replaced by root vegetables, particularly turnips, which were grown in increasing quantity from the middle of the eighteenth century and were chopped and added to cattle feed.

HORSES

By the end of the eighteenth century, motive power, for ploughing, harrowing and drawing carts, seems to have provided entirely by horses. Horses had many advantages over oxen: they were generally stronger and could work longer hours, they were easier to feed (oxen demanded more than just hay or straw), they needed less summer pasture and, above all, they were much more adaptable. Not only will horses draw ploughs, harrows, carts and sledges, they can also be used as pack-animals and for carrying humans. Horses were widely used as pack-animals for taking fleeces and other goods to market. In 1787 James Clarke wrote how they were also used for moving hay and dung: 'in carrying home their hay . . . they lay it upon their horses in bundles, one on each side . . . the traveller may even see hay carried in this manner thro' the streets of Keswick. Their manure they carried in the same manner, putting it in wicker baskets,' (these were known locally as 'holts' or 'halts'.) In 1728 John and Dorothy Wilson of Ashness Farm in Borrowdale retired from farming and passed the farm on to their son Miles. In return, as well as fuel for his parents, he had to provide for their own use one 'horse to ride to church, market and elsewhere'.

By 1800 only the poorest farmer seems to have been without a horse. The larger farms had several: one pack-animal for transporting goods, one or two for pulling the plough, and a 'fine' horse for riding. Until the mid-nineteenth century most of these horses were probably light mountain ponies, as the heavy cart-horse would have been of little advantage on the steep fields of many fell farms. In 1797 it was recorded that many Cumberland farms bred these mountain ponies, selling the surplus to light horse regiments of the army. Each year horse fairs were held on the outskirts of the Lake District, at Appleby in the spring and at Brough in the autumn, and travellers in horse-drawn 'vardos' gathered from far and wide to buy and sell horses. In Appleby, horses for sale were exercised to display their prowess and the business transaction was invested with a great deal of showmanship. Needless to say, there is a tale told of a farmer who sold a horse in the morning and unwittingly bought back the same animal in the afternoon at a much higher price after it had been groomed.

Stables were most commonly sited along with the cow-houses on the ground floor of the main multi-purpose barn. If this was of bank-barn form, the doorways to the stables opened through the same wall as the cow-house doors. It is often said that stables are similar to byres except that they have taller stalls and higher ceilings; but in the Lake District they were rarely higher, as they were positioned beneath the same barn floor as the byres and as the mountain ponies were quite small. Stables were usually fitted out with stalls, the infill being timber rather than the slate slabs used in the cow-byres. Separate tack-rooms are rarely found; instead, tack was hung on wooden pegs protruding from one wall of the stables. The horse-stalls were often positioned against a gable wall and sometimes had a food-drop above. This was a gap at one end of the barn floor which allowed food to be dropped into a rack fastened to the wall above the stalls. The average stable housed three horses; but as it has been estimated that one horse was sufficient for twenty acres of arable land, three horses would have been quite a generous complement for most Lakeland farms – two for ploughing, and one for riding and carrying panniers.

CARTS AND SLEDGES

James Clarke, writing in 1787, claimed that twenty years previously there had been no wheeled vehicles in Borrowdale. That may have

been a slight exaggeration, but it does seem that only the larger farms
had carts. Most farm produce was transported either on pack-horses
or on horse-drawn sledges, both eminently suited to steep hillsides
where wheeled vehicles would have been impractical. Evidence from
buildings tends to confirm this. Cartsheds were rare in the Lake
District before the end of the eighteenth century; they occur more
frequently around the periphery where the gradients are less steep,
such as in the Lyth valley, and are quite common in Eskdale and
Wasdale where many farm buildings were rebuilt in the late eighteenth
or early nineteenth centuries.

The local carts, at least until the early nineteenth century, were
very distinctive, bearing much more resemblance to those still found
in parts of north-west Spain than to those of lowland Britain. They
were sufficiently widespread and remarkable to be noticed by Celia
Fiennes, who wrote in 1698: 'Their little carts . . . they use hereabouts,

Drawing of clog wheels.
Each of this pair of solid wheels
was bound with an iron band
nailed on. The wheels were fixed
to the axle-tree and turned with
it. The drawing is faintly
annotated to say that they were
two feet in diameter.

the wheels are fast'ned to the axletree and so turn altogether, they hold not above what our wheele barrows would carry at three or four tymes, which the girles and boys and women doth go about with, drawn by one horse to carry any thing they want.' According to a report of the 1780s, Westmorland carts were 52 inches long, 36 inches wide and 14½ inches high, and two-thirds of their length went before the axle. The wheels were solid 'clog-wheels' made of three planks of wood joined together and with a half-moon shape cut from each of the outer planks. Such wheels apparently had a characteristic squeak. According to James Stockdale, writing in 1872, '... the revolving axle-trees of the clog-wheeled carts, scantily greased, make each a most unnatural squeak', which he thought was 'disagreeable music'. Perhaps to the farmer it was more pleasant, a hallmark of his trade. The clog-wheel carts of Spain still squeak, and they and their noise have come to be revered as proud relics of a fast-disappearing way of life. In 1988 a farmer from Cantabria in north-west Spain, having no work in his own village, moved to a neighbouring village with his ox-cart. His new employer could not stand the 'screamer': the cart had to go. It did, and so did its owner, refusing to be parted from it.

By the 1820s new-fangled carts, with iron-rimmed hub wheels turning on axles, began to make their appearance in the Lake District. They rapidly gained favour and supplanted the clog-wheeled carts almost completely by the 1850s. They were still small and drawn by one horse. Heavy four-wheeled waggons drawn by a team of horses were quite unsuitable for work in such hilly areas and it was said, at the end of the eighteenth century, to be 'a general opinion that four horses in four separate carts will draw a greater weight than if they were yoked together in a wagon'.

A cartshed was by that time normally an integral part of the main two-storey barn, being sited centrally on the ground floor between the byre and the stable, and below the threshing-floor. Farms provided with more than one cartshed (like Wha House, Eskdale, Craghouse Farm, Irton, and Dunthwaite House, Setmurthy) were most unusual. Cartsheds were normally open-fronted, doors being provided only occasionally to close off the wide opening.

PIGS

Pigsties were generally a late addition to the farmstead, being for the most part built on to the end of existing barns in the nineteenth century. This does not, however, imply the late arrival of the pig itself as a domesticated animal in the Lake District, but rather a change of husbandry and a change in the type of animals kept.

A glimpse of the role of the pig in the traditional rural economy of the Lake District can be gained by looking at other parts of Europe today. Anyone who has driven around Corsica will know that one of the main hazards on the inland roads are pigs which suddenly appear out of the thick scrub at either side of the road and run in front of the car. These pigs are quite unlike the intensively bred, slothful animals that now produce somewhat tasteless English bacon; they are small, thin and, with their longish legs, quite sprightly. Right up until possibly the end of the eighteenth century, the Lake District animals, and their husbandry, would have been very similar.

In the Middle Ages pigs were pastoral animals, and grazed for much of the year on acorns, grubs and carrion in the oak-woods that so plentifully clothed the fellsides. Place-names like Swineside, Swinstybeck, Swindale and Swinescale are all reminders of this practice. Farmers were allowed pannage, the right to graze swine, on the fellsides and in the woods; for example, in 1282 pannage was paid on 250 swine on the Derwent fells and in 1337 on 251 pigs in Inglewood Forest. The amount paid for pannage in Lowick woods in Furness is recorded in a document of 1256: 'For the pigs which they might adjist in Lowyk Woods every tenth pig or the tenth penny of the value thereof' was payable by the tenant to the lord of the manor, Alan de Steynton.

Across the mediaeval centuries the woodland cover shrank quite dramatically with more intensive settlement of the higher reaches of the fells and the accompanying increase in levels of stock-grazing. Much open common land was denuded of trees; pigs were confined to the woodlands of the lower slopes, and pannage ceased in many manors. By the late fifteenth century, restrictions on pig-keeping had come into force in some areas – either limitation of numbers, as for example in Applethwaite and Undermillbeck where tenants were only allowed two pigs each, or ringing of noses so that the pigs 'wrut nott' (this would stop them uprooting self-sown seedlings). By 1600 few farmers kept pigs and those that did had only one or two.

It seems unlikely, both inherently and on the strength of evidence from elsewhere, that the pig moved directly from being a woodland animal to one that was confined to the farmyard. As the tree cover shrank, pigs were probably grazed for part of the year and fed for the rest, perhaps initially in the woodland. A possible relic of this practice can be seen in Finsthwaite, where there is still a pigsty in the wood at a little distance from Townend Farm. These early pig shelters may have been insubstantial structures, similar to the brushwood shelter pens still in use in Corsica today.

During the eighteenth century selective breeding of pigs produced several distinct types. Up until that time the pig population throughout the country seems to have been largely homogeneous, being similar to but smaller than the wild pig. 'Heavy whites' and 'Gloucester old spots' were the new breeds that became generally popular with small farmers. In the Lake District a Cumberland breed was also developed but has since become extinct.

Inventories of the seventeenth to nineteenth centuries show that the numbers of pigs kept remained small, most farmers having only one or two. This did not stop a few owners (it may even have encouraged them) from apparently becoming attached to their pigs. When Thomas Harrison of Glencoyne Farm, Ullswater, died in 1665, he bequeathed to his son John a named pig, 'one swyne Alick'; and in 1790 George Browne took the trouble to record in his account book the demise of a pig: 'June 19th Taffy died. Sent Taffys skin to Mr. J. Holme, Ambleside.'

It is difficult to give a precise date for the earliest pigsties with attached yards in the Lake District. In Cheshire the use of pigsties was regarded as an innovation in the early nineteenth century; at the same time in Shropshire the need for pigsties was noted. Evidence from the actual buildings suggests a similar early nineteenth-century date for many Lake District pigsties. The earliest documentary evidence so far noted is an account dated 1798 for building a 'Pig-sty, Necessary [privy] and Ashes House' at Knipe Fold, Hawkshead.

The new buildings came in two forms. Perhaps the more common were pairs of 'in-and-out' sties, one-storey buildings divided into two sleeping-stalls which each had a doorway opening on to a small feeding-yard. These were usually built on to the end of bank barns, the yards projecting forward from the front of the buildings. This type predominates in the south and west of the area; Wasdale has the largest number per farm, most having either two or three double sties and at Crag House Farm, Irton, as many as five. The second type were two-storey dual-purpose buildings, the lower half of which was used for pigs while the loft either provided shelter for hens or was

Barn at Mislet Farm, Windermere.
The two-storey lean-to on the right of this bank barn was a hennery-piggery, with pigs housed on the ground floor and chickens above.

used as a privy. The 'hennery-piggery' types were often detached and some, such as the one at Townend Farm, Troutbeck, were built on sloping ground with access for the hens at ground level at the upper end of one of the long sides. Others, such as the buildings at Mislet Farm, Windermere, and Lane End Farm, Sizergh, were two-storey versions of in-an-out sties attached to the main barn. A few combined pigsties/privies survive such as the ones at Wads Howe, Longsleddale, Troutbeck Park, Troutbeck, and Beckstones, Patterdale. The two functions are now separated at Wads Howe and Troutbeck Park, and provision was made, presumably at a later date, for the privy to be served by a bucket. A peculiar elaboration is found at Kilnstones, Longsleddale, and How Green, Hartsop, where small buildings had all three functions on separate levels: hen-houses, privy, and pigsty in order of descent.

BEES

One final, albeit small, creature must be mentioned because of its delightful architectural consequences, bee-boles and bee-alcoves. In 1787 it was said of Cumberland that domesticated bees were 'found in every part of the county', and indeed beehives are commonplace in inventories from the eighteenth century onwards. On his death in 1744, Michael Satterthwaite of Cragg Farm, Colthouse, had (as well as thirteen head of cattle and three horses) a typical complement of 'two hives of bees'. Both George Browne of Staveley and George Browne of Townend, Troutbeck kept bees and recorded their various apiarian transactions. On 21 December 1767, George Browne of Staveley 'Pd sister Anne for a swarm of bees 8/6 She gave again 1d 8/5'. On 15 June 1776 beehives cost George Browne of Townend two shillings, and a further twopence was paid to Richard Dobson for 'Carriage of bee hives'. On 2 November in the same year he recouped some of his outlay when he received six shillings for four pounds of beeswax (at one shilling and sixpence a pound, just over three times the price paid for tallow). Presumably the honey was kept for home consumption as it does not appear in his account books.

Bees were not only kept for honey and beeswax, but also to pollinate plants. In the spring they fed off early-flowering orchard trees; in June white clover in the hay-meadows provided their main food supply. By August the hay had been gathered and most of the flowers in the valley bottom had been exhausted, but the heather on the fells was just coming into flower. In the first week of that month hives were customarily moved to higher ground, between 600 to 1,000 feet, where the best heather was considered to be. The move was started at around five o'clock in the morning, to avoid the warmth of the day which might have excited the bees. In 1864 E. Lynn Linton wrote of the move to Revelin Fell overlooking Ennerdale Lake:

Every Summer and Autumn hundreds of hives are brought up to Ennerdale and set on Revelin for the bees to get strength and sustenance before winter time. Carts come early in the morning laden with beehives, and 'A vast o' good honey gets shakt oot ont' road . . .'

The hives were returned to the lower ground in the autumn to be housed in bee-boles or bee-houses near the farmhouse. The hives themselves were skeps constructed of coils of straw or sometimes ling, and unlike modern wooden hives they needed protection from the weather. Bee-boles are rectangular recesses, some fifteen inches square and about twelve inches deep in the thickness of a stone wall; each bole would have housed one small hive. At High Yewdale Farm, Coniston, there is a double row of boles. A more widely spaced arrangement is found at Low Wray Farm, where the boles have backs formed of one thin piece of slate flush with the back of the wall. More elaborate shelter was provided at both Nab Scar Cottage, Rydal, and also at Tower Bank House, Sawrey, in the form of bee-houses or bee-alcoves. These were recesses in a stone wall, protected by small projecting slate roofs and with a raised slate shelf to take the hives. A drawing of Nab Scar, Rydal, by Robert Hills (1769–1844) shows the bee-alcove complete with two hives, each of which is much taller than would have fitted into bee-boles.

A complete change in bee-keeping practice in the nineteenth century produced stout wooden hives, rendering bee-boles and bee-houses obsolete. At Hill Top, Near Sawrey, Beatrix Potter put one of the new hives in an old bee-alcove in the wall of the vegetable garden just outside her house, and immortalized it in *The Tale of Jemima Puddleduck*. This strange combination cannot now be moved.

In most parts of England, bees have produced a wealth of folklore and superstition; the Lake District is no exception. When someone died it was customary to 'tell the bees'. The hives were gently tapped and the bees told who had passed away. To placate them further, after the funeral, crumbs from the funeral feast were brought to the hives and fed to the bees. It was believed that unless the bees joined in the mourning, they might fly away or become unproductive. As recently as 1916 this custom was enacted at a farm near Underbarrow.

Bee-boles, Holme Ground Farm, Coniston.
These boles, or recesses, were set within the wall of the orchard next to the farmhouse and each housed one bee-skep.

5

Crops

RING-GARTHS

I<small>N</small> MEDIAEVAL times the boundary between open fell and enclosed
cultivated land in the valley bottom was a communally maintained
stock-proof barrier. This barrier could be either a fence or a wall
and was known locally by several names including fell-garth and
ring-garth. It was far more than just a line dividing two types of land
management; it also demarcated tenanted land in the valley bottom
from fell-land over which all the tenants had grazing rights, and
enabled the manorial courts to regulate movements of stock in and
out of the enclosed land.

These ring-garths probably developed slowly from small enclosures
after the Norman Conquest, but came to encompass much larger
areas as land settlement gained pace in the twelfth and thirteenth
centuries. Early in the sixteenth century the manor court at Crosby
Ravensworth ordered the rebuilding of the ring-garth into a substantial stone wall five feet high. In Great Langdale the ring-garth is first
mentioned, or implied, in the thirteenth century when the manor of
Baysbrown was given to the priory of Conishead and the benefaction
speaks of the 'enclosed land of Great Langden'. A recent survey of
all the stone walls at the head of Great Langdale has identified the
line of the ring-garth: it runs in an arc around the head of the valley
and is some four miles in length. About a third of the ring-garth is
still standing, some 200 yards of it apparently to its original height
of about five feet. It is built dry of large river-washed boulders on
even larger foundation stones. Similarly, a recent survey of walls
around Watendlath has revealed a ring-garth wall encircling Watendlath tarn and the adjoining flat valley-bottom fields.

In thirteenth-century Langdale fifteen tenants farmed 136¼ acres
in the valley bottom within the ring-garth, giving each farm about
nine acres. Grasmere at that time had precisely the same number of
tenants and only three acres fewer. In both these valleys the farms
would have been scattered throughout the enclosed land. A similar
pattern seems to have obtained in most valleys, although the size and
density of settlement depended to a large extent on the configuration
of the landscape. At one end of the spectrum some single farms lay

Field walls, Great Langdale.
In the valley bottom can be seen walls and hedges dividing up former open fields. Stretching up the fellside are cattle intakes with an outgang, or track, between them giving access to the unenclosed fell land above.

within a small area of enclosed land, while in other valleys as many as fifteen to twenty farms lay within the ring-garth. The pattern of small undivided enclosures is illustrated in a survey dated 1570 of three farms on the east side of Coniston Water. At that time, Park-a-Moor, Waterside Park and Lawson Park each had a 'ring hedge' and provision was made on each farm for a specified amount of underwoods and saplings to be set aside and tended 'to maynteyne the Ringe Hedge of the said parke'.

The land within the ring-garth was subject to strictly controlled seasons. In the closed season, often from 'Mid-April-Day' until All Saints' Day (1 November), stock were excluded and had to be taken to pasture on the high open fells whilst the enclosed lands were cultivated for grain and hay. In the open season the stock were allowed back to graze the stubble and to be housed or sheltered during the winter months.

Where there was room within the ring-garth, the cultivated land seems to have been organized on a communal, common-field or town-field basis. This meant that each farmer had several parcels of land within one or more common fields. Such systems have been recorded at Coniston, Grasmere, Great Langdale and Buttermere. The common fields were divided either into strips or small blocks of land. In 1624 the inventory of Nicholas Hunter of Buckbarrow Farm, Wasdale, listed two yokings of arable land, which suggests two long strips each as wide as one pair of oxen could plough. Whether in strips or blocks, the land within the common fields would have been unenclosed, so that in the winter months stock grazed the whole area communally. Some common fields would have been cultivated continuously for crops, while others would have been kept as meadows for hay. (A lease to Thomas Barrow for land at Meathop in 1690 includes the constraint that he 'shall not plough up any of the ancient meadow grounds'.)

By the seventeenth century many of the common fields had been subdivided, hedges and walls having been raised to demarcate the parcels of land or 'dales', as they were then known (from *deylen*, to distribute), within the common fields. The name 'common field', however, remained; in 1745 a mortgage mentions 'two dales called Flooded Leys within Great Langdale common field'. The communal grazing seems also to have persisted, at least in some valleys. The boundaries of the old common field in Mickleden, Great Langdale, have recently been surveyed together with the network of paths and tracks linking it with the farm buildings around its periphery. There are far more lines of communication than would have been necessary merely for linking farmhouses – perhaps physical proof of the communal use of these fields in the winter months.

In many areas, the dividing of the common field simply perpetuated a pattern of patchy landholding, each farm having many small parcels of land scattered throughout the common fields. Pringle, writing of Westmorland in 1797, noted that 'the whole cultivated land is divided by hedges or stone walls into inclosures, many of which do not contain half [an] acre; there are a few of eight or ten acres; and in general they may contain three to five acres'. It took many generations to rationalize land-holding by sale and exchange until each farm was more or less surrounded by its own land; in some valleys, such as Buttermere, this has still not been completely achieved.

CROP ROTATION

By the eighteenth century a system of crop rotation on enclosed fields was being recorded by several writers. The standard regime seems to have been to cultivate fields for approximately three years out of twelve, sowing oats first of all, then barley, then oats again. Hay was then taken off until, between seven and ten years later, the grass was 'mossed over'; it was then ploughed up and the cycle repeated. Not all fields, however, seem to have been subject to this type of rotation – some seem to have been kept for pasture and not ploughed, while others were cropped and mulched continuously.

GRAIN AND HAY HARVESTING

'The only singularity is, that the occupiers of small farms, in some parts of the county, put the whole of their hay into barns.' These words were written in 1797. In the central Lakes all the hay and all the grain went into barns. Stacks and ricks were unknown, and the main crops of hay and grain were housed together in the main barn on the farm. As we have seen, these barns were often two-storey, the ground floor accommodating cattle, horses and sometimes carts, while the upper floor was used for grain and hay and also straw and bracken.

Until the early eighteenth century, grain, hay and bracken were harvested in a manner largely unchanged since prehistoric times. The crops were cut with a small hand-held sickle or reap-hook, a curved blade about two and a half feet long fitted into a short wooden handle. It was a slow process and entailed leaving fairly lengthy stubble in the fields. During the eighteenth century reaping was gradually replaced by hand-mowing with a scythe, a heavier curved blade fitted into a long wooden handle, which could be swung through the crop, cutting it faster and closer to the ground. In 1775 George Browne paid a 'sythemaker for sythe for self 5/-', the entry perhaps indicating an innovation. The following year he paid fourpence to have the scythe laid in a new shaft and on 7 August 1777, a week before the hay harvest, he wrote, 'sythemaker came in all night with me' (by that time he was perhaps sharpening more than one scythe).

By the mid-nineteenth century scythes were commonplace but still fairly highly prized and obviously worth stealing, for on 16 July 1846 Benjamin Browne wrote: 'Took Jas Biggland at Low Wood Inn for stealing a syth belonging to N. Wilson. Committed to Appleby [Court].'

Hay was apparently sometimes moved into the barn 'with great celerity', being only left in the field for three or four days if the weather was warm and dry. More often the weather was wet and the hay had to be left much longer. Sometimes, in desperation, the farmer reduced his hay to 'foot-cocks' which could be flipped over with one foot each day. In exceptionally wet summers the hay was black with mould by the time it was put into the barns. The cut oats and barley were dried more slowly, being bound into sheaves, propped into stooks and left to dry in the fields for three Sundays before being taken to the barn either in carts or on sledges.

In most two-storey barns the upper floor was entered across a ramp

Harvesting bracken, c.1930.
Bracken used for cattle-bedding and thatching was usually gathered from the higher intakes or the open fell. Sledges were often used to transport it down to the valley bottom.

or bank leading to a pair of double doors placed just off the centre of one long wall. The whole of this first-floor space was usually undivided by partitions. Its exact use is still a matter for some speculation. Hay was the first crop to be harvested and was stored in the barn all winter, being pushed down as needed to the cattle and oxen or horses beneath. It was presumably all stored to one side of the main doors. The second harvest was grain, and the unthreshed grain must have taken up part of the space on the other side of the main doors. The remaining space could then be filled with the third harvest, bracken, and with straw, as and when the grain was threshed.

Threshing and Winnowing

Threshing and winnowing are the processes whereby the ears of corn are stripped from their stalks and then separated into chaff and grain. The waste products of these processes also have their uses: the stalks, or straw, are used as animal fodder, and the chaff for stuffing mattresses.

In the central Lakes hand-threshing with a flail, a method largely unchanged since biblical times, persisted in some places until as recently as the 1950s. Mr Brockbank, of Pool Bank Farm, Crosthwaite, was still threshing by hand in 1953. Flails were normally made with a wooden handle, usually of ash and about eighteen inches long, fixed rather like a whip to a slightly shorter piece of hard wood, such as holly, yew or blackthorn, with a piece of leather, often eelskin. The thresher used the flail to beat sheaves of corn spread out on the threshing-floor. In the barns, the space between the double doors in one long wall and the single door opposite was used as the threshing-floor. In barns built along the slope the floor was of timber and at first-floor level; whereas in barns built down the slope the threshing-floor was sometimes at ground-level and was then paved with stone flags. In large one-storey barns, any threshing-floor was always flagged. When in use the threshing-floor was apparently sometimes covered with a dried horse-skin or 'burying skin'.

In many of the smaller one-storey barns it is sometimes difficult to determine whether there was any special threshing-floor, as the floors, apart from where animals were housed, were often of rammed earth. Portable threshing-floors may well have been used in association with

below

Bank barn, Holme Ground Farm, Coniston.
The upper floor of this bank barn is entered through double doors sheltered by a pentice roof. These lead on to a threshing-floor. Access to the underhousing is gained through doors in the lower long wall.

these barns, either in or out of doors. Such floors, made from thick planks braced together underneath with oak 'ledges', were known in south-west Wales.

After threshing, the straw was taken for bedding and fodder while the grain was first of all raked, then sieved several times and finally put into sacks ready for winnowing. For winnowing, a good draught was needed to blow the lighter chaff away from the heavier kernels while the threshed grain was being tossed into the air. Winnowing was usually done within barns, both the large double doors and the small 'winnowing-door' opposite being opened to provide a through draught. The grain was then tossed into the air using a shallow basket or swill, or a weyt, a flattish tray made of sheepskin fixed over a narrow hoop, and the wind blew the chaff out through the small winnowing door. On fine days the grain was sometimes taken outside to a piece of sloping ground and there 'deeted' (winnowed), the field being called the 'deetin' hill'. Wind could not of course be whistled up to order and not all barns were either built to

below
Hand-threshing, Lyth Valley, c.1900.
This somewhat posed picture shows hand-threshing with a jointed flail taking place on a threshing-floor behind closed double barn-doors.

catch the prevailing wind or in a sufficiently exposed place to make use of it, in which case draught had to be made by flapping cloths. Such winnowing-cloths are mentioned fairly commonly in inventories along with sacks and pokes, and were presumably flapped within the barns to blow the chaff out through the winnowing-door, though they may also have been used outdoors.

Threshing and winnowing (or 'dressing') the grain was usually started around October just before the cattle were tied up for the winter, and when straw was needed for bedding and fodder. Not all the crop was threshed at once; the process seems to have been carried out as and when straw and grain were needed during the winter months. Grain was apparently left on the stalks as long as possible, as a letter written on 23 March 1693 to James Grahme of Levens Hall by his agent, Hugh James, explains: 'I have given over threshing because it will keep better in the sheaves than threshed.' After threshing there again seems sometimes to have been a delay, so that winnowing did not necessarily follow on straight away. The inventory of William Rigg of Hawkshead Fields, taken on 5 February 1662, includes:

Oats, threshed and unthreshed £2 13s
Bigge winnowed and unwinnowed £4 2s 6d

A more detailed picture emerges from George Browne's account book. Between 1778 and 1791 he records several payments for threshing and dressing both oats and bigg, and these all occur between 8 October and 20 December. For instance on '18th Nov paid J. Hayton by coat 3/6; by cash 2/1 in full for 11 days threshing 5/6'; (whether J. Hayton agreed in advance to this curious method of payment is not recorded).

Mechanical Threshing

A mechanical threshing-machine was invented in Scotland in 1786 and its use spread rapidly over the next twenty to thirty years in the lowlands of Scotland and in Northumberland, areas where labour was relatively scarce, farms large and grain produced in large quantities as a cash crop. These machines hardly caught on in the central Lake District, where much of the grain was produced for home consumption and the advantage of mechanization must have been marginal; only a few farms show evidence of mechanical aids.

Threshing-machines needed a source of power. The early ones were powered by horses, wind or water; later in the nineteenth century steam-power was also used, and in this century oil-powered engines were introduced. Only horses, water and oil were harnessed in the central Lakes. Water was the cheapest and most readily available source of power but could, of course, only be used in existing buildings if they were conveniently sited near to a stream. Such buildings were rare, and very few new barns were built in the nineteenth century to take advantage of water-power. An exception is at Low Longmire Farm in the Rusland valley, where a comparatively large barn was built some distance away from the farm to make use of water-power from a stream. The barn had a small outshut at one end which housed the wheel. Outside the area, on the coastal plain and in the Eden valley, water-power was much more common. A remarkably complete example of a water-powered threshing-machine is to be found at Dunthwaite House, Setmurthy, where a large bank barn has a water-wheel built into an outshut alongside the ramp entrance to the first floor of the building.

Most farms had horses, and some farms made use of them to drive threshing-machines by harnessing them to a gin, or horse-engine. The horses were tethered to wooden cross-pieces and trod a circular path, turning a vertical axle which drove a horizontal shaft. This shaft passed into the barn and powered the threshing-machine through a belt mechanism. The earliest gins were made mostly of wood and needed protection from the elements. They were usually housed in one-storey buildings attached to one end of the main barns. These outshuts followed the shape of the gin and were thus either circular or octagonal in form. Buildings such as these were never common in the central Lakes although they were widespread in other parts of the country, notably southern Scotland and Northumberland. Very few have survived. Part of the circular building is still in place at Town End Farm, Colthouse, while Mains House Farm, Pooley Bridge, has an octagonal structure; but neither has any original machinery.

In the mid-nineteenth century cast-iron gins made by local blacksmiths began to replace the wooden prototypes. They were smaller, the horizontal shaft ran at ground-level rather than at head-height and the apparatus, being metal, did not need the protection of a building. In consequence very little material evidence of these gins remains, other than flat circular depressions or paved walkways for the horses and a hole low in the barn wall for the shaft.

The advent of the internal combustion engine brought compact oil-powered machinery which took up a fraction of the space of water-wheels or horse-gins and could be housed in tiny sheds tacked on to the back or sides of barns. At Craghouse Farm, Irton, such an engine is still in place, housed in a small stone lean-to with a corrugated iron roof.

If few 'prime movers' survive, even fewer actual threshing-machines are still to be found in barns. The one at Harrowhead Farm, Wasdale, is a notable survivor; constructed by William Heron of Gosforth in about 1900, it is built into one corner of the first floor of the bank barn.

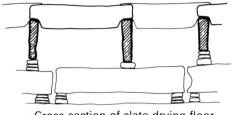

opposite above
Low Longmire Farm, Bouth.
This barn was built some
distance away from the
farmhouse – just seen on the left
of the picture – to take
advantage of a stream which
was used to power a waterwheel
housed in the lower end of the
building. The wheel drove a
threshing-machine in the upper
part of the main barn.

opposite below and right
**Corn-drier, Howe Green Farm,
Hartsop.**
One of the few remaining corn-
driers in the Lake District still
largely intact and perhaps the
only one not attached to a mill.
The drying-floor, of slatted
stone, was entered from the
upper door, the fire from the
lower door.

Cross-section of slate drying-floor

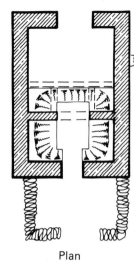

Plan

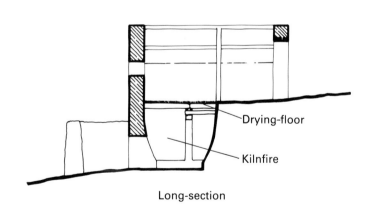

Cross-section

Drying-floor

Kilnfire

Long-section

Drying-floor

Kilnfire

Corn-Driers

After threshing and winnowing, the barley was ready to be malted
and the oats to be ground into meal. Oats are a soft, fatty grain and
need to be dried and hardened before they can be sent to the mill for
grinding. This was done in corn-drying kilns. One such kiln survives
complete, at Hartsop. It is a small two-storey structure built down

the slope, the lower end having a door into the fire-box and the upper end having access to the drying-floor. This floor is built entirely of slate, with narrow shafts of slate slotted into slate joists with spaces between. This allowed the warm air to percolate through to the grain above. The grain, spread out on the floor and resting either on straw or perhaps on a stiff hair cloth, would have been raked frequently to ensure even drying. The Hartsop kiln is placed between two farms and probably served the whole hamlet. It is quite separate from the Hartsop mills. Elsewhere corn-driers were often part of the mill complex, as were the kilns at Great Langdale, Troutbeck Bridge and Limefitt mills, which are known from documentary evidence, and the ones that still survive at Acorn Bank mill, near Penrith, at Heron mill, Beetham, and at Muncaster. In such cases the corn-driers were probably worked by the miller as part of the mill. This is confirmed for Limefitt by George Browne's accounts. In 1794 he wrote, 'paid J. Atkinson Miller [at Limefitt mill] for drying 4 years corn.' (His family had an interest in Limefitt mill, which perhaps explains why he had four years' credit.)

That so few kilns survived may suggest that substantial kiln buildings were not the norm and that more basic field-kilns were once widespread. Such kilns have been documented in parts of Wales: a fire was lit within a hollowed-out pit above which corn was laid over stone or timber slats supported on the banks around the pit. Field-names such as Kiln Mire at Little Tarn in the Newlands valley perhaps testify to such a use.

Granaries and Grain-Lofts

Once dried, a small amount of the grain was kept back for use as seed-corn in the following year. This seed-corn was sometimes quantified not in weight, but in terms of how much land it could sow; in 1624 the inventory of Nicholas Hunter of Buckbarrow, Wasdale, mentions 'seed enough for 2 yokings of arable land'. The remainder of the grain would be sent to the mill for grinding and then returned to the farmhouse for storage. Oatmeal was commonly stored in oak-plank chests in the farmhouse lofts, the meal being stamped down firmly to exclude as much air as possible. The loft-space nearest the chimney-hood was usually chosen as the cornloft, as the hood provided enough warmth to keep the grain dry. Granaries attached to barns were not common. In the eighteenth century a few were built above cartsheds added on to bank barns in the Hawkshead area; the northern wing of the main Town End barn at Colthouse housed a first-floor granary. A good complete example is at Hawes Farm, Broughton Mills, where the built-in wooden corn-bins still survive.

ROOT CROPS

The potato and the turnip were relatively late arrivals in the Lake District. Both became popular in the eighteenth century, turnips as animal feed and potatoes as a supplement to the staple diet. The first mention of turnips in the Browne manuscripts is in 1718 when Benjamin Browne paid threepence for turnip seed. Potatoes are first mentioned in 1723 when on 23 March he paid two shillings for two packs of them. By the end of the eighteenth century observers were able to report that in Cumberland 'potatoes were cultivated by almost every farmer'. George Browne seems to have gone to extremes: on 28 March 1783 he recorded 'planting potatoes round trees in orchard'.

Root vegetables need to be stored in the dark. A simple field-clamp was commonly used, a depression dug in the field and filled with potatoes bedded with straw, the whole covered over with more straw and earth. A few barns were built with root stores, others had parts adapted. At Wha House, Eskdale, part of the ground floor of the end bay of a bank barn became a root store with a chute next to the ramp, while at Grove Farm, Windermere, a small root store was built under the ramp of a bank barn. At Staveley Park, Staveley, there is one of the few detached root stores: a small rectangular drystone building built into the slope, and roofed with a rubble barrel-vault under a low-pitched roof. Similar vaulted potato stores are not uncommon in the Yorkshire Dales.

FLAX AND HEMP

By the end of the eighteenth century, hemp- and flax-growing had almost disappeared in the central Lakes. One observer writing at that time about Westmorland said that flax and hemp were 'rarely seen

Boon Crag Farm, Coniston. The small building to the right of the barn-door was built as a root store with loft above. The arched entrance, just visible, provided access to a chute to the lower floor.

growing here, though, 50 years ago, a little hemp was sown by almost every cottager and statesman'. Cumberland presented a similar picture, with only farmers in the 'northern extremities of the county' growing a little flax for family use, and 'much less less than formerly'.

Seventeenth-century inventories certainly testify to a fairly widespread growing of flax and hemp, and as early as 1578 tenants in Nether Wasdale had enclosures called hempgarths. Flax was used for weaving linen cloth, hemp for making ropes, sacks, and coarse fabric for pokes and winnowing-cloths. The name 'harden' was given to cloth made from the coarsest parts of both plants. Unlike wool, hemp and flax seem to have been produced in the central Lakes mainly for domestic use; but any surplus would have been sold to Kendal weavers to be woven into 'linsey', a 'union' cloth with linen warp and wool weft, made alongside the more common woollen cloths. 'Hemp, Hemp Yarn and Hemp Seed' valued at 6s. 8d. appear in the inventory of William Rigg at Hawkshead Field in 1662. This is not an unusual entry.

To extract the usable fibres from both hemp and flax, the stems, after separation from the seeds by threshing, have to be 'retted' to break down the tough outer covering and release the supple fibres within. Retting was either done by soaking the stems in a pond or dammed stream known locally as a 'dub' (the field-name 'Hemp Dub' survives in Longsleddale) for up to three weeks, or laying them out on the grass to catch the dew and rain for between four and six weeks. Either way the outer covering was broken down by bacterial fermentation. Once separated from their outer covering the fibres were hung up to dry, then 'scutched' or beaten to loosen all the fibres from the central pith or straw. Retting is a messy business and the strong-smelling residue can pollute streams. For good reasons was it decreed, in 1610 at Shap, that 'non henceforth shall wash any hempe or line in the Crooked Sike upon pain of default'; similar orders were widely imposed by manorial courts.

After retting, the hemp and flax fibres were dried and then stored somewhere in the main barn till such time as they were spun into yarn. It is quite possible that until the eighteenth century this spinning was still done on a whorl-spindle, a wooden rod weighted by a small disc of pottery or stone, which was twisted by the spinner. Spinning-wheels, turned first by hand and later by a treadle, are mentioned in inventories from the seventeenth century onwards. 'Wheels and cards' are a common combination, the cards being spiked boards for carding or straightening the fibres in preparation for spinning. Some inventories also refer to 'lines' or 'line wheels'. John Pearson of Buttermere, who died in 1674, had 'one spinning wheel and a line wheel 4/6d'; and again the inventory of George Rigge of High Yewdale in 1661 lists 'wheels and cardes with a line 2s.'. A line wheel was probably a yarn-winder, a reel on which the spun yarn was wound.

Spinning-Galleries

Spinning-wheels would have been used for wool as well as for flax and hemp. But where were they used? Several barns in the central Lakes have covered galleries projecting above the byre door at first-floor level, and these are known almost universally by the name 'spinning-galleries'. It is worth while to examine the evidence provided by the galleries themselves and in written records in support of this name. Apart from one or two just over the west Yorkshire border, these galleries are unique to the central Lakes.

The galleries are usually formed by an extension of the roof, supported on wooden uprights which are fixed to a platform canti-levered out from the wall on the first-floor level. A few are further supported by stone piers. The barn threshing-door usually opens on to the gallery and stone steps sometimes lead down from one end to ground-floor level. Galleries were attached to houses as well as to barns. As many as forty galleries survive in Cumbria and of these only half are attached to barns, the remainder being extensions of houses.

Galleries nearly always face north or north-east; this orientation was probably determined by the alignment of the barn – the gallery was on the opposite side to the main threshing-doors, which usually faced the prevailing south-west wind. Written references to these galleries are few and far between: an early allusion was made in 1840 by De Quincey, who spoke of 'a very interesting feature of the elder architecture annually becoming more rare, viz. the outside gallery, which is sometimes merely of wood, but is much more striking when provided for in the original construction of the house and completely enfoncée in the masonry'. Adam Sedgwick, writing about Dent in 1868, mentioned the use to which the galleries were put: 'the galleries were places of mirth and glee and active happy industry for there might be heard the buzz of the spinning wheels and the songs of those who were carrying out the labours of the day.' But Sedgwick was writing about town rather than farm galleries, as was H. S. Cowper in 1899 when he wrote in similar terms about Hawkshead galleries being used for spinners and weavers. Rather surprisingly, considering how attractive and conspicuous the galleries are, and the fact that they are specific to this area, very little else has been written about them; where the name 'spinning-gallery' came from is unclear.

What then was their use? It is hard to imagine even the most hardy spinner sitting on these galleries facing away from the sun when everywhere else in the country domestic spinning was carried out inside the house near the warmth of the fire. On the other hand, the decline of the galleries does seem to have coincided with a decline both in flax- and hemp-growing and in spinning as a farmhouse industry. More probable uses for the galleries were as drying areas, perhaps for flax and hemp after retting, or as places to prepare yarn for the looms. The textbook method of drying is either to lay out the fibres flat on a grassy field or to arrange bundles upright in a conical 'gait'. Either way, success would hardly have been guaranteed in the wet climate of the Lakes. If kilns were not used, could the galleries have provided covered drying areas? The nearest parallel that has so far been found is a biblical reference to house-roofs used as drying areas: Rahab hid the spies 'with the stalks of flax which she had laid in order on the roof' (Joshua 2: 6). Another possible use, and one that better explains the name, is suggested in a comparison with Devon linhays – open-fronted cattle-stalls which in the eighteenth century were apparently sometimes converted to other uses such as '"galleries" or "chain linneys" for "warping the chains", that is, preparing the yarn for the looms'. Or some galleries on barns may

right
Galleried barn, Yew Tree Farm, Coniston.

above right
Galleried barn, Boon Crag (High Waterhead), Coniston.
The lower doors lead to the underhousing. The gallery gives access to the hay- and grain-storage areas.

right
Dalehead Farm, Martindale.
Sadly this gallery no longer survives. When this picture was taken in 1934 the timber flooring had recently been dismantled. Inscribed on one of the piers was the date 1666. The gallery covered the entire front length of the house and appears to have been entered from first-floor level.

be merely covered walkways giving access to the first floor on the opposite side to the ramp and main doors, thus enabling farmers to reach the grain which had been dressed first and stored in the bays furthest away from the main doors. The galleries were probably also used for a variety of other purposes: both tanning and swill-making have been recorded as uses for two galleries in the recent past, and peat is said to have been seasoned in them.

Galleries on houses are no longer confined to smaller houses – indeed they occur more frequently on larger houses, especially around the margins of the region, such as Pool Bank, Crosthwaite, and Hodge Hill, Cartmel Fell. Many of these are sited above porches and are small and quite decorative, and could merely have been sitting-out areas.

PEAT

By the sixteenth century, woodland cover in the Lake District had declined to such an extent that it could only provide a small proportion of domestic fuel; peat was used instead, and remained in common use until coal became readily available in the nineteenth century.

Peat was largely cut from the open fell-land; and turbary, the right to cut peat for fuel, was carefully controlled by the manor courts in a way similar to the right of pasturage. Peat was only to be cut after a fixed date, some time between late April and late May, and each commoner was only allowed to dig on a limited number of 'day works' each year. Also, it seems that certain areas of peatmoss were delineated for the exclusive use of certain farms, for on 14 June 1780 George Browne wrote 'Rec. of Thos. Holme for trespassing on my peat moss on Kirkstone 12/6'.

Once dug, the peat was usually left to dry on the peatmoss or 'peat pot' for a month or two and then transported down to the farmhouse for storage in June or July. To keep a house in fuel for a year required a considerable volume of peat. In Buttermere in the eighteenth century each household provided the priest with a 'darrack' (a day-work) of peat each year, (which, presumably, he would have had to sell or give to his hosts). As they also provided board and lodging for two weeks at a time, there seem to have been about twenty-six households, giving the priest twenty-six day-works of peat each year. When Charles Middlefell sold Blea Tarn Farm in 1698 he reserved the right to 'dig 40 loads of peat in the Blea Tarn mosses'; in 1786 George Browne took forty carts from the Woundale mosses.

Peat from the highest mosses was often transported to lower ground by sledge. The hazardous job of sledding loads of peat down to the valley bottom was described by Thomas West in 1778:

The manner of procuring it [peat] is very singular. A man carries on his back a sledge to the top of the mountain and conducts it down the most awful descents, placing himself before it to prevent it running amain. For this purpose, a narrow furrow is cut in the mountain side which serves for a road to direct the sledge and to pitch the conductors heel in – a sledge holds one half of what a horse can draw on a good road.

The description of a 'narrow furrow cut in the mountain' belies the sophistication of many sledge tracks; they were well-engineered trackways, sometimes dug in, sometimes revetted, and furnished with clapper bridges to span becks and ditches. These furrows or peat-tracks seem to have been restricted to certain farms just like sheep intakes and demarcated peatmosses, and were just as jealously guarded.

Once down in the valley bottom, the peat was stored in peat-houses, small one-storey buildings that stood near the farmhouse and main barn. Many have now been converted to other uses, such as coal-places, although in Finsthwaite, for example, they are still invariably known as peat-houses. In a few areas the routine of digging, drying, sledding and storing was varied, the peat being stored for part of the year in small buildings at the edge of the open fell-land whence it had been gained. In parts of Eskdale, above Rawhead in Great Langdale, in Mardale and in the Duddon valley there are clusters of abandoned buildings near tracks on the lower slopes of the open fell-land. There are also documentary references to similar peat-storage buildings on

Peat-scales, Eskdale.
These peat-scales are on the open fell just above the highest intake. A sled track leads down from them to the lower slopes of the valley. The scales were used for drying peat harvested from the 'peat pots' nearby. Each peat-scale would probably have served a different farm.

the moss at Underbarrow in the Lyth valley and at Lorton in the Cocker valley, and one peat-hut still stands on the moss near Lane End Farm, Sizergh.

In Great Langdale the peat-huts themselves and their associated trackway appear to predate 1691, for the lower parts of the track lie between two fields which are mentioned in a document of that date. The brief for a lawsuit in Eskdale in 1795 describes the use of such huts: 'As it is often difficult to win their peats in summer, every tenant has a House or Peat Scale in some suitable place where he can conveniently go in winter to fetch his peats from when they are wanted and where they are deposited in summer and stored for that purpose.' In Eskdale many of these huts continued in use until about 1920, and local people remember a routine similar to the eighteenth-century one described above; semi-dried peats were stored in the huts and transported down to the farms in the winter as and when they were needed. And documentary evidence suggests that their use goes back as far as the sixteenth century, because in 1587 the Eskdale Commons award mentions 'Guddum Peat Skales' between Taw House and Cat Cove Beck. These buildings have been tentatively identified with remains still visible.

The thirty-five remaining peat-huts in Eskdale have recently been surveyed and mapped. They fall into two distinct types. The first is a low one-storey building built on a level patch of ground and having one entrance. The second is similar to many of the small field barns, being built down the slope and having two entrances, one at high level from a ramp or bank and the other at a lower level at the

below
Peat-scale, Eskdale.
Peat was put in through the small upper door and shovelled out from a door on the lower side.

opposite end of the building. Peats were tipped in through the higher door and dug out from the lower one. Both types are also found above Mardale and in Great Langdale.

In Eskdale there is some evidence that the two-storey type superseded the one-storey type, and that this change was associated with a change in transport arrangements. The bank buildings are all slightly lower down the slope and near sled-tracks, while the low buildings are not near any recognizable trackways. This suggests that horse-panniers preceded sledges as a way of transporting peat. Certainly, in the late seventeenth century, Celia Fiennes noticed 'horses on which they have sort of pannyers . . . that they strew full of . . . turff [peat]' as well as hay, lime and dung.

CHARCOAL AND BARK

Woodlands not only provided resources such as shelter and forage for pigs, fodder for cattle and sheep and timber for house repairs, but also two important crops with industrial uses: charcoal, widely used for smelting iron and other ores, and bark for tanning hides. The agricultural products of the woodlands were enjoyed by the farmers under various systems of tenant rights; the industrial products, on the other hand, remained under the control of the lord and were exploited under licence.

Furness Abbey worked 'cole pittes' and 'cole pots' in the Furness woods, south of Hawkshead and Coniston, using the charcoal to smelt haematite. Until the mid-1940s charcoal continued to be made for use in iron-smelting throughout the region, in forges, and as a component of gunpowder. In the 1990s charcoal-burners are active again in the Furness woods, providing fuel not for the local smelt-mines but for barbecues. In the Middle Ages the burners seem to have relied on underwood or dead-wood which could be cut from the oak-woods without warrant. In 1565 the inhabitants of Hawkshead were allowed to make charcoal 'using the shreddings, tops, lops, crops and under wood but not timber'. By the eighteenth century the charcoal industry had become more systematic, and banks of woodland were planted and coppiced on a regular rotation of between thirteen and fifteen years, the straight coppice-poles providing top-quality charcoal. Oak was the tree most commonly planted, but alder, sycamore, ash and even birch were also occasionally coppiced.

The charcoal-burners were known as 'collies' or 'colliers'. Their work of converting wood to charcoal demanded constant attention: the pits needing filling, firing, rearranging or dousing and finally extinguishing and raking-out, and as one pit was burning out another would be loaded up. The colliers and their families were often peripatetic, living in the woods for the duration of the burning and building temporary huts for themselves. They first cleared an area large enough for their hut and usually three pitsteads – level areas

top

Charcoal-burner's house, c.1898.

The sod roof was weighted with thick coppice poles. Slender woven poles surrounded part of the base and the rest was stone, framing the doorway. The door was constructed like a hurdle with broom or bracken sandwiched between poles.

above

Charcoal-burner's house, c.1900.

Notice the small squat chimney attached to the oval hut.

cleared of moles or rabbits and protected by windscreens, hurdles six to eight feet high and made of wattles interwoven with bracken.

Between November and April the wood was felled, except for the oak-trees which were harvested in the spring when the sap was rising, after which the bark was peeled and sent for tanning. The wood was cut into two-foot lengths and stacked in preparation for the burnings which took place in the spring and summer.

The colliers' huts were 'thacked' conical houses built on small, level platforms near to the pitsteads. Coppice-poles, arranged either in an oval or circle with the top ends bound together, were used for the main frames of these huts. This framework was covered with sods laid overlapping and weighted down with poles or stones. Sometimes a short wall of wattle hurdles protected the first few feet at the base of the hut, or occasionally a drystone retaining wall was built.

Inside, the huts were sparsely furnished: two beds either side of the low door, and between the beds a hearth in the centre of the floor. The inside of one such hut on the east side of Lake Coniston was immortalized by Arthur Ransome in *Swallows and Amazons* as the home of 'the Billies':

> On each side of the hut a stout log divided off a place where there were rugs and blankets. Between the two logs there was an open space, where it looked as if there had been a small fire. The open light came through the door holes. Not a speck of light came from between the poles of which the wigwam was made. Every chink had been well stuffed with moss . . . high above . . . was pitch darkness, where the poles met each other at the pointed top of the hut.

A few huts, especially those with drystone walls round the base, incorporated chimneys – short stumpy structures, interestingly circular in form, standing upon rectangular bases and projecting from the back of oval-plan huts.

These huts were not always the property of their occupiers, but seem sometimes to have been provided for their use. An account of expenses for setting up 'coling' and bark-peeling in a wood near Troutbeck in 1770 included amounts for:

Making a new pit stead	0 – 2 – 0
To heaping up Cabbin	0 – 2 – 6
To hurdles & bringing to	0 – 3 – 6

– the workers providing, and being paid for, labour only.

6

Barn Plans

I<small>N SEVERAL</small> parts of England excavations have shown that on medi-aeval farmsteads a longhouse tradition prevailed, with men and beasts sheltered under one roof. The family was at one end of the house, the animals at the other, separated either by a walled through-passage or by some less substantial partition. From the thirteenth century onwards men and beasts were progressively separated, so that by the sixteenth century the longhouse seems to have disappeared through-out much of the country. In the Lake District, the evidence for pre-seventeenth-century farmhouses is sketchy and as chapter 3 shows, very few longhouse plans remain.

By the sixteenth century, some Lake District records mention both houses and barns, and also, in a few cases, cow-houses – implying that by that date separate farm buildings were being constructed. A 1570 survey of three farms or 'Hardwykes' on the east side of Coniston Lake recorded that both Park-a-Moor Farm and Waterside Park Farm consisted of 'one olde mansion house, one olde barne' while Lawson Park had merely 'one olde mansion house'. All three were lived in by people defined as 'hirds'; perhaps Lawson Park was still a longhouse while the others had separate cow-house/barns.

Nearly all surviving barns show signs of mixed use, with rooms both for animals and for hay and grain storage. The main arrange-ments found are described below.

SINGLE-STOREY BARNS

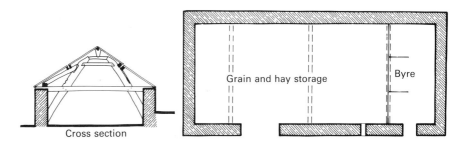

Wall End barn,
Great Langdale.

Cross section

Grain and hay storage

Byre

The simplest kind of barn is a single-storey building standing on level ground. Such structures are now in the minority and many appear to have been superseded by two-storey bank barns. Typically, the single-storey buildings are of drystone construction, three or four bays long, and many have roofs supported on pairs of full crucks. Some, such as the barn at Low Hallgarth, Little Langdale, have a threshing-floor and an adjacent walled-off cow-byre. Others, such as Wallend, Great Langdale, and High Hallgarth, Little Langdale, are undivided but have a second entrance at one end. In this case the entrance presumably once led into a small byre, although all fittings have now been removed. In some there is no evidence of any threshing-floor; the floor of the barn at Wallend, for example, is cobbled. Threshing may well have been done outside these barns on portable wooden threshing-floors.

The dating of these small cruck barns is problematic. Their style and form suggest a mediaeval date, but the available evidence suggests that in a few cases they were still being built in the early seventeenth century. At Low Hallgarth the cruck barn clearly predates the adjoining house in which stands a cupboard dated 1682. At Wallend an earlier date can be suggested with reasonable certainty, for in 1612 one of the four farmsteads at Wallend belonged to a Charles Satterthwaite who made his will on 11 November that year. He wrote that 'Robert my brother shall builde one Barne at the Walend in Langdale of three paire of trees within the terme and space of three yeeres followinge, and to the buildinge thereof I give unto him all my wood and tymber both at Walend and hackeath [Hacket] and xs which he oweth me'. Charles Satterthwaite was buried at Grasmere on 17 November 1612 and his will was proved on 8 December. Although it cannot be said with absolute certainty that the surviving cruck barn at Wallend is the one specified in the will, it does have three pairs of crucks and it seems more than likely that it was built by Robert Satterthwaite under the terms of his brother's will.

above
Barn, Wallend Farm, Great Langdale.
A four-bay barn, with the roof supported on three pairs of full crucks. The far end would originally have been partitioned off for a small byre. This barn was almost certainly put up in accordance with instructions in a will dated 1612.

right and opposite above
Bank barn, Townend Farm, Troutbeck.

Bank Barns Built down the Slope

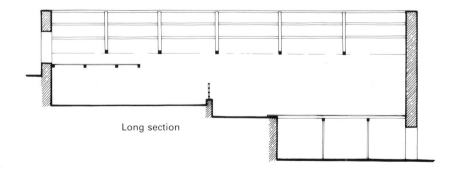

Long section

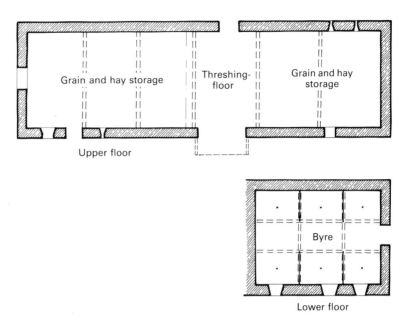

Bank barn is the name coined by R. W. Brunskill to describe two-storey barns built on sloping land with access to the upper level from a ramp or bank. These barns took two main forms, according to whether the longer axis ran along the slope or down it. Bank barns are the distinctive type in the Lake District. Although found elsewhere in small numbers – for example in the west of Scotland, parts of Wales and Devon (and also in considerable numbers in the United States of America, north-west Spain and eastern Switzerland) – in England their concentration in the upland areas of the Lake District is a notable example of a peculiarly regional style of building and one that is particularly well suited to the climate.

Barns built down the slope generally rose one storey above ground at the upper end and two storeys at the lower end. The first floor was used for storing grain and hay and was divided by a threshing-floor running across the width of the building. The underhousing was usually taken up by cattle-byres, with access through the lower gable-end into a central manure/feeding-passage. This type of bank barn is more common in the eastern than in the western valleys and is particularly prevalent in Troutbeck and Kentmere. It does not, however, belong exclusively to one area and is often found in association with the second type. At Beckstones Farm, Ullswater, two barns, one of each type, stand next to one another. Nor can the two types be separated chronologically. Although there is evidence that some bank barns built down the slope were medieval in date, this type persisted alongside the second pattern until well into the nineteenth century, as is shown by the substantial mid-nineteenth-century example at Townend Farm, Colthouse.

above
Bank barn, High Oxenfell Farm, Coniston.
This bank barn is built down the slope. The steepness of the slope means that the underhousing runs beneath only half its length.

right
Bank barn, Townend Farm, Colthouse.
A nineteenth-century barn with a central passage under half its length. The outshut to the right of the door was built to house a cartshed with granary above.

There are remains of two bank barns which are possibly mediaeval in origin. The first is Low Park barn at Rydal rebuilt by Sir Daniel Fleming in 1659, and a detailed account of his building activities survives. The barn is a large six-bay structure some 74 feet by 24 feet running down the slope, with an entrance to the cow housing through the lower gable-end and access to the first floor via a ramp at one side. Fleming's accounts show that the new barn was built around the remains of an earlier one and on a similar alignment, for his waller John Holme was paid for walling 'beside 16 yards of old wall which was not meddled with all'. Meticulous detective work by Blake Tyson has identified the pre-existing walls as being the foundations, most of the lower gable and part of one long wall against the ramp, thus showing that the older – possibly mediaeval – building was also a bank barn built down the slope.

At Rydal Hall there are two other bank barns both built down the slope. The earlier 'old barn' can only be dated tentatively through papers recording extensions made to it. In 1673 a brewhouse adjoining the barn had its chimney reconstructed, which suggests that the brewhouse predated 1673 by a considerable period. Moreover the brewhouse blocked one of the narrow windows at the side of the barn, indicating that the barn itself was of sixteenth-century date or earlier. It is 55 feet long by 25 feet wide. Now much altered, it originally had underhousing for fourteen cows each side of a central manure/feed-passage entered through a central door in the lower gable.

The second bank barn at Rydal can be dated with certainty, for on 28 June 1670 Sir Daniel Fleming wrote, 'this day was raised ye home barn at Rydall.' This barn is 85 feet 9 inches long by 25 feet wide and is of eight bays. Its layout differs from the two barns described previously in having underhousing beneath only half its length, the threshing-floor being at ground-level. Also the underhousing was originally without stalls, being used presumably as a loose-box and only later fitted out. This barn is unusual in having a small elevated door, approached by a ramp, leading into one end of the upper storey. Perhaps this gave access to the first crops put into the barn – a necessary measure in a barn of such immense length and storage capacity.

The Rydal corn-barn pattern, with underhousing under only half the length, became the most common for bank barns built down the slope. The great advantage of this arrangement is that if the building is aligned south-west–north-east to catch prevailing winds across the threshing-floor, loop-lights in either side of the under-housing will also catch the wind and give cross-ventilation for the cattle, while the door into the manure/feed-passage remains relatively sheltered. Admittedly, many barns of this design are not thus aligned: for instance, two at Colthouse are built at right angles to one another.

Bank Barns Built along the Slope

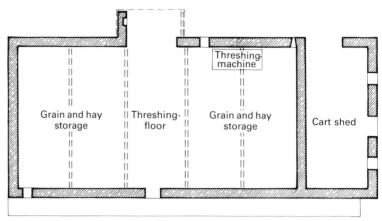

Upper floor

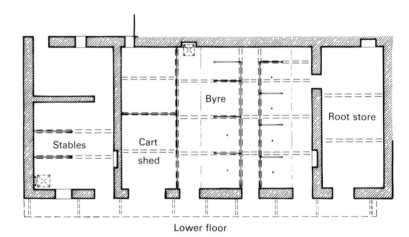

Bank barn, Wha House Farm, Eskdale.

Lower floor

Bank barns built along the slope have access to the upper storey from the bank on the higher side and to the underhousing from ground-level on the lower side. This style of bank barn became the most common type in the Lake District, and was sometimes built on almost flat ground by constructing a large ramp to reach the double doors opening on to the first-floor threshing-floor.

With access to the underhousing being through one of the long walls, it became possible to subdivide the ground-floor space and have separate doors into the 'rooms' so created. Most bank barns built along the slope had at least three doors at the lower level. In some valleys such as Great Langdale, all three doors characteristically opened into the manure/feeding-passages running across the width of the building with byres either side. Elsewhere, and especially in Eskdale and Wasdale in the nineteenth century, the underhousing was divided between three different uses: a wide central door opened into a cartshed which was flanked by a byre on one side and a stable on the other. Byres usually had one or two single passages running from front to back of the barns which served as manure- and feeding-passages and off which opened the stalls. Only in very large, late nineteenth-century bank barns were separate manure- and feeding-passages commonly provided. In the eastern and southern valleys the doors to the underhousing were often sheltered by a small projecting pentice roof.

The earliest reliably dated bank barn of this type is yet another built by Sir Daniel Fleming, this time at Coniston Old Hall. On 20 March 1688 Fleming wrote, 'this day was laid the foundation of the Great Barn etc. at Coniston Hall.' The barn was finished in the summer of that year and still stands, albeit much altered. The barn measures 90 feet by 28. Originally the underhousing had five entrance doors, two into byres, one for a loose-box, one for a stable and one for an ox-house. The upper storey was approached along an artificial ramp. Barns of this type continued to be built throughout the eighteenth and nineteenth centuries and a few were put up in the early twentieth century. Perhaps the latest dated example is the barn at Moor Farm, near Keswick, with a date-stone of 1909. Unfortunately, barns which are dated are in the minority; but several appear on stylistic grounds to be of the seventeenth century or earlier. However, unless and until more documentary evidence is forthcoming, the genesis of bank barns must remain uncertain.

The basic rectangular form of these barns was sometimes augmented by lean-to cartsheds, granaries and pigsties. Pigsties were most common in the western valleys, and almost every farm in Wasdale had a pair of 'in-and-out' sties added to one end of its bank barn in the nineteenth century. Around Hawkshead, cartsheds with

right
Wha House Farm, Eskdale.
A very large mid-nineteenth-century barn. The underhousing has provision for stables on the left, cartshed and byre.

above right
Holme Ground Farm, Coniston.
Two bank barns on either side
of the house, both built across
the slope with access to the
underhousing through doors in
the lower long side.

right
Crosslands Farm, Rusland.
The left door in the
underhousing led to a stable, the
others to byres. The central
door has been made into a
window at a later date.

granaries above, located in a wing to one side of the double doors, were especially prevalent. Townend barn, in Troutbeck, is unusual in having a two-storey wing added to each end of the ramp side, the upper part of one wing being originally fitted with bins for a granary. Pool Bank, Crosthwaite, and High Grigg Farm, Underbarrow, both have barns with a single projecting two-storey wing.

BARNS WITH GALLERIES

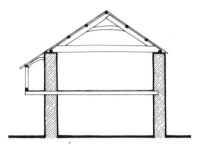

Galleried barn, Yew Tree Farm, Coniston.

Cross section showing gallery. Yew Tree Farm barn, Coniston.

The most distinctive and a much-debated addition to barns is that of covered galleries known as 'spinning-galleries'. These first-floor projecting galleries covered by short pentice roofs were not confined to barns but were also found on houses. As relatively few survive on barns it is difficult to make generalizations. Well-preserved galleries are found at Yew Tree Farm, Coniston, Boon Crag Cottage, Coniston, Low Tilberthwaite Farm, Coniston, Stangends Farm, Coniston, Bellman Houses, Winster, Townend, Troutbeck, Low Fold Farm, Troutbeck, and Thorn House, Hartsop (although the building here is now in domestic use). Despite the many differences, some similarities emerge. All except the Townend gallery are on the opposite side of the building to the main doors, and shelter the doors to the ground-floor underhousing. All are on bank barns built along the slope, and all have access from ground-level up external stone steps as well as internal access. The gallery at Townend is the odd man out as it covers the main double doors and provides covered access to two projecting two-storey wings (in themselves an unusual feature). Two other barns, however, are known to have had similar galleries in the past. Barns at Pool Bank, Crosthwaite, and High Grigg Hall, Underbarrow, each had galleries leading from the main ramp to two-storey wings.

The use to which these galleries were put is discussed in chapter 5. It seems highly unlikely they really were spinning-galleries, and more probable that they provided space used in several different ways – as drying-areas, for swill-making, for beehives, or to give access to the rear of the grain-storage area for extracting small quantities of grain for threshing. This was the general conclusion reached by H. S.

above
Galleried barn, Bellman Houses, Winster.
A particularly lofty gallery with access from the ground up stone steps.

right
Galleried barn, Townend Farm, Troutbeck.
This gallery gives covered access to the two wings of the barn. The wing on the left has the granary at first-floor level. The barn has a date of 1666 carved on one of the lintels.

above
Galleried barn, Townend Farm,
Troutbeck.

Cowper in 1899 when he wrote: 'no other explanation is necessary than the wetness of the climate . . . under these galleries . . . were stored . . . produce and effects which should be kept from the rain.'

Threshing-Floors

Whether the barn was built down or along the slope, the off-centre position of the threshing-doors and floor in relation to the overall length of the barn was remarkably consistent, forming more storage bays at one end than at the other. Usually the threshing-floor was just one bay in from one end. Thus in a five-bay barn the threshing-floor was normally positioned to leave a single bay to one side and three bays to the other, while in a four-bay barn the spaces either side were of one and two bays respectively. The reason behind this asymmetrical arrangement is not entirely clear but may be connected to the fact that unthreshed grain takes up more room than straw, or that hay needs more room than grain.

Long Barns

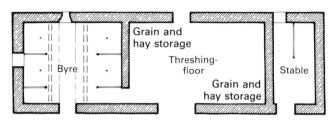

opposite top
Wasdale Head.

opposite below
Wasdale Head.

right
Barn, Fold Head Farm, Watendlath, Borrowdale.

below
Barn, Fold Head Farm, Watendlath, Borrowdale.
A one-storey barn with grain storage areas in the centre and a byre to one side and a stable to the other.

Although bank barns were the dominant plan-type, mixed barns, for both storage of grain and housing of animals, were built on one level in some valleys. Their plans fall into two main types, a simple rectangle and an L-shape. The rectangular barns had a threshing-floor with storage for grain and hay either side, the arrangement being

top
Yew Tree Farm, Coniston.

above
Wall End Farm, Great Langdale.

right
Troutbeck Park Farm,
Troutbeck.

above
Troutbeck Valley *by W. Taylor-*
Longmire.

similar in form and size to the first floors of bank barns. Housing for
cattle, or for cattle and horses, was either at one end or at both ends
of the building and had lofts over, reached from within the main
barn-space.

L-Shaped Barns

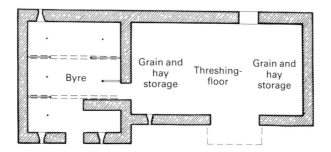

On a few farms at Wasdale Head a distinctive type of L-shaped
barn-plan is found. Built on a single level, such a threshing-barn has
flanking byres which are slightly deeper than the grain-storage area,
the extra depth being covered by a small outshut roof, usually at the
back. A door in the centre of this outshut leads into a central manure/
feeding passage with byres on either side. This type of barn has
similarities with some Lancashire barns, but also marked differences.
In the Lancashire type, one end is broadened to take two rows
of stalls served by a feeding-passage and two manure-passages, each
entered through a separate door in the gable-end; the outshut is
always at the front, with a pentice roof over the main doors. At

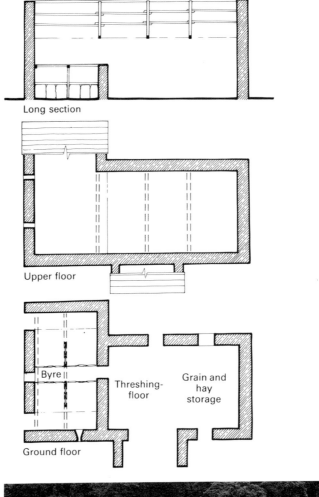

Long section

Upper floor

Byre

Threshing-floor

Grain and hay storage

Ground floor

above
Barn, Beckstones Farm, Patterdale.

right
Barn, Beckstones Farm, Patterdale.
This unusual L-shaped barn has doors in the gable-end leading to byres with a loft above.

Beckstones, Patterdale, an L-shaped barn more nearly approaches this plan with doors in the gable-end, albeit with a rear projection. At Hazelhead Farm in the Duddon valley there is a strange hybrid — an L-shaped barn with underhousing beneath the wider end.

TWO-STOREY FIELD BARNS

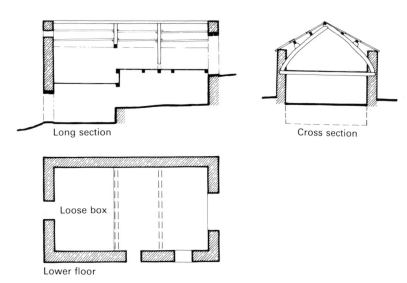

Long section

Cross section

Loose box

Lower floor

right
Field barn, Hartsop Hall Farm, Patterdale.

Many of the smaller farm buildings, despite having widely diverse uses, had largely similar forms. Size and position were the main distinctions between, for example, peat-houses and hogg houses, or bark-houses and hennery-piggeries. Many smaller structures were of two storeys and built on sloping ground rather like miniature bank barns. Field barns were no exception and most had housing for animals beneath storage for hay. They were built both along and down the slope. In the first case, access to both the hay-storage areas and the underhousing was in the long walls, whereas in the second case access to the storage loft was usually through the gable-end while the underhousing was entered through a door at one end of one long wall. This second plan is the type most commonly found.

A few field barns were larger in size so as to accommodate grain as well as hay, in which case they were similar in form to bank barns built along the slope and had threshing-floors and threshing-doors.

7

Construction:
Materials and Techniques

It is often said that before the seventeenth century many buildings in the Lake District were 'cabins' with wattle walls and thatched roofs, insubstantial structures that hardly outlived a generation. Such evidence as there is, however, tends to point the other way: buildings may have been less substantial and less well finished than their successors of the seventeenth and eighteenth centuries, but they were built of permanent materials, stone and oak, which were locally available.

STONE

When a new house was built in Outgate in the early years of this century, the walling stone came 'from just behind the house', pieces off a natural outcrop. Both archaeological and early written evidence suggests that wall-building with readily available stone, either taken off an outcrop or surface-gathered, was a practice long followed. Stone was probably much more readily available than timber which was tightly controlled by manorial rights, and which, by the end of the sixteenth century, had become a relatively scarce resource.

Deserted settlements and remains of shielings reveal buildings with walls of locally gathered stone. The study of field-boundaries has also yielded valuable evidence for an ancient stone-building tradition. The ring-garth wall in Great Langdale could be as early as the thirteenth century; the ring-garth wall in Crosby Ravensworth was rebuilt in stone in the early sixteenth century. In other areas it has been suggested that stone walling for houses and for field-boundaries went together naturally, so that a change from hedges to stone walls tended to be contemporary with a change from timber-framing to masonry construction.

As will be shown later, tenants had a customary right to the supply of timber for house-building and repairs. In the mid-seventeenth century these, by then ancient, customs were enunciated by Mr Gilpin. What the timber was supplied for was carefully set down. The Lord 'was to allow only principals ... Riggin tree, sparres, Ribbs and Laths'. No mention is made of any timber for wall construction, which suggests that masonry walls were then the norm.

Such early written records as exist confirm this general picture. Celia Fiennes, in 1698, mentions a remote village (probably Hartsop) as being 'of sad little hutts made up of drye walls only stones piled together'. A few years later Thomas Machell wrote, 'in these Dales are not many villages nor towns, but for the most part stone houses which stand very frequently one from another half a mile distant.'

In the heart of the Lake District the predominant rock is slate, divided geologically into the Borrowdale Volcanic Series, the Skiddaw Slates and Silurian gritstone, and varying in colour from watery green to deep blue-black with occasional outcrops of red, brown and shades of grey and black. After a century or two of weathering, it is sometimes hard to distinguish between blue and green stone in a building, as the damp climate favours the growth of lichens. So pervasive is the lichen cover that all stone walls tend to end up looking grey-green. The exceptions lie in part of the western valleys of Eskdale and Wasdale, where a pinkish Eskdale granite weathers to a dull brown.

Building stone came in two forms, surface-gathered and quarried.

Surface-Gathered Stone

Boulders or cobbles, rounded by water or glacial action, are widespread in becks and rivers or loosely embedded in the subsoil. In many valleys there was a superabundance of such stones and clearing them to provide meadows and arable fields must have taken much effort over several generations. Many were incorporated into field-boundaries. In a few places walls and buildings could not absorb all the available stone. Heaps or clearance cairns were left in the corners of many fields, as in parts of Great Langdale and Wasdale Head and also further east in Dentdale. In other places, for instance parts of Eskdale and Wasdale, where walls five feet thick are found, the walls were enlarged.

At least until the seventeenth century, stone boulders were in most places not a scarce resource to be shared amicably, but a commodity that was readily available. They seem, therefore, not to have been subject to the same rights and controls as timber and peat. In 1682 Michael Bowness of Dale End Farm, Little Langdale, was enfranchised with the right to get slate for repairs – a common occurrence. Stone very rarely appears as an asset in wills or inventories, at least in its unbuilt form. The will of John Mawson of Silverhowe, Gosforth, dated 1740, is unusual. In it he bequeathed to his eldest son Joseph 'all free stone both upon the premises and also on the common'.

Cobbles were either laid whole, if roughly rectangular, or else the bulge at the front was knocked off to form a face, as no other form of dressing was possible. In some of the earlier buildings, boulders of enormous size, sometimes as much as three feet across, were used as corner-stones and foundations beneath walls of lesser, but still

substantial, boulders. The oldest barn at Stool End, Great Langdale, and Thwaite House near Ashness Farm in Borrowdale, both exhibit foundations of Cyclopean proportions. Also built of huge boulders are the pele tower at Yewbarrow Hall, Longsleddale, the abandoned Scales Farm in Netherwasdale, the remains of the older walling at Low Park barn, Rydal, and the identifiable remains of the mediaeval ring-garth wall in Great Langdale. By the time Wallend barn was built in Great Langdale in 1617, much smaller cobblestones were being used. A century and a half later walls built solely of cobblestones had largely given way to a mixed construction: cobbles interspersed with quarried stone, some of the larger pieces of which provided 'throughs' to bind the two outer surfaces of the wall together. In Langdale this construction is characterized by the use of strategically placed cobblestones above windows and doors, wooden lintels being covered first by a course of thin slates projecting from the face of the wall, and then by a course of cobbles holding the slates in place.

On the higher reaches of the open fells as well as on some of the lower land there was an abundance of sharp, angular surface stone which had flaked off from the sheer rock faces over several millennia. This stone was used for hogg houses on the higher intakes, and for peat-huts, shielings and shepherds' huts on the open fells. It was also transported down into the valley bottoms to be used with cobbles for field-walls and buildings.

Quarried Stone

Although by the nineteenth century quarried stone had almost entirely replaced surface-gathered stone as the common building material, the two types subsisted side by side from the seventeenth century onwards. Stone for walls was obtained from dozens of small quarries, the remains of which are visible on the lower slopes of the fells. In the nineteenth century larger quarries were opened up, and these provided stone not only for the new tourist resorts within the area but also for export to the rapidly expanding towns and cities elsewhere in England.

The few building contracts which survive from the seventeenth and eighteenth centuries include requirements such as the contractors' 'finding and providing all stones', and payments offered to named wallers for days' work in 'stone-getting' or 'finding stone' or occasionally for work at 'ye quarry'. No payments are made for the stone itself, only for the effort involved in retrieving it. All this is in contrast to the details in such contracts for roof-slates, which were bought by the load direct from the quarry or from slate-dealers. The inference from these phrases seems to be that building stone was either surface-gathered, or reused, or was worked by wallers from small quarries not continuously manned. Quarries for walling stone thus seem to have been very much domestic affairs, used as and when they were

opposite top
Barn, Stool End Farm, Great Langdale.
This barn has walls built mainly of river-boulders laid dry without mortar.

opposite below
Barn, Hartsop Hall Farm, Patterdale.
The walls are built of surface-gathered stone laid dry without mortar.

above

Barn wall, Low Park Farm, Rydal.
The main part of this wall was built in 1659 of a mixture of quarried and surface-gathered stone laid dry. The wall was raised in the eighteenth century when quarried stone was used.

needed, until the walling-stone industry expanded in the nineteenth century to the point of exporting stone out of the area.

Many of these small quarries were sited on the lower slopes of the fells on common land. They appear to have been common quarries with common rights to take stone. A lease of Mythop (Meathop) at the end of the seventeenth century emphasizes the link between common land and quarries: Thomas Barrow in 1690 was prohibited from 'Delving any in the enclosed ground'.

Stone-getting, even from a nearby quarry or outcrop, had to be paid for in man-hours; so clearly the cost of a new building would be less if stone from an earlier building could be reused. This practice seems to have been relatively commonplace. In 1758 Jonathan Birkhead wrote to William Birkett, about a proposed new building in Troutbeck, that 'there was an old Hoghouse in the Nothern end of my Fathers Intack from which [we] might have had stones . . . [but] if that be removed . . . some remains of old Houses or Walls . . . [may] be had at a reasonable rate . . . At the worst . . . they might . . . be had out of a quarry in Geo Jonies Bank, or elsewhere . . .' From extant documentation, it would appear that the size of the buildings and the wealth of the owner were no bars to such practice. Sir Daniel Fleming's new barn at Low Park, Rydal, already mentioned, reused some walling from an earlier building. Stone for the great barn at Sockbridge, built in 1699, came partly from Penrith Fell and partly from demolishing two barns built only forty years previously. At Skirwith Hall in 1773, a barn was built partly with new stone and partly with reused stone; and although this is a little outside the central Lake District, the building accounts do give some idea of the possible savings from using second-hand walling materials. The estimate allowed for 'taking down and Removing 300 [square] yards [of] Stones of the old Building @ 2d' and 'Quarrying and carting 500 [square] yards of new stone @ 1od'. The reused stone therefore cost only one-fifth the price of new stone, a considerable saving. Moreover the reused stone would have required less building time, as quarried stone needs hammer-dressing to square it up and put a face on it.

By the end of the nineteenth century, the increase in building activity had led to a reliance on new stone from the numerous local quarries by then open. But the price was not low and the purchase of such stone still represented a substantial part of the total building cost. When Ashleigh, a house in Little Langdale, was put up in the 1920s, it was said that it 'cost as much carting stone [from Hodge Close Quarry] with horses and carts belonging to farmers – that it did for putting house up'. The accounts for Sir Daniel Fleming's barn in 1659 show that very little had changed; even though he reused much stone, the cost of stone- and slate-getting came to almost 60 per cent of the total cost of the new barn. Today many of the smaller Lake District quarries have closed and supplies of second-hand stone and slate are once again being sought as a cheaper alternative to

quarried stone. This has the unfortunate consequence that the countryside is being denuded of redundant stone walls and small underused buildings – many of which have great historical significance.

Wall Construction

Wall stone was sometimes laid dry and sometimes with a mortar which could be made of either lime and sand, or of clay. Drystone construction of both surface-gathered and quarried stone was widely used for barns and other non-domestic buildings until the end of the eighteenth century. For smaller and remote buildings, it continued occasionally until well into the nineteenth century. The shepherd's hut built on Woundale in about 1838 had 'Walls . . . walled without lime' specified. The great advantage of drystone construction is that any ingress of water will have less effect than in a mortared wall, where the clay or lime mortar can be washed out causing subsidence. There are two main disadvantages. The first is that the absence of mortar allows draughts through the cracks and holes; the second is that drystone construction calls for good-quality stone. Most house-walls seem to have been built with some sort of mortar core, but generalizations are difficult because so many houses are now rendered on the outside as well as being plastered within, and because in ruined buildings the core tends to wash out. There does not seem to be a neat progression from clay to lime mortar. Although clay cores appear in some smaller, earlier houses, (such as Hoathwaite Cottage, Coniston, which was probably built in the early seventeenth century), many other houses of a similar date have lime mortar in their walls. But by the late seventeenth century clay mortaring seems to have become all but obsolete as a technique.

Stonework techniques vary from valley to valley. Broadly, though, it can be stated that by the mid-eighteenth century most walls were constructed with intermittent layers of large flat through-stones binding the two outer skins of the wall. This was something rarely thought necessary by earlier builders, even on substantial buildings. At Sizergh Castle, in the 1940s, one of the (probably) sixteenth-century barns suddenly collapsed; the then owner, Henry Hornyold-Strickland, noted laconically in his diary 'no throughs'. Throughs were sometimes arranged decoratively, on house-fronts as an undressed 'drip course'

Lane Foot, Troutbeck, by William Green, 1809.
A large Brathay flag supports one side of the porch, others form part of the wall of the small outbuilding. Notice the gable entrance with its studded door, and the cantilevered chimney detail.

LANE FOOT

above window-heads or on barns symmetrically in rows on the gable-end.

Some stones, when quarried, split naturally at an angle between the bed and the face. When laid flat, such stones give buildings a distinct sawtooth profile. The barn at The Bield, Little Langdale, is a good example. By the late eighteenth century many stonemasons laid such stones at an angle, tilting them downwards towards the outside face of the walls. A wall constructed in this way is said to be 'watershot', the tilt allowing any moisture in the wall to drain outwards. The other obvious advantage of this technique is that it produces a wall with a flat outer surface. Many such watershot walls, with tightly fitting stones and well-recessed mortar, give the impression of being built dry.

In the Hawkshead and Ambleside areas, huge stone flags, up to eight feet in length, are a prominent feature of many buildings. They were also used to provide shard fences, stock-proof field-boundaries of rows of interlocking upright stones embedded in the ground. Known as Brathay flags, they derive from the bed that runs along the limestone fault that crosses the central Lake District from south-west to north-east. The quarry from which they mostly came was above the banks of the river Brathay. A prominent building with flag walls is the west wing of Bend-or-Bump Cottage in Hawkshead. Upright flags some 2 feet by 6 feet support a slightly jettied and gabled first floor of timber construction, clad in smaller, vertically hung slates. Pictorial evidence shows that such flags were also used at first-floor level as balustrades on galleries, such as the one that used to exist at Low Fold, Ambleside.

ARCHITECTURAL DETAILS

Crow-Steps

Crow- or corbie-steps are the names given to a distinctive stepped projection of the gable-end wall above the level of the roof-slates. This arrangement functioned in the same way as dressed coping-stones, protecting the ends of the rows of slates from being whipped up by the wind. False crow-steps were also put on buildings. These had a similar profile, but were built up on top of the slates rather than being continuations of the gable wall.

Crow-steps are found both on houses and on some of the smaller agricultural buildings, such as the remote shepherds' huts built for the Brownes near the Kirkstone Pass in the mid-nineteenth century and the much earlier hogg house in Dovedale above Hartsop Hall. Crow-steps are now more widespread in the eastern valleys than in the west. In some cases they may have been added in the nineteenth century to earlier, plainer buildings. An early nineteenth-century drawing of Glencoyne Farm by the remarkably accurate Ambleside

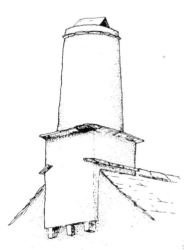

artist, William Green, shows no sign of crow-steps, whereas the house now has well-finished, prominent steps. On the other hand, William Green's local *œuvre* records many instances of crow-steps in Coniston, Troutbeck and Ambleside which have since disappeared. Like some other distinctive architectural details of the area, crow-steps seem to have been 'discovered' by the early nineteenth-century *cognoscenti* and reintroduced to decorate not only lodges and villas but also existing houses and farm buildings.

Chimneys

In his book *Wordsworthiana: Reminiscences of Wordsworth*, Canon Rawnsley recalled a local mason saying, 'Wordsworth was a great 'un for chimleys . . . And he'ed a great fancy an 'aw for chimleys square up half way, and round t'other. And so we built 'em that how.' Of these chimneys, built with a circular shaft set upon a rectangular base, Wordsworth himself wrote that they 'give to the cottage chimney the most beautiful shape ever seen'. Such chimneys were a distinctive feature of some Lake District houses particularly around Troutbeck, Ambleside and Kendal. Although they were placed in quite a different position on the houses (projecting from one long front wall), similar chimneys are also found in Dyfed (Pembrokeshire) and in a small part of Devon and Somerset, where, for some obscure reason, they are often referred to as Flemish chimneys. It may be that many prosperous merchants in Pembrokeshire were Flemish and used their wealth conspicuously;

certainly Flanders does not boast anything comparable.

In the Lake District, the number of such chimneys has diminished rapidly over the last hundred years. In Troutbeck only a dozen are now left; in 1880 there were more than thirty. The same story is told by a comparison of William Green's drawings with the same views today. Often built of small, almost flake-like pieces of stone they are vulnerable first of all to the ravages of the weather, if not properly pointed, and secondly to salts of sulphur from the smoke. They can be extremely expensive to rebuild. The top halves were thus often removed and replaced with something simpler and lower. Oddly enough, the flues within are all always rectangular in section, not circular, so the form cannot have been created as a means of making fires burn better. This is also true of the Somerset, Devon and South Wales examples.

Some of the circular shafts are of immense height, far higher than one would have thought necessary to gain a good draught. They seem to be primarily for display, particularly on the larger houses such as Nether Levens and Coniston Hall, where they are the local (but much more massive) equivalents of the elaborate Elizabethan stacks found on houses in the south of England.

Essentially similar in form to these large chimneys, but with short stumpy shafts upon a low rectangular base, are the diminutive chimneys recorded as having been built as rear extensions to the charcoal-burners' thatched oval huts.

One or two houses still possess chimneys which are almost the antithesis of the obtrusively tall cylindrical ones; they project only slightly above ridge-level, with the top few courses of stones corbelled inwards to produce a narrow aperture so that the chimney has a roughly dome-shaped profile. Perhaps it was these that had caught Celia Fiennes' attention when she wrote of a village: 'There seems to be little or noe tunnells for their chimneys.'

Chimney-stacks were often corbelled out from the gable-wall a short way below the ridge either on the outer wall or within, especially if they served or had served a timber-framed hood. On an inner wall, the stack was usually held by a wooden lintel supported on two wooden corbels; on an outer wall there was a similar arrangement, sometimes constructed in stone.

Ceramic chimney-pots are a fairly recent introduction into the area and have gradually supplanted various forms of slate chimney-covering which were put on to allow smoke to escape whilst stopping rain and wind blowing down the flue. The most common arrangement was a flat stone flag, the same shape as the cross-section of the chimney, supported on three or four stones and sometimes held in place by a stone weight above. Another arrangement was to have two flags resting against each other to form an inverted V, and yet another involved four vertical flags shaped to a point at the top, supporting a flat flag with a pyramidal stone weight above.

ROOF-COVERINGS

By 1797 Pringle was able to say of Westmorland that the houses were generally covered with slates. He went on, however, to say that there were a few houses still thatched with wheat-straw. Of the many hundreds of paintings, sketches and engravings made of the Lake District in the hundred years following 1750, almost none showed thatched buildings; so Pringle may have been referring to thatched houses in the lowland parts of the county, east of Penrith, where thatch persisted until the end of the nineteenth century. In the upland areas, thatch seems largely to have given way to slate by the middle of the eighteenth century.

Thatch

References to thatch and thatching are relatively common in the sixteenth century. In 1560 manorial court records mention a house belonging to John and Thomas Harrison in Great Langdale as being 'without thatch', and 'thatching of Mill for Troutbeck out of repair'. And a survey of three farms on the east side of Coniston Water in 1570 described the buildings at Park-a-Moor, Lawson Park and Waterside all as 'Olde Mansion Houses and olde barns' covered with 'Brackens'.

By the seventeenth century references to thatch become less common. Celia Fiennes noted 'Sad little hutts made up of drye walls only stones piled together and the roofs of same slatt'. This suggests that in some parts, by that date, even the smallest buildings were slated. Similarly in 1692 Thomas Machell could write of Rydal, 'There are quarries of slate at Whitemoss near the Town, by reason of which convenience most of their houses are slated.'

Undoubtedly there were many variations in thatching techniques and materials, although very little evidence for either has survived. Pringle mentions straw being used and gives prices: 'From one shilling and tuppence to one shilling and eight pence a threave of twenty four sheaves'. This was for wheat-straw. There is, however, a reference to barley-straw being used for thatching at Levens at the end of the seventeenth century. By far the most common material recorded is 'Thack Brackens' grown on bracken 'dalts' on the commons, but no indication is given of how this was put on to the roofs. There is a possible parallel with the bracken thatch recorded as being used in a few parts of Scotland. How it was applied there was described by Ure in 1794. The bracken was pulled up complete with its root in early October before it had begun to wither (if left later, the fronds became too brittle and the leaves tended to fall off). The stems were laid on the roof in rows, roots downwards, some three to four inches apart. The roots were therefore left exposed whilst the fronds and leaves were almost entirely covered. It was said that bracken thatch would last only about six or seven years on the exposed side of a roof, while on the sheltered north side it could survive for upwards of thirty years. It was, nevertheless, a much better proposition than straw thatch which, in wet areas, was reckoned to last only some two to four years.

Heather or ling thatch, which is particularly durable, was widely used in the Yorkshire Dales and parts of Scotland; but there is very little evidence for its use in the Lake District. There is no obvious reason why it seems to have been avoided, especially as supplies of heather were fairly plentiful on the open fells.

Slate

Unlike walling stone which could be surface-gathered on the lower slopes of the fells or in the valley bottoms, roofing slates had to be manufactured – mined from the rock face, then riven or split, and finally dressed into suitable shapes. This was skilled work. The cost of riving and dressing had to be added to the considerable cost of transporting the dressed slate from the quarry to the site, making slate a very expensive alternative to thatch. Nevertheless from the seventeenth century onwards slate gradually came to replace thatch as the common roof-covering. By the middle of the eighteenth century it had all but ousted bracken as roofing material.

Only some stone in the area is capable of being worked for slate. The geological fault running from Millom to Shap provides some good quarrying opportunities, and quarries or the remains of quarries can be picked out along its length from Walna Scar in the west, through Coniston Old Man, Tilberthwaite and Elterwater to the eastern valleys of Kentmere and Longsleddale. All these produce green slates in various colours from bright blue-green to soft grey-green. Apart from these exposed sites of the Borrowdale Volcanic Series, the other main workings are in the Silurian rocks that are found on the other side of the fault. These produce blue or dark grey slate.

The job of transporting the slate to lower-level trackways from the quarries was arduous and hazardous. It was generally taken down

Barn roof, High Birk Howe Farm, Little Langdale.
The thick, uneven but graded slates, and the interlocking or 'wrostler', slates forming the ridge-piece, were once both commonplace details but are now fairly rare.

rock and scree slopes on sledges, the man in charge running in front, trying to regulate the speed of the load.

In the late eighteenth century and early nineteenth century many quarries expanded to supply the needs of developing industrial areas, and the product began to be tailored to meet these needs. Three standard grades of slate were produced; the best was called 'London' slate; the next best 'country' slate, and the lowest grade 'Neum Tom' slate. These three grades were characterized in terms of thickness, flatness and size: London slate was generally the thinnest, smoothest and smallest; Tom slates were rough, thick and fairly large. As its name suggests, London slate was mostly sold out of the area, whilst country and Tom slates were supplied to local customers. The difference in price was considerable: in 1753 a contract with the Troutbeck Park Quarries fixed prices as one shilling and sixpence a load for London slates, one shilling and twopence for country slates and sixpence for Neum Tom slates. On top of these prices the local customer had to pay carriage. (Analysis of the accounts for the Troutbeck Park Quarries shows what tardy payers these local customers were: out of eighty local transactions over five years, only one customer paid in less than six months and most took just over one year.)

Many local customers bought a mixture of Tom and country slates. On 23 February 1758 twenty-one loads of country slates and thirty loads of Tom slates were sold for re-roofing part of a barn destroyed by fire at Low House, Troutbeck. The building accounts for this work survive and they show that the amount delivered (recorded in the foreman William Birkett's accounts as '2 Tuns and one Load of Cuntry slate' and '3 Tuns of Tom slate') re-roofed a section of the barn twenty feet wide and forty feet long.

The country and Tom slates were laid on the roof in diminishing courses, the largest Tom slates being put on the lower edge of the roof above the walls, while the country slates were used for the smaller courses towards the ridge. Some Tom slates were enormous – as big as three feet square and up to two inches thick – whilst the smallest slates next to the ridge could be as small as twelve inches by eight inches. The slates were usually dressed so that they were rounded at the head: there was no attempt to make them all equal in width.

Each slate had a small hole in the centre of the shaped head through which it was fixed to the roof. Oak pegs were commonly used, resting on the laths spanning the rafters. Occasionally small pieces of bone are found fastening the slates and such material does not seem to have been considered inferior to oak – being used, for example, on Barton church when repairs were carried out in 1699: John Robinson was paid 1s. 1¾d. for 'Five hundred and fifty sheep shanks for slate pins used in the repair thereof at two and a half pence a hundred'. Similarly at Sockbridge Hall barn in 1699 3,600 'bone pinns for the slate at two and a half pence per hundred' were supplied. Nowadays

above left and above right
Boon Crag (High Waterhead), Coniston.
Two photographs showing this house before and after re-roofing in the 1950s. The old thick slates with their wrostler ridge and swept valley have been replaced by regular 'tile' slates, a tile ridge and a leaded valley, changing the whole character of the roof.

bone is never used and oak pegs only rarely, the majority of re-roofing work being carried out with nails fastened through the slates into the slate laths.

The method of hanging is not the only change to have affected roofs in the last hundred years: supports have also undergone a radical transformation in both material and method. However, the most marked influence on the external appearance of roofs has been the shift away from thick, heavy and uneven Tom and country slates towards thin, even London slates, a change accelerated by the shortage of Tom slates. This loss of substance in the roof-covering can alter the whole feel of a building. London slates also require less skill on the part of the slater: he needs to spend less time organizing his slates for an even gradation from eaves to ridge, and in manhandling large, heavy slates for the lower courses. It can also reduce job satisfaction: 'Today slating is more or less size slating, it all comes one size so to me it is not slating, it's tiling,' was the comment of one Windermere slater interviewed recently.

Ridges

Sandstone or tile ridges or rigging are now more or less ubiquitous on Lake District roofs. But these imported V-section ridge-pieces have only taken over in the last hundred years or so from a rather curious local arrangement for finishing off the ridge. The local slate cannot be dressed easily, so a watertight capping for the join between the tops of the two highest courses was formed by interlocking notched slates, giving the ridge a sawtoothed profile. These slates were called 'wrestler' or 'wrostler' slates, as they appear to wrestle with one another. The specification for the Woundale shepherd's hut in 1839 included the detail that the roof was to be 'Ridgen'd with wrestlers'. Wrestler slates are now very rare and a determined effort will be needed to keep the tradition alive; the Lake District is now virtually its only home in this country. There is evidence (albeit scant) that a similar practice was once followed in parts of Northumberland, and a few interlocking ridges survive in North Yorkshire. (Interlocking slates are still used quite extensively in some parts of Europe, however, notably the Ticino canton of Switzerland and Cantabria in north-west Spain.)

Mossing

Slates make a more or less waterproof covering for a roof, but they do not stop wind or driving snow unless all the cracks between the slates are sealed in some way. This was achieved either by mossing or tiering. Mossing seems to have been the standard method at least until the eighteenth century. There are numerous records of payments for mossing the roof of Hawkshead church. For Rydal Hall an agreement was drawn up on 30 April 1669, by which six shillings and eightpence was paid annually on 30 November for mossing the house roof at fourpence a day. The moss seems to have been gathered in the autumn, presumably from swampy areas, and used straight away. We can only guess at which type of moss was used, but it would probably have been a variety of sphagnum, which can be compressed and will absorb moisture. From the inside of the roof,

Barn roof, High Oxenfell Farm, Coniston.
The slate-pegs rest on split laths supported by riven rafters which in turn rest on purlins made from small ash-trees roughly dressed with an adze. Some of the bark is still in place.

the moss was stuffed down into the spaces between the slates. The problem with mossing was that the process had to be regularly repeated and, as wetlands were drained and improved in the eighteenth century, moss was less readily obtained.

Tiering

Tiering, or applying a type of plaster to the underside of the slates, was the longer-lasting alternative that gradually superseded mossing. The disadvantage of tiering is that, unlike moss, it is heavy and adds significantly to the total weight of the roof. As a local builder recently explained: 'For every ton of slate that went on there was also a ton of under-drawing that had to go on, or tiering underneath.'

The plaster used was a mixture of lime, sand and hair and it was applied to the horizontal joints between the slates, care being taken to avoid covering the slate laths. The tiering firmly anchored the slates in position, stopping movement caused by wind or by warping of the oak pegs. It was thus much more effective than the sheets of roofing-felt that have now taken its place; felt may be impervious to snow and wind, but it does not stop the slates shifting nor does it allow the roof-space to breathe – the latter characteristic being particularly important in barns where hay and straw are stored.

TIMBER

The right of tenant farmers to cut timber for building and repairing houses was tightly controlled by the manorial courts. Stone could be gathered or worked in small quantities without specific permission, but tenants were constrained not to cut timber, even off their own holdings, without the consent of the lord of the manor. In normal circumstances, however, that consent would not be unreasonably withheld; either custom imposed constraints on the lord of the manor as well as on his tenants, so that he had to allow timber to be cut for certain building work and repairs, or he agreed as a gesture of goodwill.

The lord of the manor controlled all timber and underwood growing on his own land. Tenants had considerable freedom to cut underwood for fuel, and to lop pollards for thatching-poles and fodder according to the 'law of greenhew'. Much tighter control was exercised over what were called 'woods of warrant', namely mature timber trees, usually oak or ash, which could only be cut with permission. Tenants were allowed wood for building, but the system enabled the lord to control the size and type of the building as permission had to be sought before wood could be cut. In the mid-seventeenth century it was said that permission was given not for 'all sorts of building but only for a convenient dwelling house, barn, bier [byre] or cow house' and that 'the dwelling house, barne or bier should not exceed three pairs of bindings and for small tenements fower [fewer] might serve'. Further, 'if the tenant would build larger houses for his own pleasure or conveniency rather than for necessity . . . the tenant was to provide tymber at his own charge, for it were an unreasonable custom that the Landlord should find his tenant tymber for building for his pleasure or vain Glory.' It has been suggested that in some areas there were even stricter limitations and that timber could not be provided for the erection of a new house unless it 'rose again on the old site'. In other areas timber was available only for repairs. In the Furness fells in 1559 it was said that the tenants 'Clayme of Custome to have sufficient tymber for repayre and maynetence of their houses [?save] hit be no newe buyldinge . . .' A similar rule seems to have prevailed in Derwentwater. In 1774 a certain Jeremiah Waine was chastised for building a 'New house with ye Timber he pretended to want to repair his Old housing: This we think is breaking in upon ye Antient Custom . . .'

Timber for repairs – 'housebot' or 'houseboote' as it was called – was provided only if the lord's bailiff could be satisfied that the need was genuine. It fell to elected representatives of the tenants, called 'Bierlawmen' or 'House Lookers', to argue the tenant's case. In the seventeenth century the procedure at the manorial court was that

> If any tenant complain'd for want of Timber to repaire his houses; then these Bierlawmen were to view the decay, and see whether it came by the Tenant's default or by accident; and they were also to view what trees would be needful and sufficient for the repair; and if it came not through the Tenant's default, then the Lord's Bailiff Upon the Bierlawmen's presentiment was to sett out for the Tenant upon his own Tenement such and so many trees as the said Bierlawmen did or should say to be sufficient.

With such an entangled and closely watched system, it was inevitable that both sides should at times seek to free themselves of constraint. In 1534 the abbot of Furness accused John, Robert and Nicholas Fisher of cutting down oak-trees without permission in Furness. In their defence, they referred to the custom that allowed them to fell the trees when their houses were in need of repair. During the Civil War many tenants seem to have cut wood at will, which led in the later seventeenth century to a stiffening of the system in favour of the lords. A century later several lords of the manor sought to extend their right in order to profit from the sale of timber; one such was Sir Gilfred Lawson, who succeeded in extending his own rights over his customary tenants at Stonethwaite in 1766–7.

Nevertheless, in many areas the customary arrangements persisted well into the nineteenth century. As late as 1846 timber was supplied from woods in Derwentwater for repairs and for a new building on a customary tenement in Keswick, after a lengthy exchange of correspondence between the tenant and the agents for the estate-owners, the trustees of John Marshall, although the tenant only got larch instead of the oak he had requested.

Oak-trees needed for building and repairs were always felled or cut in the spring, just as the sap was rising, so that the bark could be harvested and sold for tanning. The bark on customary timber was not the tenant's property but the lord's perquisite and had to be surrendered to him for sale. The value of bark can be gauged from the seventeenth-century accounts of Sir Daniel Fleming. On 9 May 1679 Fleming 'Sold Christopher Dixon the bark of eleven trees which William Dennisson had at Yewdall for his new barne for four shillings and six pence'. This was an example of trees being supplied as a customary right to the tenant, with the lord benefiting from the sale of bark. Nine years earlier Fleming was building his own large barn at Rydal using his own timber. There he sold the bark from twenty-five trees for £1 8s. The total cost of the barn was £12 16s. 3d. The sale of the bark thus recouped some 11 per cent of the total cost. A slightly higher figure of 13 per cent was recorded for another of his barns, at Low Park, built in 1659.

As soon as the timber had been debarked, it was used for building in its green state without seasoning. Until the late eighteenth century, roof-timbers were not normally sawn but split and dressed with axes and adzes. The main cruck-blades or trusses were formed from the trunk split into two (perhaps sometimes roughly pit-sawn), or occasionally quartered, while the purlins and ridge-pieces were formed from smaller branches adzed into shape. The rafters came from branches or small trees split several times into pieces approximately four inches square in section. Laths to support the slates were the only part of the main roof not to come from standard trees, being more commonly worked from coppice-poles and split with a sharp knife. This was skilled work. In 1794 Benjamin Browne wrote, 'April 12th T. J. finished this evening making in the whole sixteen days in which he rove 6,100 lathes.' If T. J. worked a ten-hour day, he was producing laths at the rate of almost forty an hour, or one every minute and a half! Laths for roofs were usually described as heart laths or heartwood laths. (Laths were also used as part of a framework for plaster walls. Plastering laths were usually known as sap laths and were often riven from ash-timber rather than oak.)

Saws were used to plank timber for floorboards and doors. A distinction thus often seems to have been made between the carpentry work for the roof structure and floor-joists and the sawing work for boards. At both Low Park barn and Rydal Hall barn, the contracts let for the main woodwork did not include the sawing of boards, this work being let separately.

Roof-Trusses

Roof-supports fall into two broad types: cruck-frames and triangular trusses. Crucks are long, curved timbers standing on the ground and leaning inwards to meet at the apex of the roof. They are strengthened either by a tie-beam or by a collar near the apex, or sometimes by both. The purlins and ridge-piece rest directly on the cruck-blades and in turn carry the rafters, laths and roof-coverings. The cruck-trusses therefore transmit the weight of the roof directly to the ground independently of the walls, which are merely infills and not load-bearing. Roof-trusses, on the other hand, rest on load-bearing walls. They are basically triangular in shape and, like crucks, carry the purlins and ridge-pieces which in turn support the smaller roof-members and the roof-coverings.

There are two intermediate types, known as upper and raised crucks. Upper crucks have their feet supported part of the way up a load-bearing wall. Raised crucks sit on a tie-beam, which in turn is supported by a masonry wall. Raised and upper crucks are widely found on small two-storey hogg houses.

Crucks are usually formed by splitting a curved tree in half, so that each cruck has a mirror-image twin. As no two trees are precisely the same, cruck profiles vary widely. Some form a smooth curve while others are almost straight, and others again are sharply elbowed. Most cruck-trusses have a tie-beam lap-jointed on to one face of the crucks, level with the top of the wall and extending beyond the outside edge of the blades and into the wall to join up with the wall-plate. Two rows of purlins lap over the blades and either rest in a groove on the back of the blade or are held in place by blocking-pieces or occasionally by outer blades. Lateral stability was provided in some, but certainly not all, cruck buildings by braces between the purlins and the cruck-frame.

The apex of the frame was treated in a variety of ways, the most common arrangement being for the top of the two blades to be lap-jointed together diagonally, with a notch cut out of the top to support the ridge-piece. Another common apex form is for the top of the blades to be held apart by a saddle or yoke which supports the ridge-piece. A third form has the top of the blades rising to form a cradle for the ridge-piece and held together by a collar a short distance below the ridge. Cruck-framing is generally considered to be an earlier form than truss construction; in many places the former seems to have been superseded by the latter at a comparatively early date. In the central Lake District, crucks are now most commonly found in the central valleys of Hawkshead, Coniston and Duddon. Much more rarely are they found in Wasdale, Borrowdale and the eastern valleys. But in all valleys reused cruck-blades are commonplace, indicating that crucks were formerly much more widespread. What is significant is the large scale of many remaining full cruck houses – both the massive size of the timbers and the floor area covered. These are not small, humble dwellings, relics of a primitive form of construction. Indeed they account for some of the largest farmhouses studied, both in floor area and in height. Around Hawkshead and Coniston no fewer than eight houses remain with crucks as large as eighteen feet high and with a base of similar dimensions, amongst them High Yewdale Farm, Coniston, Old House, Hawkshead Fields, and Boon Crag Farm, Coniston.

Apart from their large size these cruck-framed houses have several other distinctive features. First, they are usually two and a half bays in length; the half-bay at the chimney end of the firehouse was taken up by the firehood, and the tie-beam of the cruck became the firebeam. This arrangement seems to have been associated with a curious window layout in which the fire-window and the firehouse window were separated solely by an upright timber which was visible on the outside of the house. Only in the Coniston and Duddon valleys is the dual window met with, coinciding with part of the area of surviving cruck-frames. In some cases the upright timber dividing the window is no longer part of a cruck, but seems to be a relict arrangement which persisted after the cruck-frames had been replaced by trusses or by upper crucks. Both Hoathwaithe Farm, Coniston, and Boon Crag Farm, Coniston, display this pleasing window layout.

There is the further problem of dating the substantial cruck-frames which are such a prominent feature of houses in Coniston and

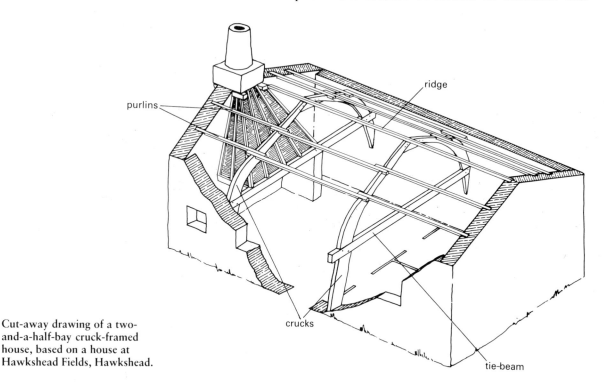

Cut-away drawing of a two-and-a-half-bay cruck-framed house, based on a house at Hawkshead Fields, Hawkshead.

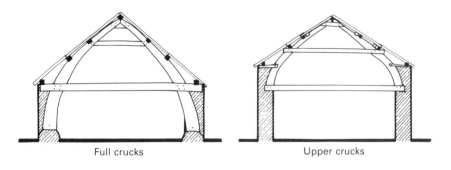

right
Diagrams showing full-cruck and upper-cruck roof construction.

Full crucks   Upper crucks

below
Cruck-trusses at Boon Crag Cottages, Coniston.
This photograph was taken during restoration work in 1948. It gives a good idea of the construction. Note the arrangement of collar- and tie-beams, the way the ridge is notched into the apex of the cruck-truss, and how the purlins lap at the truss.

above
**Cruck-truss, High Yewdale
Farm, Coniston.**

right
**Diagrams showing a simple
roof-truss with angle-struts,
carrying two rows of purlins,
and a nineteenth-century king
post roof-truss, carrying three
rows of purlins.**

Roof-truss with angle struts   Nineteenth-century king post truss

High Yewdale Farm, Coniston.
The house in the foreground was abandoned in 1936 after it had been condemned by an over-enthusiastic sanitary inspector. A casual glance at these two houses suggests that the smaller one was superseded by the larger, more prosperous-looking one. The reality is otherwise. The earlier house is a large cruck-framed building dating from the early seventeenth century or maybe before.

Hawkshead. Studies elsewhere have indicated that smaller and less substantial houses usually decay first, the survivors from an earlier era tending to come from the upper end of the social scale. On this reasoning, the large cruck-frames of the Lake District could be seen as survivals of the grander efforts in this style and could date from any time within the period when cruck construction flourished. Despite apparently being the houses of the more prosperous members of a community, they contain very few datable features such as moulded panelling or cupboards. Only one house has so far been found to have a date: on a window-sill at one of the Boon Crag cottages are the words *William Sawrey built this house 1631*. This is a comparatively late date for cruck construction. If others are of a similar date, then perhaps these large cruck houses were simply constructed for much longer in the Coniston-Hawkshead area by extremely conservative builders, or perhaps it was a status symbol to live in a large cruck house at a time when other houses were being constructed with truss roofs. Until more evidence is available (perhaps from dendrochronology), the precise position held by these buildings in the cruck hierarchy will remain undetermined.

Some smaller cruck houses do survive. Notable is Windsor Farm, Wasdale, which has a date of 1704 on the tie-beam of its one upper cruck-truss. Thrang in Little Langdale and Cothow in Martindale (with remains of three full crucks) are two further examples and there are two more in Loughrigg. Cruck-framing also survives in barns and hogg houses (see chapter 4). Vast numbers of reused cruck-timbers can be found in seventeenth-century and later roof trusses. In some valleys, almost every roof examined had evidence of a former cruck building. Taken with the surviving buildings, these reused timbers attest to a once widespread cruck-building tradition which was gradually displaced by the collar-truss roofing technique.

This change did not mean that houses were all built or rebuilt to progressively more generous proportions. Indeed in some farmhouses the opposite occurs, the later building being considerably smaller than its forerunners. High Yewdale, Coniston, is a case in point. The main farmhouse is now a large, prosperous-looking building. Immediately in front of it and next to the road stands a much smaller house no longer used domestically. The small house has a plain truss roof, the larger one cruck-trusses. Whereas at first glance the smaller house appears to have been abandoned in favour of the larger, the reality is probably otherwise. The smaller one was built in the eighteenth century and was lived in until the early 1900s.

The pattern of roof-trusses, which gradually superseded crucks, is remarkably similar across the region. They also varied little through time until sawn softwood trusses appeared in the nineteenth century. Most are simple tie-beam trusses, triangular frames with the bottom ends of the principal rafters morticed into the tie-beam, and with the top ends either lap-jointed diagonally or tenoned together with a seating for the ridge-piece at the apex. Purlins, two rows along each side, are almost invariably lapped over the truss and supported in trenches cut in the backs of the principal rafters. Some trusses have light lap-jointed collars and others light angle-struts tenoned in between the tie-beam and the principal rafters; but the majority of trusses studied have neither, being simple triangular frames.

Both cruck-frames and tie-beam trusses, together with their associated ridges, purlins and rafters, were until the nineteenth century made either from oak or less commonly from ash. Ash is mostly found in barns rather than in houses, and it is not unusual to find that it has been dressed with the bark unstripped, as ash bark (unlike oak bark) has no value for tanning. Many trusses made use of reused

above right

Barn trusses, Yewtree Farm, Coniston.
Most trusses are of plain triangular form; but sometimes, in both barns and houses, they are strengthened with collars or braces. The purlins usually lap at the trusses and the rafters at the purlins.

right

Brotherilkeld Farm, Eskdale.
In the late eighteenth and early nineteenth centuries wider barns were built and some houses were extended at the rear to form 'double pile' dwellings. In both cases, a much wider roof span was needed. The new trusses were designed to take account of the greater weight, as well as the greater span, and had king post trusses and three rows of purlins on each side.

cruck-blades: the blades were inverted, cut short and used as principal rafters, the recess for the collar lap-joint indicating their previous use. During the course of the nineteenth century, larch and other softwoods gradually came to replace oak or ash as the most common material for roof-timbers, especially on the larger barns and houses. With the change in material came a change in technique, and sawn timber replaced riven or split timbers. The new woods did not, however, become universal until well into the twentieth century. Many houses and barns which were last re-roofed about one hundred years ago still have hardwood rafters split in the traditional way.

right
Riving machine, Bowe Barn, Borrowdale.
This machine, based on the traditional technique of splitting with a wedge and a hammer, was specially designed for the National Trust. It split oak butts into sizes suitable for use as purlins or rafters in re-roofing work. Splitting the timber with the grain, rather than sawing across it, produces members which are much stronger in relation to their size than the sawn equivalent. The wood used is green from freshly-felled trees.

The gradual change from riven green oak to sawn 'tanalized' softwood, which now prevails for nearly all roofing work, has meant more than just a change in internal appearance. It has also altered the whole external profile of roofs. Split green oak seasoned slowly while it was on the roof, gradually twisting and settling and eventually giving the roof a slightly undulating profile which reflected the skeletal framework within. Sawn pine, on the other hand, stays absolutely rigid unless it sags under stress, and a roof supported with it will maintain an almost mechanical flatness throughout its life.

The high cost of splitting oak by hand has been one of the main reasons for the abandonment of traditional methods. In 1984, in an attempt to revive riven timber at a lower cost, the National Trust commissioned a machine for splitting oak mechanically with a hydraulic wedge. This can be used for splitting large trees into suitable sizes for purlins or for splitting smaller thinnings into rafters. Once split by the machine, the wood is then hand-finished with an adze and is ready for use. Riven hardwood is gradually being reintroduced into those buildings where most of the original roof structure, that is the trusses and purlins, is intact and where riven rafters would once have been used. The next generation should be able to reap the visual benefit of this process.

The necessity of felling oak trees in the spring in order to harvest their bark, combined with the desirability of getting a new barn roofed before the harvest, suggests that, at least for barns, there was a definite building season, from mid-May until the end of August. Certainly Sir Daniel Fleming's two barns at Rydal and Low Park Farm fit into this pattern: work started in April and the barns were weather-tight by August (a considerable achievement given the size and scale of the buildings). There is no reason to suppose that smaller barns built with customary timber did not fit into a similar time-scale. By the eighteenth century Benjamin Browne's barns at Lane End and Crostenriggs show a slightly different pattern in which work began as early as January, using timber bought the previous autumn. This was not customary timber, however, but material that had been bought at Benjamin Browne's expense from various suppliers in the area, some of it possibly reused.

Surviving accounts for buildings record a certain amount of conviviality, the owners of new buildings oiling the wheels of their transactions at various local hostelries. When Finsthwaite church was built in the 1720s the church was charged for some entertainment – one shilling and sixpence paid for ale to Thomas Denny, who kept the inn at Newby Bridge. Similarly, when Benjamin Browne was building Crostenrigs barn he set down accounts for entertainment in his memorandum book under the heading 'Expenses'. Between 4 January, contract day, and 17 October, he recorded eleven separate occasions when he spent money, mostly on ale at the Black Cock Inn, for various workmen.

By far the most expensive occasion, and the one obligatory time for entertainment, was the raising of the roof. This involved hoisting the prefabricated roof-trusses on to the top of the newly built walls. The owner not only had to provide food and drink for all who helped but also customary pairs of gloves for the joiners and others who took part in the lifting. The numbers of pairs of gloves, when they were recorded, give a useful indication of how many 'bearers' were involved. At Crostenrigs barn in 1733 there were thirteen, and at Lane Barn in 1731 sixteen. The food provided seems to have varied from job to job. Benjamin Browne provided beef (twenty-seven and a half pounds), bread and sugar at Crostenrigs, and twenty-eight pounds of cheese and two and a half dozen loaves of bread at Lane End. Two meals as well as tobacco were provided for the Rydal barn by Sir Daniel Fleming, who has left a fairly complete account of the proceedings:

> This day [28th June, 1670] was raised ye corne barne at Rydall, they began at about nine in ye morneing, at twelve all ye bearers had a dinner, about five in ye afternoon they had a great cheesecake, four s [shillings] in ale (besides which was sent and two pales full of our owne) and five pounds of tobacco (vis). I gave one pound to ye rights, one pound to ye wallers and two pounds to ye other bearers and my wife gave one pound amongst ye women (which comes to four shillings and two pence, in all eight shillings two pence).

Joinery

Most houses, at least until the late eighteenth century, were constructed precisely like barns in that nearly all internal partitions were

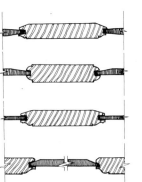

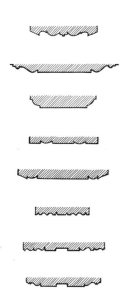

opposite and above
Drawing of muntin-and-plank panelling.
Muntin-and-plank panelling, with alternate thinner planks slotted into grooves in thicker panels, was once found widely in farmhouses as partitions for both ground-floor and first-floor rooms. In a simpler version, planks are lapped rather than grooved. Sometimes the planks were merely finished square or with a simple chamfer. Many, however, were finished with moulded edges such as these.

right
Plaster-and-plank partition, Heelis office, Hawkshead.
An uncommon alternative to muntin-and-plank panelling, was plank-and-plaster partitions. The laths were slotted into grooves in the planks and then plastered on both sides.

of timber and non-load-bearing. The construction of these partitions took several forms, the most basic being a framework of woven wattles plastered on both sides with a daub of clay and straw. Other houses had a framework of roughly shaped vertical posts set up between the floor and the ceiling, with laths nailed across one side and plastered over. An alternative timber-and-plaster partition was formed from equally spaced upright planks, the interstices being filled in with laths which were slotted into grooves down the sides of the planks and plastered over on both sides. Finally, and perhaps most commonly, walls were formed of muntin-and-plank panelling, thin planks with chamfered sides slotted into thicker planks, or occasionally lapped together.

Until imported timber became more readily available at the end of the eighteenth century, planks for walls were nearly always of oak and only very occasionally of elm. Oak planks were also used for floorboards in the upstairs rooms of houses as well as in barns. These boards were either pegged into the joists with pegs some half an inch in diameter (two pegs across the width of one board), or nailed down. Nails seem to have superseded pegs eventually, but from the mid-seventeenth century to the early eighteenth century both methods appear to have been employed. For instance, the extension built at the back of Townend, Troutbeck, in about 1670 has nailed boards whereas Townend Cottage, Colthouse, built in 1703, has pegged boards. Rather like roof-timbers, many boards seem to have been sawn from green timber and used straight away without seasoning, at least in some agricultural buildings. At Rydal, the wrights were paid in September 1663 for 'Sawing boards and planks for the new

above
Detail of a barn-door, Townend, Troutbeck.
This door is 'harr-hung', i.e. the thick end plank is supported top and bottom in U-shaped metal cradles pivoted between the threshold and the lintel above, so that the doors can open either inwards or outwards. The thick oak planks are pegged into the rails.

opposite above
Studded door, Ashness Farm, Borrowdale.
The studs are wooden and join the two oak skins of the door together, the outside vertical planks and the inner horizontal planks.

opposite below
Door to stairs, High Birk Howe Farm, Little Langdale.
Three oak planks are pegged into three supporting cross-rails. Top, bottom, sides and joints all have applied moulded pieces also pegged on. The latches, too, are wooden, raised by twisting the semicircular peg.

stables' and a month later for fixing them. In 1678 two wrights were paid for 'seventeen dayes work in sawing boards and laying them over ye slaughter house at 4d ye day'. One detailed account of laying a new floor in a house, Hartsop Hall, suggests that the boards were left some eighteen months to season before laying – whether intentionally or unintentionally is unclear. On 15 February 1703 Richard Dalton was paid 'For a rood of inched boards lately sent to Hartsupp' but it was not until December 1704 that payment was made for 'Smiths nails had the last summer for lyeing the floor at Hartsupp' and to Richard Dalton for 'Laying the floor'. A similar picture is presented by the documents relating to the rebuilding of Skirwith Hall barn in the Eden valley, although here the intention is much clearer. In spring 1773 it was recommended that felling should be commenced 'With all speed' so that 'Some of the wood work . . . such as boards, sawing for floors and doors and such like . . . would have time to dry and be fit for using'. Only at Levens Hall is there evidence of newly felled and sawn boards being sent to a kiln for drying. In 1693 the steward wrote to Colonel Grahme, 'Pray lett me know if you would have the new flowres [floor] laid with yor own oake boards . . . if soe I must gett them kiln dried . . .'; he went on to say he had 'Two hundred and eighty furr dailes [fir deal] which I intend to kiln dry too'.

At the end of the eighteenth century, with the development of the Solway and west coast ports, imported deal became readily available and was widely used for floorboards in both barns and houses – indeed in some cases it was preferred to home-grown oak for better-quality floors.

Doors

Planks of elm and oak, and later deal, were also used for doors in houses and barns, but very few hardwood barn-doors survive. The one or two old plank doors that do survive (such as the pair at Pye Howe, Great Langdale) are of oak planks some twelve inches broad and one inch thick pegged into three thick horizontal battens, the planks being butt-jointed together. Later, deal doors were constructed in a similar way but with nails instead of pegs. As the nineteenth century wore on the planks became narrower and thinner, the strength coming from diagonal bracing rather than the thickness of the planks. Such doors are found at Seathwaite Farm, Borrowdale. There were two methods of hanging barn-doors, either from jambs or by pivoting them between the lintel and the sill. For the first method, large strap-hinges were attached to the door-battens and hung from spigots driven into the rear of the door-jamb. Doors attached by the second method were usually said to be harr-hung, the end planks of the door nearest to the jambs generally being thicker than the rest and supporting iron pins which pivoted in sockets above and below the

doors. The great advantage of this method was that doors could open either inwards or outwards, as they were held in place by a removable central vertical timber which was socketed into the lintel and sill.

Oak external doors on houses are not quite so rare as barn-doors but are still unusual survivals. A particularly interesting cluster of pegged doors exists in Borrowdale, including the ones at Ashness Farm, Stepps End and Caffle House, Watendlath, and Nook Farm, Rosthwaite. Whether these have survived in this valley by chance or whether they were a particular feature of Borrowdale is difficult to say. The doors were constructed of two pairs of planks, the outer ones placed vertically and the inner ones horizontally, held together by faceted oak pegs projecting from the face of the door. They were hung on strap-hinges fastened against the wooden door-surround. A few single-skin oak outer doors also survive, such as the ones at Causeway Farm, Windermere, and Cropple How Farm, Ravenglass, where thick oak planks are butt-jointed and held in place by wide battens pegged into the planks.

By contrast, hardwood internal doors have survived in large numbers. Many are constructed in a distinctive way, a local variation of a simple plank-and-batten door. The three main planks are held in place by three horizontal battens nailed to the planks. The central plank is, however, thinner than the other two, and three cross-pieces, similar in width to the outer planks, are applied to the top, centre and bottom of the central plank. This gives the effect of two recessed panels. On many doors the edges of these 'panels' were chamfered or moulded, adding further to the illusion of 'post-and-panel' construction. Where these doors open off muntin-and-plank panelling, similar mouldings were used both for the doors and for the leading edges of the panelling. Simple plank doors are also found, sometimes made of elm such as the set at High Skelghyll Farm, Ambleside, where all the doors match. In larger houses these plank doors were often embellished with faceted cover-strips applied on the face of the door over the butt-joints between the planks and also across the top and bottom.

Most internal doors of these designs were hung on thin strap-hinges, about twelve to fifteen inches long, nailed on to the door-battens and jambs. A few, however, had very small spigots driven into the jambs on which hung spiked iron rings, which were themselves driven into the ends of the battens.

The local name for an iron latch-fastening is a sneck. The form of the handle side of snecks changed over the years from a simple hoop, held in place by two plates (often shaped like clubs on a playing-card), to a more substantial arrangement with the handle fixed on to a shaped backplate. Very few of these handles can be dated; one of the exceptions is at Yew Tree Farm, Coniston, where it is initialled and dated *CWA 1743*. Some doors had wooden, rather than metal, latches and these appear not just on simple doors but on some of the more

carefully finished examples in larger houses such as Staveley Park, Staveley, and Causeway Farm, Windermere: a shaped peg on the outer face of the door is twisted to raise a wooden latch on the inside.

During the nineteenth century, imported deal began to be used when doors were replaced and for doors on new buildings. In 1841 William Coward of Low Loanthwaite Farm, Hawkshead, put in – as well as a new 'House door', or main external door into the houseplace – two new room-doors of 'foreign deal'. On older buildings the replacement doors often followed the local pattern with two mock recessed panels. Gradually, though, framed and panelled doors with either four or six panels began to appear, following the national trend. Hill Top at Near Sawrey has only two oak doors, the rest having been replaced in the nineteenth century by six-panelled softwood doors. And when panelled doors were put in they were generally hung on L-shaped hinges to close into shaped jambs, thereby gaining a much better fit. Fastenings were also changed, brass knobs turning to lift latches fixed to a small square metal backplate.

Stairs

Timber was only used in a few houses for spiral staircases, most of these being constructed of stone. Where timber was used, the technique was usually similar to building in stone, large blocks resting on top of one another as at Townend, Troutbeck, or Holeslack Farm, Sizergh. 'Dog-leg' staircases on the other hand were constructed in a much lighter fashion, thin planks of oak for both treads and risers supported on a timber framework, with balusters separating the flights. These balusters gave the joiner much opportunity for display, an opportunity that was not wasted: most of the balusters were turned, or thrown on a lathe, and some were worked into wonderful flights of fancy. No two designs are precisely the same and many bear only a passing resemblance to pattern-book designs. By the nineteenth century, as with doors and floors, deal had begun to be used for staircases. Fortunately, many of the earlier staircases were still in good condition and were not replaced by plainer softwood versions.

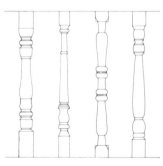

above top
Doors, High Arnside Farm, Coniston.
These are typical Lake District doors which give the appearance of being panelled but are in fact constructed of butted planks. The centre planks are thinner than the outer two and have applied pieces along the top, bottom and centre. On the right-hand door, the centre and bottom pieces have fallen off, revealing the wide centre plank.

above
Drawing of a variety of baluster turnings.

Windows

In 1794 William Hutchinson, commenting on Skirwith Hall, near Penrith, wrote, 'The Hall was a miserable mansion [with] loupe holes rather than windows.' The Skirwith Hall he was describing seems to have remained unchanged after extensive alterations in 1617 until around the time of his visit, but it is impossible to be sure what the windows were like. As we noted in chapter 2, whether window-glazing appeared at the same time as window-frames is far from clear as many early frames show no evidence of glazing. The

right

Oak spiral stairs, Townend, Troutbeck.
In more prosperous houses, spiral stairs were constructed of blocks of oak, rather than stone, and these were tenoned into a faceted newel-post.

far right

Stone spiral stairs, High Birk Howe Farm, Little Langdale.
Stone flags are supported on random stones and the risers plastered over.

below

Iron 'snecks', Orrest Head Farm and Causeway Farm, Windermere.
Front and back views of snecks, one of which has a lift mechanism and the other a turning mechanism.

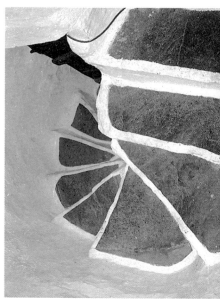

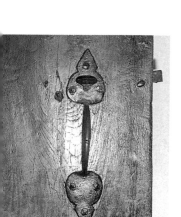

'loupe holes' could have been slits in the stonework, or more likely were small unglazed windows with wooden mullions.

The earliest surviving window-frames are of oak with one or more mullions; the members are fixed together with pegged mortice-and-tenon joints. Mouldings are usually simple, flat splays on the frames and mullions. In the centre of each opening were one or more vertical, diamond-section wooden bars, to which any leaded glazing panels would have been tied. Taller windows divided by transoms were also installed in more prosperous houses, but rarely did their frames display anything but the simplest chamfer.

Towards the end of the eighteenth century, the availability of softwood and the more ready availability of glass encouraged many householders to increase the size of window-openings. Small, squat, mullioned windows were replaced by larger windows of numerous small rectangular panes of glass fixed into thin frames. Opening lights were few: at Beckside Cottage, Colthouse, only one small pane of glass, out of as many as forty-eight in the whole window, was fitted with a tiny metal frame. Elsewhere the top row of lights opened inwards on a hinged casement such as at Stepps End, Watendlath. Other houses were fitted with sash-windows and the openings were rearranged to give house-fronts a semblance of symmetry. The earliest sashes were eight or even ten small panes. Later examples had two or three larger panes. These changes in pane size were made possible by improved glass-making techniques. Crown glass (blown in a sphere and cut into pieces) gave way first to cylinder glass (blown into a cylinder shape, then cut and rolled flat), later to drawn glass, and finally in this century to float glass.

right
Dog-leg stair, Brimmerhead Farm, Grasmere.
The turned posts are a mixture of bobbin and baluster shapes, symmetrical about their mid-points.

below left
Staircase, Townend, Troutbeck.
This stair has slightly more conventional baluster shapes. The upper flight only leads into the roof space.

below right
Staircase, Hill Top, Near Sawrey.
An elegant eighteenth-century oak staircase in Beatrix Potter's farm home.

top left
Windows, Beckside Cottage, Colthouse.
This eighteenth-century window has paper-thin glass and very slender glazing-bars. Only one of the forty-two panes opens to provide ventilation.

top right
Mullion window, Low Millerground, Windermere
The moulding on wooden window mullions was rarely anything but the simple chamfer shown here.

Towards the end of the nineteenth century the fashion for reviving local building traditions percolated down to some of the larger farmhouses. As well as having crow-steps restored to their gables, several houses had sash-windows taken out and replaced within the same opening by large mullion-and-transom windows with metal opening casements. The eighteenth-century wing at Townend, Trout-beck, was 'improved' in this way, with the sash-windows replaced by mullion-and-transom windows to match those in the newly built downhouse/wash-house. Similar changes were made at Mislet Farm, Windermere. These new windows differed markedly from their proto-types not only in size, but in the way they were glazed with large plain sheets of glass instead of smaller panes in leaded panels.

LIME RENDERS, MORTARS AND PLASTERS

After stone and timber, the main building materials were clay, lime and sand. These were combined in various ways to make mortars, plasters and renders. Many early barns used none of these substances; walls were often constructed dry and roof-slates weather-proofed with moss. A good draught through stone walls may be useful in a barn, but is not such an asset in a house. So house walls seem generally to have been constructed with a mortar bedding and with some sort of plaster on the inside. Clay marl (sammel) was a readily available local material and appears to have been used quite frequently as a mortar for inside walls, at least until the end of the seventeenth century. It was probably also widely used as a plaster when mixed with straw and dung. Few such plasters survive; the old cottage at

Hoathwaite, Coniston, is one of the few extant examples – or rather one of the few visible examples, as many others must be covered with layers of paint.

By the seventeenth century, however, lime had become fairly commonly available and gradually superseded clay as an ingredient of mortars. There were three main sources of limestone. First the extensive outcrops around Kendal, in the south of the area; secondly those near Penrith in the east; and thirdly the thin band of limestone running across the centre of the Lakes from Broughton in the south-west, through Coniston, and stretching almost as far as Shap in the east. Known as Coniston limestone, this band follows the Lake District's main geological fault and neatly divides the two types of slate rocks (the Borrowdale Volcanic Series to the north and the Silurian rocks to the south).

Throughout most of the Lake District, therefore, limestone was only available if transported. Local legend suggests that burnt lime brought in for building purposes was initially treated with a certain amount of suspicion. The story goes that the first consignment of it that went into Borrowdale ran into difficulties. The bearer carried the lime across his saddle bow in a bag. A thunderstorm came on and the lime began to fizzle. Whereupon 'the astonished rustic dismounted and poured water over it, the effect of which so alarmed him that he thought the devil was in the sack and throwing it into the beck rode for home as fast as his horse could carry him.'

Lime has to be burnt before it can be slaked and used for mortar. This burning was mostly carried out in a kiln near where the stone was quarried. At least five kilns were built on the central part of the Coniston limestone belt: at Yewdale, at Sunny Brow below Black

Lime-kiln, near High Yewdale Farm, Coniston.
A simple pot-kiln built into the hillside with a ramp leading to the top for filling.

Fell, between Brathay and Black Fell, at Lake Head and at Low Wood. Kilns were also fairly plentiful around the Kendal area, such as the one at Holeslack Farm and another large one just outside Levens village. Further east, in Ravenstonedale, nearly every farm had a kiln. Coniston limestone, which contains impurities, is grey in colour: the Kendal and Penrith limestone is Carboniferous Limestone, a much purer and whiter form. A trade carrying the purer Kendal limestone into the central Lakes seems to have developed fairly early, the lime being transported by boat up Windermere and from the head of the lake by pack-horse.

Lime-Kilns

The earliest types of kiln were called 'sough' or 'sow' kilns. These were often little more than depressions in the hillside on which limestone and fuel were heaped, the whole being covered with turf and clay and allowed to burn out into a small heap of lime. Such sod-kilns leave little or no trace on the ground and their use can only be surmised from parallels elsewhere, such as Northumberland and parts of Wales. Remaining farm-kilns built on the Coniston limestone were 'pot-kilns' – a cylindrical shaft reducing to a narrower neck at the top and set within a rectangular or circular frame against the hillside. The main body of the kiln was of slate or limestone; the lining of brick or red sandstone. The kilns often had a ramp leading to the upper edge for loading from the top. A combined fire- and draw-hole at the bottom was used for lighting the fire as well as for emptying the kiln after firing. The simplest way to fire a kiln is to charge it with alternate layers of wood (short oak coppice-poles) and limestone, freshly quarried in small lumps about four inches across. The mixture is then ignited and left to burn out over three or four days. Most farm-kilns would have been fired in this way, the lime they produced being used either for building purposes or as a fertilizer for arable fields and grasslands.

Coal could also be used for firing. In this case a grate was constructed at the base of the kiln, coal was heaped in, and the rest of the kiln was filled with limestone resting on a roughly formed arch above the coal. Peat also served as a fuel. For the building of a new wing at Levens Hall in the 1690s, whatever fuel was to hand seems to have been used for burning lime, kilns sometimes being fired with 'coales', at other times with peat and once with 'all the routs [roots] and knotty stuff that came out of Ninesor hedge'.

Larger kilns could be fired continuously for several days once they had got going, the lime-burners feeding them with limestone and fuel from above. Lime was extracted from the draw-holes in the base after four or five days' burning. At Sockbridge, for example, Sir John Lowther wrote in 1686 that there was a man 'whose sole business is

Fired lime-kiln, Jack Scout Land, Silverdale.
This small pot-kiln was restored from a near-ruin in 1987 and then fired with wood and limestone as a trial.

lime burning for all the Neighbour Villages'. Clearly this man must have used some sort of continuously fired kiln. If it stood around, the freshly burnt 'quicklime' began to absorb water, so after burning it had to be transported without delay either to the fields where it was scattered in small heaps for the rain to slake before it was spread out as fertilizer, or to the building-site where it would be slaked for mortar.

Slaking involves combining burnt lime with water. A chemical reaction ensues, generating large quantities of heat and breaking the lime down to a kind of slurry which is fed into a tank through a riddle and allowed to settle. When cool the resulting substance is called lime putty and is the basic ingredient for mortars, plasters and renders. Lime putty improves after being left to mature for several months or even longer; the Romans advocated keeping putty for around seven years, and the durability and quality of their plasters testify to the soundness of that precept. Rarely, it seems, did that happen in this area. Most lime for large building jobs was used almost immediately after burning and slaking. At Levens Hall in the 1690s, letters written by the steward about the building of the new wing show that in that instance lime was certainly slaked and used almost immediately, for one of the steward's main headaches was persuading the lime-burners to burn sufficient lime so as not to hold up the building work.

At Levens Hall the lime-kiln was apparently owned by the estate, the limestone and fuel were gained by the builders, and the lime-burners were employed to fire the kiln. At the smaller lime-kilns, some were no doubt built by tenants for their own use; but in at least one case tenants seem to have shared the use of a kiln. In 1772 a complaint was made about 'the tenants' liberty to burn lime in our in-pasture' near Kirkland Hall, probably at a kiln in Wittons Field, which suggests that tenants burnt lime as and when they needed it. And in Northumberland there is evidence for kilns being constructed on commons, and for tenants exercising their rights to quarry and burn limestone for their own use. Perhaps there were instances of a similar arrangement in the Lake District; in 1684 the manorial records for the Five Towns area, west of the River Cocker, refer to a tenant being fined for pulling down a lime-kiln which, to be within the jurisdiction of the court, must have been on common land.

For larger jobs lime was not always burnt on site; sometimes it seems to have been bought in when needed and used almost immediately after slaking. In 1773, when building work was being carried out at Skirwith Hall, it was agreed to 'Build a new lime killn at Kirkland . . . to have the lime at a lower rate both for the buildings and Improving both Estates'. But extra lime was also bought in 'off the field'. For work at Sockbridge Hall in 1699 and at Barton church in 1702 payments were made for 'getting lime'; and for building work at Hartsop in 1701 payment was similarly made for 'twenty loads of lime carried to Hartsupp'. In all these cases one presumes the trade was in burnt lime ready for slaking, probably transported in barrels (as is recorded in parts of Wales) by boat and pack-horse, and then slaked on the building-site and used almost immediately.

Mortars and Renders

To make a render, an outside plaster or a mortar, lime was mixed with sand. Sand was obtained either from the beds of becks, rivers or lakes or from suitably located holes in the ground. All these sources produced coarse, slightly gravelly sand which sometimes had to be washed clean. For the building of Finsthwaite church, for example, payment was made to 'Rownson Taylor for washing sand'. Digging holes to find the sand was obviously fraught with uncertainty at times. When the work of building a ramp against a barn at Sockbridge Hall was in progress in 1699, a certain John Talbot received a payment of ninepence for 'Digging a hole where we hope to have found sand and for filling it up again'. Dredging also had its problems: in February 1693 the steward in charge of building operations at Levens Hall wrote, 'But the waters is soe high, cann gett noe sand.'

Surviving mortars and renders indicate that the proportions of lime to sand varied considerably, some mixtures being rich with about one part of lime to three or four parts of sand, others being very lean with as little as one part of lime to twelve parts of sand, as is recorded for building work at Skirwith Hall in 1773. There it was noted that the mortar mix consisted of a part load ('less than sixteen cubic feet') of sand with each bushel of lime.

right

The Wyke, Grasmere.
This house was built with boulders and rough slates bedded in clay mortar and left unrendered. This photograph was taken in 1934. The house is still unrendered, but some windows have now been altered.

below

House wall, Glencoyne Farm, Ullswater.
This photograph was taken when the house was being re-rendered. Notice the small size of much of the wall-stone which is embedded in lime mortar. This wall would almost certainly have been rendered when first built.

Building work was usually carried out only in the summer months when the risk of frost was at a minimum, as new mortar is very susceptible to frost. Unexpected and quite sharp frosts could, however, still strike even as late as June and as early as September, so newly mortared walls had to be protected in some way. A covering of bracken seems to have been used in some instances, for in October 1692 Colonel James Grahme of Levens Hall sent the following instructions: 'When the wallers have done worke to let the walls be well covered with brackens.'

Where walls were to be left unrendered the joints were made fairly tight and the mortar was kept well back from the surface of the wall. Walls built to be rendered, on the other hand, often showed generous joints and in some buildings, like Coniston Old Hall, no great care was taken to arrange the stones on the face of the wall, triangular and other odd-shaped stones being set rather awkwardly amongst small regular blocks.

Renders

Barns were almost never protected by a shelter-coat unless it was applied at a later date to cover defective stonework. By the mid-eighteenth century, however, most houses seem to have had at least their front walls rendered. Wordsworth noted, 'Frequently the Dwelling or Fire house as it is ordinarily called, has been distinguished from the Barn or Byer by roughcast and white wash.' It is hard to say when this practice became the norm. A few abandoned houses such as Scales Farm, Netherwasdale, showed no evidence at all of rendering (or of lime mortar, the walls being built with clay mortar); this is equally true of several other surviving houses which probably date from the seventeenth century such as The Wyke, Grasmere, and Rooking Farm, Patterdale. And in 1692 Thomas Machell described Hartsop Hall as a 'low blackish building', which suggests that at that date it was not rendered. On the other hand a few early cruck buildings have lime-mortared walls, clearly built to be rendered, such as the end of Fell Foot Farm, Little Langdale. And larger and grander houses used mortars and renders from an early date: Coniston Old Hall was rendered when it was originally built in the sixteenth century.

As renders became more generally used so the techniques of applying them changed. From a rough and ready shelter-coat, which reflected the irregularities of the stones beneath, there gradually developed an all-obliterating render which tends to make walls look unnaturally flat and smooth. The earlier method of applying the render was to give the walls a one-coat finish with a thick mixture of lime and coarse sand, incorporating a good proportion of pea-sized pebbles. This render was laid on roughly, more being put into the

above
The Crag, Troutbeck.
Another example of unpainted
render. In this case the stones
are more or less completely
covered. Only the surround to
the front door is limewashed.

opposite above
Howe Head, Ambleside.
This photograph was taken in
1897. Notice the sparing use of
limewash and the scanty nature
of the render on the house-
front: it barely covers the stone.

opposite bottom and below
Flag Street, Hawkshead.
Two photographs taken about
twenty years apart at the end of
the nineteenth century. The old
one-coat render shown in the
earlier photograph was replaced
by a thicker, smoother render
finished with a pebble-dash
finish.

cracks and less on to the face of the stones, and the whole was smoothed out only here and there with no attempt at ironing out the imperfections of the stonework. This method was aptly called 'ruff-casting'. Photographs of Hawkshead taken in the 1880s show many buildings finished in this way. Around the turn of the century roughcasting began to be replaced by a two-coat pebble-dash treatment. First the walls were covered by a thick coat of render, which smoothed out the face of the walls and left the corners sharp and straight. Then a thin dash-coat of pebbles was thrown on or mixed with a thin final coat of sand and lime. The illustration shows the changes this new technique made to the appearance of houses.

Limewash

If left unpainted, render weathers to a brown-grey colour. On a few houses the render was left in its natural colour or was merely whitened around the main door, as can be seen in a photograph of Robin Lane Cottage, Troutbeck, taken in the 1880s. On most houses the render was protected, and given colour, by a coat of limewash. Limewash is lime putty thinned with water to a milky consistency and applied with a large brush. Two or three coats are usually put on to new render, and thereafter one coat is applied every time the house needs painting. Sometimes the lime is mixed with tallow or boiled oil to help it to adhere or to throw any rain landing on the surface. Tallow is often added when the lime is being slaked, the heat of the slaking dissolving the tallow. Wordsworth noted that the limewash, which 'inhabitants are not hasty in renewing . . . in a few years acquires, by the influence of weather a tint at once both sober and variegated'. By the end of the nineteenth century whiteness seems to have become desirable, and householders apparently vied with one another to get the whitest limewash. When the lime-kiln was emptied after burning, the purest pieces were put on one side to be slaked separately for limewash. A good coat of limewash lasts four or five years and will sometimes last for as long as eight or ten, depending on how anxious the owner is to keep the house pure white. Some farmers put on a coat of limewash each year as a spring routine.

Limewash was by no means applied only in its natural colour. Pigments of various sorts could be added to tint it blue, yellow, red or buff. On the whole, farmhouses tended to be white while colours were most common for village houses and in small hamlets. Nevertheless there were exceptions. Scraps of the limewash at Low Yewdale Farm, Coniston, showed that for a while it was a fairly bright blue colour, and The Bield Farm in Little Langdale was for many years coloured dark pink. Pinks and reds were usually obtained by adding red ruddle or raddle, a soft red ironstone, used not only for colouring limewash but also mixed with whale-oil for marking sheep. In the nineteenth century at least, ruddle was sold by gypsy women sitting around the market cross at Carlisle market. It was also dug by farmers for their own use from such places as Red Tarn near Wrynose Pass. Damson juice was also used for making a slightly sharper pink colour. In the nineteenth century other pigments became fairly readily available, such as red and yellow ochre (both earth colours which gave muted yellows, reds and creams) and lime blue. A paler blue was also made with 'dolly blue bags' manufactured at Backbarrow from the 1880s. In the 1820s what Wordsworth called 'Flaring yellow' (a colour which he thought was censurable), a deep bright yellow made with copperas (copper sulphate), enjoyed a certain popularity; it was used in particular on cottages in Rydal, a tradition that persisted until very recently.

Internal Plastering

Internal house walls were plastered either directly on to the stone where they were of masonry construction or on to laths on ceilings and on internal partitions. For both, the mix of plaster was usually

above right
Decorative plasterwork, Fell Foot Farm, Little Langdale. In the seventeenth century, when the main bedroom or chamber of a larger house was moved to the first floor, it was sometimes provided with a small fireplace surmounted by a decorative plaster panel.

right
Causeway Farm, Windermere. Decorative plasterwork is rare in all but the grandest farmhouses. The most common position for ornament was above the fireplace, either in the main chamber, or in the parlour, as this one is.

similar: lime and coarse sand to which was usually added chopped hair for strength. The hair was usually horsehair, but sometimes cowhair was used instead. Only inside flues was the mixture varied by the addition of well-rotted cow-dung. The plaster was applied thickly and smoothed off with a wooden board or float. On a few houses a second, finer coat was added of lime and fine sand only, sometimes gauged with gypsum. This finer mixture was also used for moulding plaster into decorative patterns fixed as panels over fireplaces or as friezes running along the top of the fire-house wall.

Whether these decorative panels were picked out in colours is not clear. On only a few houses is there evidence of paint being used as a decorative medium. The floor-joists at Thrang, Little Langdale, had the soffits decorated with a pattern of running foliage. At Wood Farm, Troutbeck, a first-floor room had painted inscriptions in black letters along the frieze, one of which read *Oh God of thee one thing do I require, thine holy place for that is my desire.* At Low Tock How, Hawkshead, a mural, uncovered during building work in 1966, probably once filled at least one wall of a first-floor room. About a square yard is now left exposed; it is in yellow, blue, black and red and depicts flowers and foliage in a free-flowing design.

Wall-plasters inside houses were finished with coats of limewash, usually tinted with similar pigments to those used on the outside of the building. Red ruddle was probably the most common colour – traces of it seem to occur wherever old paint is scraped, and it was used particularly in the firehouse – while blue was chosen for larders as it was thought to deter flies.

Today in very few houses is limewash still used. Townend, Troutbeck, and the solicitor's office, Hawkshead (now the Beatrix Potter Gallery) are two buildings where the practice of limewashing is still followed and all the rooms are decorated with colours made from natural pigments.

8

Looking Forward

MANY WRITERS agree that the closing years of the eighteenth century
were a watershed for the way of life of Lake District farmers: some
prospered, many more did not. This so-called decline of the yeoman
farmers is a subject that has been much debated. Recently it has been
claimed that studies of trade directories of the early nineteenth century
suggest that the yeoman did not decline so much as migrate into a
different category – farmers no longer calling themselves statesman or
yeoman but just plain farmer. Evidence from the studies of farmhouses
and the families who lived in them leads to a rather different conclusion. There does not seem to have been a decline in the prosperity
of those farmers who survived, or those who fought their way in, but
certainly the numbers of both people and buildings diminished at a
much more rapid rate between the years 1750 and 1820 than had
happened in the previous 200 years.

There were several economic factors working against the small-
scale farming economy at this time. Many of the part-time, secondary
occupations such as spinning, fulling and quarrying, which had
supplemented farming income, were in decline as a result of industrial-
ization; there had been a run of severe winters in the 1780s and
1790s; and inflation, fuelled by the Napoleonic Wars, meant that
the real value of farming produce had declined sharply. All these
circumstances favoured the larger-scale rather than the small-scale
farmers, who could not ride out the lean years. Also, the rapidly
expanding towns lured some with the promise of an easier life than
that of the shepherd/farmer; and some sons did not wish to run small
farms which only just provided enough to live on, preferring instead
to sell up and move away. Wordsworth's poem 'Michael' vividly
describes the anguish of an old man whose son does not want to
follow in his footsteps.

In 1797 all this was succinctly summed up by the report to the
Board of Agriculture:

> This class of men [statesmen] is daily decreasing. The turnpikes have
> brought the manners of the capital to this extremity of the kingdom.
> The simplicity of ancient times has gone. Finer clothes, better dwellings
> and more expensive viands, are now sought after by all. This change
> of manners combined with other circumstances which have taken place

within the last 40 years, has compelled many a statesman to sell his property, and reduced him to the necessity of working as a labourer in those fields, which perhaps he and his ancestors had for many generations cultivated as their own.

Some farmers struggled to stay on, but in order to survive 'began to mortgage their lands. After bearing the burden of these mortgages till they could no longer bear it, their children have sold their lands.'

The mortgaging of land is certainly a constant theme in the story of land ownership at this time. The impetus may have been provided by debts from lean years, by rising expectations, by the desire to expand operations or take advantage of the growing market economy. For these and doubtless other reasons, large mortgages became a regular occurrence, followed inevitably by defaults in payment, forced sales, and the prospering of solicitors and opportunist money-lenders.

High Snab Farm was sold in 1817, High Birk Howe Farm, Little Langdale, was sold in 1834. The examples could be multiplied. A dramatic and extreme case is Stangends Farm in Netherwasdale. Robert Wilkinson inherited the farm in 1780 and went to live there. He also owned Netherwasdale mill and houses at Wright How, Easthwaite, and Howend. In 1800 he began to raise money by a mortgage on all his property. In 1812 he raised £1,300 on the farm from a London merchant, John Moore, formerly of Whitehaven. In 1813 he increased his commitment to £1,500. In 1814 he raised another £2,200 and by 1819 his debt was £4,797. In 1820, both Stangends and the rest of Wilkinson's property were handed over to the mortgagee, Nicholas Nicholson, a Cockermouth solicitor, and when all the loans were finally added up in 1829 they amounted to the staggering sum of £14,083 6s. 4½d., over ten times the original amount borrowed.

A few farmers managed not only to prosper agriculturally but also to enter the money-lending business themselves (or perhaps prospered because of their diversification). Brotherilkeld Farm in Upper Eskdale seems to have been the base of one of the more notable money-lenders; evidence has come to light of its owner providing mortgages for (amongst others) farms at Sidehouse, Great Langdale, Tower Bank, Sawrey, and Brimmerhead Farm, Grasmere, which had a £1,200 mortgage in 1859.

In all valleys the pattern was similar: the larger farms prospered, the smaller ones sold out. As John Fisher of Townend, Grasmere, told his neighbour Dorothy Wordsworth, soon there would only be two ranks of people in the dale, the very rich and the very poor: 'for those who have small estates are forced to sell, and all the land goes in one hand'.

A detailed survey of two valley heads may give a clearer picture of the effect of these economic upheavals on the land holding pattern. At Wasdale Head in 1578 there were eighteen separate holdings, each with arable land and pasture, a house and barn, and, in most cases, a little garth next to the homestead. By 1808 only six farms covered the same land, the remaining twelve having been absorbed into the larger units. This process of amalgamation was fairly gradual for the first 180 years, the numbers reducing first to fifteen in 1675, and then to twelve in 1750, on average one farm being absorbed every thirty years. The pace of change quickened thereafter, for in the next fifty-eight years the number of farms fell by 50 per cent, six farms disappearing in just under sixty years. Both William Hutchinson in 1776 and William Green in 1819 wrote about the resulting ruins visible in the valley head. Ruined cottages seem to have been a common sight in many valleys. Wordsworth used the theme for his story 'The Ruined Cottage' in the first book of *The Excursion*.

A similar pattern emerges in Great Langdale. In 1750 the head of the valley supported eleven farms: four at Wallend, four at Stool End, one each at Ash Busk and Middlefell Place, and one at what is now the Old Dungeon Ghyll Hotel and was then Low Millbeck. A hundred years later, only four farms remained: one each at Stool End, Wall End, Middlefell Place and Low Millbeck.

As well as decline and amalgamation this period brought with it a certain amount of agricultural improvement. Those farms which survived benefited from the effects of the so-called agricultural revolution – improved animal breeds, improved crops, and the mechanization of some farm processes – as well as in some valleys from the enclosure of certain fells as a means of controlling and improving grazing. The common at Wasdale Head was enclosed in 1808, the Troutbeck Hundreds in 1842, and the fells around Hartsop in 1865.

These new enclosures changed the method of farming but little, with cattle and sheep still being grazed on the high land in summer. They did, however, bring about a fundamental change in the system of mutual co-operation which had underpinned Lake District farming life for at least seven or eight centuries. Where the land was enclosed, common rights were extinguished and replaced with a system of freehold fells divided up amongst those who had previously had common rights. Only in the very heart of the Lake District did the old system prevail and the fells remain unenclosed.

Even so, by comparison with other parts of England, these agricultural changes touched the area lightly. Few farms were sufficiently large, diverse or prosperous to be completely replanned and rebuilt along 'model farm' lines. What brought very much greater change to the area was the arrival in the 1840s of the railway, which began to break down the isolation of the region and to open up the area to visitors. The trickle of leisured tourists in the late eighteenth century, who out of necessity had 'discovered' the area as an alternative to the Grand Tour, no longer possible in war-torn Europe, rapidly turned into a flood in the late nineteenth century. Many people chose not only to visit but also to live in the area, creating a demand for villas and houses near the Lakes. By the 1890s real concern was beginning to be expressed about the breakdown of traditional farming life and the overdevelopment of roads and railways. Despite some agricultural improvement, grain prices had fallen sharply after 1815 and the market economy continued to have a destabilizing influence on small farmers throughout the century. Many small farmers borrowed beyond their means to tide them over lean years. After the 1850s developers began to arrive in the wake of tourists, and farmland began to have a value quite divorced from the potential returns of agriculture. All these factors seem to have encouraged many small farmers to sell up and move away. The growing towns of Lancashire provided opportunities for people to find work and establish businesses.

Fortunately the natural beauty of the area, which drew visitors in the first place, also provided the means for its salvation. The Lake District had the ability to attract attention to itself, and it had amongst its adopted residents those eloquent enough to bring notice of its impending plight to a national audience. Wordsworth and Ruskin predicted the demise of the region's distinct way of life in the early and mid-1800s, but it was left to those who followed to come up with the means to stem the tide of change.

In 1894 at a meeting in London a society was formed to hold places of historic interest or national beauty for the benefit of the nation. The following year the association was registered and the National Trust was born. Its creation was mainly due to three people – Octavia Hill, Sir Robert Hunter and Canon H. D. Rawnsley. Canon Rawnsley was then vicar of Crosthwaite, near Keswick, and both Octavia Hill and Sir Robert Hunter were frequent visitors to the Lake District.

The National Trust was formed in response to a nation-wide concern over the loss of footpaths, the enclosing of commons and open spaces, and the threat of building on amenity land. Its aim was to 'keep for her people for ever, in their beauty, accessible to all, some of England's fairest, most memorable places'. In 1900 it launched its first Lake District Appeal to buy Brandelhow Park on Derwentwater.

Through ownership the young National Trust set about trying to preserve the essential character of the Lake District. First it purchased small pockets of land threatened by development, and fells such as Gowbarrow. Only in the 1920s did it begin to acquire significant tracts of farmland such as the head of Great Langdale and with it the ability to do something positive about nurturing traditional husbandry. The world-wide economic depression of the 1920s and 1930s forced many farmers out of business, bringing much land on to the open market. But even at the extremely low prices of the day, there were insufficient funds to purchase everything under threat. Fortunately, there emerged in the figure of Beatrix Potter someone who had a single-minded devotion both to the preservation of the landscape of her adopted home and to the ideals of the National Trust. She also had the means, through the proceeds of her successful children's books, to buy up farms under threat. Between 1905 and her death, Beatrix Potter bought fifteen farms; through loans, she also helped the National Trust to acquire a further 2600 acres. On her death in 1943, all her estate of 4000 acres passed to the National Trust.

The Trust has since continued to acquire land and buildings in need of protection. In the intervening years controls over the whole area have tightened in several ways. First of all, in 1951, the Lake District was given National Park status, and one of the stated aims of the newly formed National Park Commission was to maintain the farming pattern of the area. Secondly, large areas of meadows, woodlands and fells have been designated as Sites of Special Scientific Interest by the government and their management is now closely monitored by the Nature Conservancy Council. Thirdly, in recent years, government relisting surveys of historic buildings have identified many farmhouses, cottages and farm buildings as being of national importance and worthy of protection. Fourthly, several hamlets have been given the added protection of 'conservation area' status.

Nevertheless, despite these safeguards the area is still under threat. The threat now comes in smaller and in some ways more insidious forms than the large-scale depredations of roads, railways and sub-urban housing developments that loomed in 1900. These new threats are not cataclysmic, but still eat away at the basic underpinning of the rural economy and traditions. The rise of the motor car has led to a dramatic growth in the numbers of people wanting to live in the area and commute to work outside the Lake District. Even more people want to move into the area when they retire or visit for holidays. Second homes for weekend or holiday use or as an investment for letting to other holiday-makers are now sought after on a scale unimagined even in the 1950s. The advent of caravan parks, time-share complexes and centres for field studies or outdoor pursuits has further inflated property and land prices. The property market is now largely unconnected with the local farming economy. This has led first of all to the breaking-up of family farming units, as land and buildings command a much higher price when sold separately; secondly, it has led to the pricing of cottages at such a level that few locally employed people can afford to buy them.

Similarly, changes in the agricultural economy have led to the almost complete disappearance of mixed farms. Crops, pigs and horses are now no longer part of the farm scene and even cattle are scarce. This change in the pastoral economy has had a far-reaching effect on the landscape. Cattle formerly grazed the steep enclosures on the lower slopes of the fells and effectively kept bracken under control through trampling; bracken was also cut for bedding. With fewer cattle, bracken has spread throughout the intakes, sheep being too light to trample it down. With less cow manure, many hay meadows have had to be fertilized with chemicals and in the process herb-rich meadows have given away to fields of uniform green grass.

Sheep-farmers have been supported by a 'headage' payment from the Ministry of Agriculture. This arrangement has tended to promote overgrazing on the high fells as farmers have maximized their grants by increasing the number of sheep they run. Even where commons remain unenclosed, the farmers are not limited in the number of sheep they may graze (the power of the manorial courts having long since faded away) and overgrazing has led to the decline of the heather moorlands and with it the loss of valuable habitat for wildlife.

Despite grant support, the changes have not necessarily led to increased prosperity. Herdwick wool is dark and coarse. Traditionally it was used for short-pile, durable carpets as well as for coarse cloth. Latterly it has commanded only the lowest of prices as the fashion in clothes has moved away from rough tweeds, and as carpet styles have increasingly favoured softer, shaggier finishes. As a result many farmers have been tempted to change to Swaledales and Swaledale crosses even though they are less hardy than the Herdwick breed.

The change away from a mixed farming system towards a sheep monoculture, and the changes in the way sheep are managed, have in some valleys taken away the purpose of the numerous stone walls and hedges which once separated arable land from meadows, valley-bottom land from the intakes, and the intakes from the open fells. It has also left hogg houses, pigsties and two-storey barns redundant. Changes in the farming economy have reduced the number of people working on farming units and many farmers now manage without any additional labour. The maintenance of stone walls, hedges and hedge-trees has become an onerous business with few benefits to the individual farmer.

The threats to the landscape cannot all be attributed to the new farming practice. The way buildings are maintained has, over the last generation, changed from a specifically local tradition to a universal one, partly as a result of economic considerations and partly because of the shortage of traditional materials and craftsmen. Traditional building techniques have tended to give way to materials and methods which could be applied anywhere.

The examples could be multiplied. What is clear, however, is that a change in any aspect of Lake District life has far-reaching repercussions both for the landscape and for those who work it. Landscape and society have not been static in the past; the changes affecting them now, however, are more profound and irreversible than anything that has happened before. It is perhaps not putting it too strongly to say that what is at risk is the way of life of the upland farmer and the landscape and buildings which his forebears created. If the Lake District valleys are to remain populated, farmhouses lived in, farm buildings used, and the land farmed in a way that has persisted for probably more than a thousand years, stronger controls are going to be needed than exist at the time of writing. The present system of grants and subsidies, taken together with the forces of the property market, is driving traditional practice to the verge of extinction.

Few people would want to see a totally controlled landscape; few farmers would want to farm without any incentives. Three things are needed at minimum. First, new specialized outlets for farm produce must be created; secondly, positive recognition must be given to the value of the buildings and historic landscapes and the way in which they provide the basis for a system of farming which works with, rather than against, the geology, vegetation and climate of the valleys; and thirdly, financial encouragement must be provided in the form of grants and subsidies for those ends.

The Lake District landscape reflects not so much the dramatic impact of monarchs, barons and lords, but the gentler, more persistent impression made by countless generations of small-scale farmers who have eked out a livelihood from the narrow valleys and inhospitable fells in an often intemperate climate. Few landscapes in Britain have changed so little since mediaeval times. The natural beauty of the Lake District has long since been recognized. Attention needs now to be given to the distinctive man-made landscapes and buildings, and to the people and systems of agriculture that produced them.

Glossary

ARK
Plank chest for storing grain.

ARVEL BREAD
Wheat bread given to mourners at a funeral.

BACKSTONE
Originally a thin flat stone and latterly an iron plate, used for baking oatcakes.

BANK BARN
Two-storey barn built either on sloping ground or against a ramp, and having access from the ground to both levels.

BARONY
The estate of a feudal lord held of the Crown.

BAY
Space in a building between adjacent roof supports or between a roof support and an end wall.

BOSKIN
Partition, between cow-stalls; usually a stone flag set within a wooden surround.

BOUSE
Cow-stall.

BOWER
Bedroom of master or mistress of the house.

BRANDRETH
Iron trivet for supporting cooking utensils over a hearth fire.

BYRE
Cow house.

CELLE-TREE
Vertical wooden post fixed between the floor and the main ceiling beam at the edge of a cow stall.

CHAMBER
Bed-chamber or bedroom.

CLAPBREAD
Flat, unleavened bread made from fine oatmeal and water, known also as haverbread (q.v.).

CLOG-WHEEL
Solid wooden wheel fixed to the axle of a cart and turning with it.

COLLAR
Horizontal roof timber near the apex of a roof truss (q.v.).

COLLIER
Charcoal burner.

CRUCKS
Pair of curved roof timbers resting on pad stones and inclined together at the top. They carry the ridge (q.v.) and purlins (q.v.).

DALE
Division of a former open common field.

DEETING
Winnowing (q.v.) of grain.

DOWNHOUSE
Back-kitchen or brewhouse.

FIRE-WINDOW
Small window, within the chimney recess of the firehouse, giving illumination to the hearth.

FIREHOUSE
The main heated ground floor room of a farmhouse.

GRANGE
Monastic sheep farm.

GREENHEW, LAW OF
An arrangement by which tenants were allowed to cut underwood for fuel and lop pollards for thatching and fodder.

HALLAN
Through passage between firehouse (q.v.) and downhouse (q.v.).

HAVERBREAD
Flat, unleavened bread made from fine oatmeal and water, known also as clapbread (q.v.).

HEAF
Part of a fell to which a particular flock of sheep will always return to graze. Such a flock is said to be heafed to the pasture.

HECK
Partition of either stone or wood separating the main hearth of a house from the mell (q.v.).

HERDWICK
A breed of sheep peculiar to the central Lake District.

HOGG
Male or female lamb before first shearing.

HOGG HOUSE
Small building for storing fodder and for sheltering sheep in winter.

HOUSEBOOTE OR HOUSEBOT
Timber for repairing buildings provided free by the lord for agreed repairs.

HOUSEPLACE
See firehouse.

INTAKE
Parcel of land between the valley bottom fields and the open fell, enclosed from the lower slopes of the fell and used for cattle grazing.

LATH
Thin horizontal roof timbers, supported by the rafters (q.v.), carrying the pegs or nails which fix the slates.

MACON
Smoked, salted mutton.

MANOR
Self-sufficient mediaeval estate under the control of a lord.

MANORIAL COURT
Court appointed by the lord to administer customary law.

MELL
Short passage leading into the firehouse (q.v.) either from the main door of the house or from the through-passage.

MUNTIN-AND-PLANK
Timber panelling formed of vertical planks, alternately grooved and chamfered.

PAN-BREAD
Leavened, wheat bread cooked in a covered pan over an open fire.

PANNAGE
Grazing for pigs in woodland.

POT-CRANE
Rotating L-shaped bracket fixed to one side of an open fire for suspending cooking pots.

PURLIN
Horizontal roof timber supported between trusses (q.v.) or between a truss and an end wall, and carrying rafters (q.v.).

RAFTER
Inclined roof timber supported on the ridge (q.v.) and purlins (q.v.) and carrying the roof covering.

RANNEL-BALK
Wooden beam spanning the chimney from which cooking pots were suspended.

RATTEN CROOK OR RECKON
Adjustable iron hangers for suspending cooking pots over an open fire which could be 'reckoned' up or down.

RIDGE
Horizontal roof timber at the apex of the roof supported between trusses (q.v.) or between a truss and an end wall, and supporting the top ends of the rafters (q.v.).

RING-GARTH
Stone wall or fence dividing cultivated valley-bottom fields from open, grazed fell land.

RUDDLE
Soft red ironstone used for marking sheep and tinting limewash.

SALVE
A protective mixture of tar and butter applied to a sheep's fleece at the onset of winter.

SCALE
Building on high fell pasture occupied during the summer months.

SCONCE
Low shelf, usually of stone, used for salting meat or storing produce.

SHIELING
Fell pasture and small dwelling used during the summer months.

SIEVE
Rush used for making rushlights.

SILES
Crucks (q.v.).

SNECK
Iron door latch.

STATESMAN
Yeoman farmer holding his land by customary tenure from the lord.

SWILL
Shallow, oval, woven, oak basket.

THRESHING
Beating or bruising corn to separate the grain from the chaff.

THRESHING-FLOOR
Floor of stone flags or timber boards used for threshing (q.v.) grain.

THROUGH-STONE
Flat stone large enough to go across the thickness of a wall and put in to bind the outer and inner surfaces together.

TIE-BEAM
Horizontal timber forming the base of a roof truss (q.v.).

TIERING
Lime, sand and hair plaster applied to the underside of roof slates.

TRUSS
Rigid, timber, roof framework resting on the walls and supporting the purlins (q.v.) and ridge (q.v.).

TURBARY
Cutting of peat.

VACCARY
Dairy farm.

WALL-PLATE
Horizontal timber laid on the top of a wall which supports the lower rafter (q.v.) ends.

'WANG' CHEESE
Hard cheese, said to be as tough as wangs – leather thongs.

WEYT
Shallow leather dish used for winnowing (q.v.).

WINNOWING
Shaking or throwing threshed (q.v.) grain to allow a draught of air to separate the heavier grain from the lighter chaff.

WOODS OF WARRANT
Mature timber trees which could only be cut with the lord's permission, for housebuilding and repairs.

SOURCES OF ILLUSTRATIONS

References

The references below show page number followed by line number.

CHAPTER 1

11.5 Coleridge, S. T., *Table Talk*.
11.23 Mason, William, DD., *Poems and Letters of Thomas Gray*, 1820.
11.25 Wordsworth, William, 'Michael'.
12.24 Wordsworth, William, *A Guide to the Lakes*, first published anonymously 1810; published in 1822 as *A Description of the Scenery of the Lakes in the North of England*.
16.7 Sandford, Edmund, 'Antiquities and families in Cumberland, 1675', *CWAAS Tracts*, 1890.

CHAPTER 2

18.6 Millward, R., and Robinson, A., *The Lake District*, 1974.
18.33 LRO, WRW/C.
20.13 Published in Scott, S. H., *Westmorland Village*, 1904.
20.15 CRO, WD/TE
20.19 Hodgson, J., 'Westmorland as it was', *The Lonsdale Magazine*, vol. 3, 1822, with notes by J. Briggs.
20.23 Information from Mrs Elias, Low House, Troutbeck.
21.5 Hodgson, J., op. cit.
21.35 Tyson, B., 'Rydal Hall farmyard: the development of the Westmorland farmstead before 1700', *CWAAS*, vol. LXXX, 1980.
22.2 Clarke, James, *A Survey of the Lakes of Cumberland, Westmorland and Lancashire*, 1787.
22.11 Briggs, John, *Letters from the Lakes*.
22.20 Gibson, A. C., 'Hawkshead Parish', *Transactions of the Historic Society of Lancashire and Cheshire*, vol. 6 (second series), 1865.
23.1 Ellwood, T., The Landnama Book and the folklore of Cumberland and Westmorland, *CWAAS*, vol. XII, 1893.
23.4 Rowling, Marjorie, *The Folklore of the Lake District*, 1976.
24.16 Morris, C. (ed.), *The Journeys of Celia Fiennes*, 1947.
24.25 LRO, DO Pd/26/32.
25.5 Pringle, A., *A General View of the Agriculture of the County of Westmorland*, 1794.
25.8 Martindale, J. H., *Toast Dogs, Frying Pans and Peat*, *CWAAS*, vol. XIII, 1895.
25.12 Hodgson, op. cit.
25.33 Brears, Peter C. D., 'Oatcake in the West Riding', *Folklife*, vol. 12, 1974.
25.41 Fowkes, R., and Ridley, S., *Our Satterthwaite Heritage*, 1988.
26.8 Brears, op. cit.
26.22 Bailey, John, and Culley, George, *A General View of the Agriculture of the County of Cumberland*, 1794.
26.26 CRO, WD/TE.
27.20 Hartley, D., *Food in England*, 1954.
27.25 CRO, WD/TE.
27.30 CRO, WD/TE.
27.38 CRO, WD/TE.
27.39 LRO, WRW/K.
28.26 'Survivals in Hawkshead', *The North Lonsdale Magazine*, vol. 4, 1901.
30.1 Martineau, H., *A Complete Guide to the English Lakes*, 1855.
30.7 'Survivals in Hawkshead', op. cit.
30.17 Waugh, Edwin, 'Cockley Beck, 1861', in Thompson, B. L. (compiler), *Prose of Lakeland*, 1954.

31.17 Information from Janet Martin, Finsthwaite.
31.21 'Survivals in Hawkshead', op. cit.
31.27 Anon., *Gentlemen's Magazine*, 1766; quoted in Walton, John K., 'The strange decline of the Lakeland yeoman', *CWAAS*, vol. LXXXVI, 1986.
31.38 CRO, WD/TE.
31.40 CRO, WD/TE.
31.44 LRO, WRW/C.
32.4 Bailey and Culley, op. cit.
32.17 Hodgson, op. cit.
32.19 Hodgson, op. cit.
32.26 Notes by John Briggs for 'Westmorland as it was', op. cit.
32.40 Palmer, J. H., *Historic Farmhouses in and around Westmorland*, 1945.
32.42 Produced by Ashdown Smokeries.
33.2 Bailey and Culley, op. cit.
33.20 Wordsworth, *A Guide to the Lakes*, first published anonymously 1810; published in 1822 as *A Description of the Scenery of the Lakes in the North of England*.
33.22 Armitt, M., *Rydal*, 1916.
33.29 'The Gleaner, no. 16: North Country Cheese', in *The Lonsdale Magazine*, vol. 2, 1821.
34.8 'The Gleaner', op. cit.
34.11 Cowper, H. S., *Hawkshead*, 1899.
34.45 CRO, WD/TE.
35.2 Bagot, A., and Munby, J. (eds.), '"All things is well here", letters from Hugh James of Levens to James Graham, 1692–5,' *CWAAS Record Series*, vol. X, 1988.
35.17 CRO, WD/TE.
36.10 Hodgson, op. cit.
36.13 Fowkes and Ridley, op. cit.
36.14 LRO, DDN/2/1.
36.16 CRO, WD/NT.
36.17 Scott, S., *Westmorland Village*, 1904.
37.2 *Rural Houses of the Lancashire Pennines, 1560–1760*, RCHM, 1985.
37.4 Quoted in *Rural Houses of the Lancashire Pennines*, 1985, op. cit.
39.6 Cowper, 1899, op. cit.
39.15 *Oak Furniture from Lancashire and the Lake District*, exhibition catalogue, Temple Newsam, 1973.
42.24 *Westmorland*, RCHM, 1936.
44.31 Martineau, op. cit.
43.5 Fowkes and Ridley, op. cit.
43.7 Scott, op. cit.
44.15 CRO, D/NT/9.
44.17 LRO, WRW/C.
44.28 LRO, WRW/F.
44.30 CRO, WD/TE.
45.11 LRO, WRW/K.
45.14 Cowper, H. S., 'A Grasmere farmer's sale schedule in 1710', *CWAAS*, vol. XIII, 1894, or CRO, WD/L.
45.19 Information from Mr John Porter, Yatters Farm, Eskdale Green.
45.23 CRO, WD/TE.
45.26 CRO, WD/TE.
45.29 CRO, WD/TE.
45.32 Gough, John, *Manners and customs of Westmorland*, 1847; originally printed in the *Kendal Chronicle* in 1812.
46.3 *Westmorland*, RCHM, op. cit.
47.10 CRO, WD/TE.

47.20 Waugh, op. cit.
47.43 LRO, WRW/K.
48.22 Walpole, Hugh, *Rogue Herries*, 1930; quoted in Rollinson, W., *Life and Tradition in the Lake District*, 1974.
48.35 Clarke, op. cit.
48.46 Cowper, 1894, op. cit.
49.3 LRO, DDPd/26/32.
49.12 Hodgson, op. cit.
49.19 LRO, WRW/K.
50.3 Cowper, 1894, op. cit.
50.17 CRO, WD/TE.
50.18 CRO, WD/TE.
50.26 CRO, WD/TE.
50.30 Cowper, 1894, op. cit.
50.37 LRO, WRW/F.
51.4 LRO, WRW/K.
52.31 LRO, DDPd/26/262.
52.36 LRO, WRW/K.
56.6 Gough, op. cit.
56.30 Armitt, op. cit.

CHAPTER 3
65.7 Clarke, James, *A Survey of the Lakes of Cumberland, Westmorland and Lancashire*, 1787.
70.20 de Quincey, Thomas, *Recollections of the Lakes*, 1840.
70.29 Ford, Revd William, *A Description of the Scenery in the Lake District*, 1839.
72.30 Cowper, H. S., *Hawkshead*, 1899.

CHAPTER 4
73.9 Bailey, John, and Culley, George, *A General View of the Agriculture of the County of Cumberland*, 1797.
73.20 Ryder, M. S., *Sheep and Man*, 1983.
73.28 Bailey and Culley, op. cit.
74.4 Ryder, M. S., op. cit.
74.9 Satchell, John, *A Kendal Weaver*, 1986.
75.20 Ryder, op. cit.
75.23 Ryder, op. cit.
75.34 Ryder, op. cit.
75.41 Ryder, op. cit.
76.6 Ryder, op. cit.
76.17 Quoted in Satchell, op. cit.
76.20 Quoted in Satchell, op. cit.
77.2 Ryder, op. cit.
77.10 Ryder, op. cit.
77.15 Mitchelmore, D. J. H. (ed.), 'The Fountains Abbey Lease Book', *Yorkshire Archaeological Society Records Series*, vol. CXL, 1981.
77.24 Raistrick, A., 'The great sheep house at Malham', *Journal of the Bradford Textile Society*, 1954–5.
78.3 Studied by the author in 1982.
78.30 LRO, WRW/C.
78.34 CRO, D/HG/107.
78.37 CRO, WD/AG/Box 5.
79.5 Winchester, Angus, 'The farming landscape', in Rollinson, W. (ed.), *The Lake District Landscape Heritage*, 1989.
79.9 Winchester, 1989, op. cit.
80.3 CRO, D/Lons/L5/2/11/15.
80.11 Bailey and Culley, op. cit.
80.44 Ewbank, J. M., (ed.), *Antiquary on Horseback: the collections of the Reverend Thomas Machell*, 1692, 1963.
81.8 Bailey and Culley, op. cit.
81.14 Ryder, op. cit.
81.16 Ambleside Sound Archives.
81.17 Ambleside Sound Archives.
81.19 *Cumbria Magazine*, 1954.
81.34 West, Thomas, *The Antiquities of Furness*, 1774.
81.38 Information from Harry Wilson.
82.8 Quoted in Winchester, Angus, *Landscape and Society in Medieval Cumbria*, 1987.
82.10 Winchester, op. cit.
83.2 Quoted in Winchester, 1987, op. cit.
83.4 Quoted in Forrester, R. M., 'Ash as Fodder', *Journal of the Lakeland Horticultural Society*, vol. VII, Spring 1985.
83.9 Ambleside Sound Archives.
83.22 Wordsworth, William, *A Guide to the Lakes*, first published anonymously 1810.
83.26 Information from Harry Wilson, Ambleside.
83.29 Ambleside Sound Archives.
83.40 CRO, WD/TE.
84.7 *Wharton's Chronicle*, Records of the Chief Magistrates of Kendal from 1575, compiled by Wharton, 1724.
84.22 Information from Peter Johnson.
84.29 Tyson, B., 'Some traditional buildings in the Troutbeck valley: a documentary study', *CWAAS*, vol. LXXXII, 1982.
85.9 Griffin, H., *The Guardian*, 28 March 1988.
85.17 CRO, WD/TE.
85.20 CRO, WD/TE.
86.1 Quoted in Ryder, op. cit.
86.23 Mitchell, W. R., *Lakeland Dalesfolk*, 1983.
86.31 CRO, WD/TE.
87.11 Ewbank, op. cit.
88.3 Mitchell, op. cit.
88.10 Ryder, op. cit.
88.38 CRO, WD/TE.
89.10 CRO, WD/TE/Vol 2/365.
89.19 LRO, WRW/K.
89.22 LRO, WRW/K.
89.37 Marshall, J. D., 'The domestic economy of the Lakeland yeoman 1660–1749', *CWAAS*, vol. LXXIII, 1973.
90.33 Winchester, 1987, op. cit.
90.37 Winchester, 1987, op. cit.
91.4 Winchester, 1987, op. cit.
91.14 Quoted in Mitchelmore, op. cit.
91.31 Winchester, 1987, op. cit.
91.43 *Camden's Britannia*, 1698 edn., translated by E. Gibson.
92.8 Winchester, 1987, op. cit.
92.19 Ravis-Giordini, Georges, *Bergers Corses*, 1983.
92.24 Wiliam, Eurwyn, *The Historical Farm Buildings of Wales*, 1986.
92.37 Whyte, Ian D., 'Shielings and the upland pastoral economy of the Lake District in mediaeval and early modern times', in Baldwin, John R., and Whyte, Ian D. (eds.), *The Scandinavians in Cumbria*, 1985.
92.40 Whyte, op. cit.
92.43 Winchester, 1987, op. cit.
92.46 Whyte, op. cit.
93.19 Winchester, 1987, op. cit.
93.28 Ramm, H. G., et al, *Shielings and Bastles*, 1970.
94.8 Information from Ian Whyte.
94.15 Quoted in Wiliam, op. cit.
94.24 Winchester, 1987, op. cit.
94.36 Winchester, 1989, op. cit.
94.38 Bailey and Culley, op. cit.
94.42 CRO, WD/TE.
94.45 Winchester, 1989, op. cit.
95.2 CRO, WD/AG 59/3.
95.9 Bailey and Culley, op. cit.
95.18 Winchester, 1989, op. cit.
96.2 For comparable material from Wales see Wiliam, op. cit.
96.14 Winchester, 1987, op. cit.
96.16 Winchester, 1987, op. cit.
96.38 LRO, WRW/C.
98.11 LRO, WRW/K.
98.14 LRO, WRW/K.
100.12 Tyson, B., 1982, op. cit.
100.20 CRO, WD/TE.
101.13 Bailey and Culley, op. cit.
101.15 Pringle, A., *A General View of the Agriculture of the County of Westmorland*, 1794.
101.19 LRO, WRW/K.
101.24 Tyson, B., 'Low Park barn, Rydal: the reconstruction of a farm building in Westmorland in the seventeenth century', *CWAAS*, vol. LXXIX, 1979.
101.30 Tyson, 1979, op. cit.
101.34 Tyson, 1979, op. cit.
101.42 Mitchell, op. cit.

102.2 LRO, DDPd/26/337.
102.9 Mitchell, op. cit.
102.21 Tyson, 1979, op. cit.
102.25 National Trust Tenancy Agreement, 20 January, 1966.
102.26 Mortimer, J., *The Whole Art of Husbandry*, 1712.
102.45 Winchester, 1987, op. cit.
103.7 *Histories of Troutbeck Park and Troutbeck*, Lonsdale Papers, Barony of Kendal, 1769.
104.2 Clarke, James, *A Survey of the Lakes of Cumberland, Westmorland and Lancashire*, 1787.
104.7 CRO, WD/TE/vol. XIV, 223–6.
104.14 Bailey and Culley, op. cit.
104.23 Mitchell, op. cit.
104.45 Clarke, op. cit.
106.3 Morris, C., *The Journeys of Celia Fiennes: through England on side saddle, 1690*, 1949.
106.6 Pringle, op. cit.
106.12 Stockdale, James, *Annals of Cartmel*, 1872.
106.20 Lewis, Norman, 'The last of the old Europe', *Sunday Times*, 20 Nov. 1988.
106.29 Pringle, op. cit.
107.14 Winchester, 1987, op. cit.
107.19 Quoted in Satchell, J. E., 'A history of Meathop Woods, part 2', *CWAAS*, vol. LXXXIV, 1984.
107.27 Winchester, 1987, op. cit.
107.28 Winchester, 1987, op. cit.
108.5 CRO, Carlisle Probate Records.
108.8 CRO, WD/TE.
108.12 Harvey, Nigel, *The History of Farm Buildings in England and Wales*, 1970.
108.16 Tyson, B., 'Some farm lavatories in the English Lake District', *Journal of the Historic Farm Buildings Group*, vol. 2, 1985.
109.18 Bailey and Culley, op. cit.
109.22 Fowkes, R., and Ridley, S., *Our Satterthwaite Heritage*, 1988.
109.32 CRO, WD/TE.
110.4 Linton, E. Lynn, *The Lake Country*, 1864.
110.35 Rowling, Marjorie, *The Folklore of the Lake District*, 1976.

CHAPTER 5
111.15 Winchester, Angus, *Landscape and Society in Medieval Cumbria*, 1987.
111.18 West, Thomas, *The Antiquities of Furness*, 1774.
111.27 National Trust Landscape Survey Team, 1988–9.
111.30 Winchester, 1987, op. cit.
112.8 PRO, DL 44/194.
113.5 Porter, R. E., 'The Townfields of Coniston', *CWAAS*, vol. XXIX, 1929.
113.7 LRO, WRW/C.
113.16 Satchell, J. E., 'A History of Meathop Woods', *CWAAS*, vol. LXXXIV, 1984.
113.19 Wordsworth, William, *A Guide to the Lakes*, first published anonymously 1810; published in 1822 as *A Description of the Scenery of the Lakes in Northern England*.
113.21 CRO, WD/AG 29/4.
113.35 Pringle, J., *A General View of Agriculture in the County of Westmorland*, 1794.
114.1 See for example Pringle, A., op. cit., and Young, A., *Six Months Tour through the North of England, vol. 3, Cumberland and Westmorland*, 1770.
114.8 Bailey, J., and Culley, G., *A General View of the Agriculture of the County of Cumberland*, 1794.
114.25 CRO WD/TE.
114.29 CRO WD/TE.
114.34 CRO WD/TE.
114.36 Pringle, A., op. cit.
114.39 Information from Harry Wilson.
116.1 Information from Janet Martin.
116.13 Lefebure Molly, *Cumberland Heritage*, 1970.
117.3 Wiliam, E., *The Historical Farm Buildings of Wales*, 1986.
118.14 Bagot, A., and Munby, J. (eds.), '"All things is well here"', Letters from Hugh James of Levens to James Graham, 1692–5', *CWAAS Record Series*, vol. X, 1988.

118.21 LRO, WRW/F.
118.28 CRO, WD/TE.
122.16 CRO, WD/TE.
122.23 Wiliam, op. cit.
122.31 LRO, WRW/C.
123.7 CRO, WD/TE.
123.9 Bailey, John, and Culley, George, *A General View of Agriculture of the County of Cumberland, 1797*.
123.11 CRO, WD/TE.
124.1 Pringle, op. cit.
124.4 Bailey and Culley, op. cit.
124.7 CRO, D/LEC/301.
124.16 LRO, WRW/F.
124.30 Quoted in Satchell, John, *The Kendal Weaver*, 1986.
124.43 LRO, WRW/C.
124.45 LRO, WRW/F.
125.27 De Quincey, Thomas, *Recollections of the Lakes*, 1840.
125.31 Sedgwick, Adam, *A Memorial to Cowgill Chapel*, 1868.
125.34 Cowper, H. S., *Hawkshead*, 1899.
126.12 Chapman, S. D. (ed.), 'The Devon cloth industry in the eighteenth century', *Devon and Cornwall Records Society*, 197.
128.24 Winchester, Angus, 'Peat storage huts in Eskdale, *CWAAS*, vol. LXXXXIV, 1984.
128.28 CRO, WD/TE.
128.33 Rice, H. A. L., *Lake Country Portraits*, 1967.
128.38 LRO, WD/AG/5.
128.40 CRO, WD/TE.
129.7 West, Thomas, *A Guide to the Lakes*, 1778.
130.15 Winchester, 1987, op. cit.
130.20 Winchester, 1987, op. cit.
130.22 Winchester, 1987, op. cit.
131.1 Winchester, 1987, op. cit.
131.6 CRO, WD/AG 59/3.
131.11 Winchester, 1987, op. cit.
131.12 Morris, C., *The Journeys of Celia Fiennes: through England on a side saddle, 1690*, 1949.
132.14 Cowper, H. S., 'A contrast in architecture, part 2: the sod hut: an archaic survival', *CWAAS*, vol. I, 1901.
132.26 Ransome, Arthur, *Swallows and Amazons*, 1930.
132.38 CRO, WD/TE.

CHAPTER 6
133.19 PRO, DL 44/194.
134.27 Higgins, Martin, and Martin, Janet, 'An early seventeenth-century cruck barn in Great Langdale' *CWAAS*, vol. LXXXVI, 1986.
137.2 Tyson, B., Low Park barn, Rydal: 'the reconstruction of a farm building in Westmorland in the seventeenth century', *CWAAS*, vol. LXXIX, 1979.
137.16 Tyson, 1979, op. cit.
137.26 Tyson, 1979, op. cit.
139.10 Tyson, 1979, op. cit.
143.3 Cowper, H. S., *Hawkshead*, 1899.

CHAPTER 7
148.11 Ambleside Sound Archives.
148.27 Moorhouse, S. A., and Faull, M. L. (eds.), *West Yorkshire: An Archaeological Survey to AD 1500*, 1981.
148.33 Bagot, A., 'Mr Gilpin and manorial customs', *CWAAS*, vol. LXII, 1962.
149.4 Morris, C., *The Journeys of Celia Fiennes: through England on a side saddle, 1690*, 1949.
149.7 Ewbank, J. M., *Antiquary on Horseback: the collections of the Reverend Thomas Machell, 1692*, 1963.
149.36 LRO, WD/NT.
149.40 LRO, WRW/C.
151.38 See for example Tyson, B., 'Rydal Hall farmyard: the development of a Westmorland farmstead before 1700', *CWAAS*, vol. LXXX, 1980.
152.8 Quoted in Satchell, J. E., 'A history of Meathop Woods, part 2', *CWAAS*, Vol. LXXIV, 1984.
152.18 Tyson, B., 'Some traditional buildings in the Troutbeck valley', *CWAAS*, vol. LXXXII, 1982.

152.21 Tyson, B., 'Low Park barn, Rydal: the reconstruction of a farm building in Westmorland in the seventeenth century', *CWAAS*, vol. LXXIX, 1979.

152.23 Tyson, B., 'Building work at Sockbridge Hall, its farmyard and neighbourhood, 1660–1710', *CWAAS*, vol. LXXXIII, 1983.

152.30 Tyson, B., 'Skirwith Hall and Wilton Tenement (Kirkland Hall): the rebuilding of two Cumbrian farmsteads in the eighteenth century', *CWAAS*, vol. LXXXI, 1981.

152.41 Ambleside Sound Archives.

152.44 Tyson, 1979, op. cit.

153.12 Tyson, 1982, op. cit.

154.23 Information from the late Mr Thomas Hornyold-Strickland.

156.13 Rawnsley, H. D., *Wordsworthiana: Reminiscences of Wordsworth*.

156.16 Wordsworth, William, *A Guide to the Lakes*, first published anonymously 1810; published in 1822 as *A Description of the Scenery of the Lakes in the North of England*.

157.31 Morris, op. cit.

158.3 Pringle, Andrew, *A General View of Agriculture in the County of Westmorland*, 1797.

158.16 Farrer, W., (ed.), 'Records relating to the Barony of Kendale', *CWAAS Trans, Record Series*, vols. IV–VI, 1923–6.

158.20 PRO, DL 44/194.

158.23 Morris, op. cit.

158.27 Ewbank, op. cit.

158.31 Pringle, op. cit.

158.33 Bagot, A., and Munby, J. (eds.), '"All things is well here", letters from Hugh James of Levens to James Grahame 1692–5", *CWAAS Record Series*, vol. X, 1988.

158.39 Ure, D., *General View of Agriculture in the County of Dumbarton*, 1794.

160.16 Tyson, B., 'The Troutbeck Park slate quarries, their management and markets', 1753–60, *CWAAS*, vol. LXXXIV, 1984.

160.21 Tyson, 1984, op. cit.

160.29 Tyson, 1984, op. cit.

160.45 Tyson, 1983, op. cit.

160.47 Tyson, 1983, op. cit.

161.17 Ambleside Sound Archives.

162.2 Tyson, 1982, op. cit.

162.19 Tyson, 1980, op. cit.

163.11 Ambleside Sound Archives.

164.7 Bagot, 1962, op. cit.

164.9 Armitt, M., *Rydal*, 1916.

164.13 PRO, DL 43/17/5.

164.17 PRO, ADM 66/106.

164.30 Armitt, op. cit.

164.35 Harrison, S. M., *The Pilgrimage of Grace in the Lake Counties, 1536–7*, 1981.

164.38 Searle, C. E., 'Custom and class conflict in Cumbria', *Past and Present*, 110, 1986.

164.42 CRO, D/Law/1/164.

165.3 CRO, D/WM/11/185-205.

165.11 Tyson, 1979, op. cit.

165.16 Tyson, 1980, op. cit.

165.19 Tyson, 1979, op. cit.

165.33 CRO, WD/TE.

165.44 Tyson, 1979 and 1980, op. cit.

173.28 Tyson, 1979 and 1980, op. cit.

174.4 Tyson, 1982, op. cit.

174.12 Martin, Janet, 'The building and endowment of Finsthwaite church and school, 1723–5', *CWAAS*, vol. LXXXIV, 1984.

174.18 Tyson, 1982, op. cit.

174.26 Tyson, 1982, op. cit.

174.27 Tyson, 1982, op. cit.

174.28 Tyson, 1982, op. cit.

174.30 Tyson, 1982, op. cit.

174.41 Tyson, 1980, op. cit.

176.2 Tyson, 1980, op. cit.

176.9 Tyson, 1983, op. cit.

176.15 Tyson, 1981, op. cit.

176.22 Bagot and Munby, op. cit.

178.7 CRO, WD/GH.

178.37 Tyson, 1981, op. cit.

182.24 Bradley, A. G., *Highways and Byways in the Lake District*, 1901.

183.17 Wiliam, Eurwyn, *The Traditional Farm Buildings of Wales*, 1986.

183.39 Bagot and Munby, op. cit.

184.1 Tyson, 1981, op. cit.

184.23 Bagot and Munby, op. cit.

184.25 Bagot and Munby, op. cit.

185.3 Tyson, 1981, op. cit.

185.10 CRO, D/Lec.

185.16 Tyson, 1981, op. cit.

185.17 Tyson, 1983, op. cit.

185.18 Tyson, 1983, op. cit.

185.19 Tyson, 1983, op. cit.

185.22 Wiliam, op. cit.

185.30 Martin, op. cit.

185.34 Tyson, 1983, op. cit.

185.37 Bagot and Munby, op. cit.

185.44 Tyson, 1981, op. cit.

187.9 Bagot and Munby, op. cit.

187.22 Wordsworth, op. cit.

187.30 Carlisle D&C, Machel mss.

189.26 Wordsworth, op. cit.

191.15 *Westmorland*, RCHM, 1933.

CHAPTER 8

192.7 Walton, John K., 'The strange decline of the Lakeland yeoman: some thoughts on sources, methods and definitions', *CWAAS*, vol. LXXXVI, 1986.

192.29 Wordsworth, W., 'Michael'.

193.4 Bailey, John, and Culley, George, *A General View of the Agriculture of the County of Cumberland*, 1794.

193.7 Martineau, H., *A Complete Guide to the English Lakes*, 1855.

193.15 CRO, D/NT/12.

193.16 CRO, D/NT/27.

193.29 CRO, D/NT/17/2 and CRO, D/NT/18.

193.37 CRO, D/Lec/30, CRO, D/Lec/94.

193.43 Wordsworth, Dorothy, *Grasmere Journal*.

194.7 CRO, D/Lec/94.

194.10 Hutchinson, William, *An Excursion to the Lakes in Westmorland and Cumberland in 1773 and 1774*, 1776, and Green, William, *The Tourist's New Guide*, 1819.

194.12 Wordsworth, William, *The Excursion*.

ILLUSTRATIONS

6 Anon. (A Member of the Scandinavian Society), *Troutbeck: Its Scenery, Old Architecture etc*, 1876.

14 De Quincey, Thomas, *Recollections of the Lake Poets*, 1840.

15 *Troutbeck*, 1876, op. cit.

26 Anon., 'Rusland Valley', *North Lonsdale Magazine*, vol. 4, 1901.

42 Scott, S., *A Westmorland Village*, 1904.

45 Information from Mr Porter, Yatters Farm, Eskdale.

170 Letters of Beatrix Potter, National Trust.

127 *Westmorland*, RCHM, 1936.

152 Tyson, B., 'Low Park barn, Rydal: the reconstruction of a farm building in Westmorland in the seventeenth century', *CWAAS*. vol. LXXIX, 1979.

Index

The black and white photographs are shown in the index in **bold**. The colour photographs which appear in sections following text pages, are indexed thus: **48***foll.*

Above Becks Farm *see* Stepps End
Acorn Bank Mill, 122
Addison, Thomas, Penny Hill Farm, Eskdale, 44
Ale *see* Beer
Ambrey *see* Buttery
Appleby, 13, 104
Arable fields, 12, 15, 17, 78, 90, 91, 95
Arvel bread, 26, 32
Ash Busk Farm, Great Langdale, 79, 194
Ash trees/wood, 14, 79, 81, 82, 83, 102, 116, 131, 162, 163, 171
Ashes Farm, Staveley, 33
Ashleigh, Little Langdale, 152
Ashness Farm, Borrowdale, 19, 29, 84, 88, 151, **176**, 177
Aspland, T. L., **28**
Atkinson Ground, Hawkshead, 15
Atkinson, J., Troutbeck, 122

Backboards, 24, 25
Backstones, 25–6
Bakestone Barrow Wood, 26
Bakestone Moss, 26
Bank barns, **48***foll.*, 88, 97, 98, 100, 104, 108, 134–43, 193, 195
Bark, 17, 81, 131–2, 162, 165, 173
Barker Knott Farm, Windermere, 44
Barley, 12, 32, 34, 35, 52, 113, 118, 121
Barn plans, 133–47
Barns (*see also* Bank barns, Field barns), 21, 66, 67
Baronies, 13, 16
Barrow, Thomas, Meathop, 113, 152
Barton Church, 160, 185
Baysbrown Farm, Great Langdale, 81
Baysbrown Manor, 111
Beckside Cottage, Colthouse, 27, 179, **181**
Beckstones Farm, Patterdale, 65, 66, 109, 135, **146**, 147
Bedding, cattle, 100, 117, 118
Bedding, domestic, 49, 50, 51
Beds, 49–50, 51, 132
    Tester, 50
Bee-boles, 109–10
Beehives, 109–10, 141
Beer (*also* Ale), 34–7, 53
Bees, 109–10
Beeswax, 47, 109
Bell, William, 16
Bellman Houses, Winster, 141, **142**
Below Becks Farm *see* Caffle House
Benches, 20, 42, 43, 44, 47, 48
Bend-or-Bump Cottage, Hawkshead, 155
Bengarth, Wasdale, 70
Bield, The, Little Langdale, 155, 189
Bigg *see* Barley
Biggland, James, 114
Birkett, George, Fold Farm, Troutbeck, 27, 86
Birkett, William, Troutbeck, 46, 152, 160
Birkhead, Jonathan, Troutbeck, 152
Birks Farm, Underbarrow, 67

Blackbeck Cottage, Hawkshead, 72
Blea Tarn Farm, Little Langdale, 78, 89, 128
Boon Crag Cottages, Coniston, 141, **161**, 167, **168**, 170
Boon Crag Farm, Coniston, 123, 127
Borrowdale Place, Eskdale, 79
Borwick Ground Farm, Hawkshead, 24
Boskins, 98
Bouses, 98, 100
Bowe Barn, Borrowdale, **173**
Bowness, Michael, Dale End Farm, Little Langdale, 149
Bracken, 17, 26, 80, 83, 95, 100, 105, 112, 115, 131, 132, 158, 159, 187, 196
Brandreth, 24, 25, 26
Brass pans, 48, 49
Brewhouses, 21, 137
Brewing, 34–7
Briggs, John, 22
Brighouse Farm, Ulpha, 31
Brimmerhead Farm, Easdale, Grasmere, 102, 180, 193
Brockbank, Mr, Eskdale Green, 45
Brockbank, Mr, Pool Bank Farm, Crosthwaite, 115
Broom, 83, 131
Brotherilkeld Farm, Eskdale, **29**, 34, 35, 36, 81, 90, 91, **145**, 172, 193
Broughton Mills, 122
Brown Cow Cottage, Hawkshead, 30
Browne family, 6, **17**, 24, 35, 45, 155
Browne, Benjamin, 1664–1748, Townend, Troutbeck, 27, 28, 31, 45, 47, 48, 50, 86, 89, 100, 114, 123, 165, 174
Browne, Ellinor, Townend, Troutbeck, 50
Browne, George, Townend, Troutbeck, 1596–1685, 50, 100
Browne, George, 1741–1804, Townend, Troutbeck, 26, 35, 83, 85, 88, 94, 108, 109, 114, 118, 122, 123, 128
Browne, George, 1834–1914, Townend, Troutbeck, 43, 74
Browne, George, Staveley, 34, 109
Brownrigg, William, 45
Brunt How Farm, Netherwasdale, 36
Buckbarrow Farm, Netherwasdale, 44, 113, 122
Bulls, 101–2
Butter, 48, 85, 90, 91
Butteries, 18, 36, 37, 48, 51, 55–71, 113
Byres *see* Cattle housing **48***foll.*, 66, 67, 98–9, 104, 134–47

Caffle House, Watendlath, 20, 23, 31, 36, 62, 177
Calder Abbey, 102
Camden, 91
Candles, 47
Candlesticks, 47
Carpets, 46
Carts, 97, 103, 104–6, 110, 114, 128
Cartsheds, 103, 105, 106, 122, 139

Cattle, 14, 17, 67, 76, 78, 79, 84, 89–103, 109, 114, 118, 131, 133–47
Cattle housing, 90, 95–102
Caudale Beck Farm, Patterdale, **48***foll.*
Causeway Farm, Windermere, 38, 44, 50, 177, 178, **179**, **190**
Celle-trees, 98, 100
Chaff, 50, 115, 117, 118
Chairs, 42–5, 47, 49
Chambers, sleeping, 18, 49, 51, 58, 64, 190
Chapman House, Finsthwaite, 27
Charcoal, 17, 131–2, 157
Charcoal burner's huts, 131–2, 157
Cheese, 31, 32, 33–4, 48, 49, 77, 90, 91, 92
Cheese-presses, 33
Cheese-shelves, 33
Chests, 23, 42, 49, 50, 51, 52, 122
Chickens, 108–9
Chimney recesses *see* Hearths
Chimney-hoods, 19, 20, 21, 22, 23, 29, 31, 32, 52, 53, 59, 60, 68, 122, 157, 167
Chimney-pots, 157
Chimneys, 14, 15, 19, 21, 28, 29, 36, 59, 60, 65, 66, 84, 85, 131, 132, 137, 156–7
Clapbread, 23–6, 31, 37
Clarke, James, 48, 65, 103
Clay, 21, 22, 153, 154, 175, 181–2, 186
Cloth, 76
Coal, 28, 29, 30, 128, 183
Cockley Beck Farm, Duddon, 30, 47
Coleridge, 11
Colliers *see* Charcoal
Collinfield, Kendal, 88
Common Farm, Windermere, 40, 42
Common fields, 113
Conishead Priory, 111
Coniston Old Hall, Coniston, 101, 102, 139, 157
Cooking, 23–8
Cooking utensils, 19, 23, 30, 47
Copper pans, 48, 49
Coppice Woodland, 71
Corn-driers, 121–2
Cothow, Martindale, 171
Coward, William, Low Loanthwaite Farm, Hawkshead, 118
Cowperthwaite, Stanley, Tarn Foot, Loughrigg, 51
Cowperthwaithe, George, Tarn Foot, Loughrigg, 50
Cows *see* Cattle
Crag Farm Cottage, Colthouse, 30
Crag, The, Troutbeck, **188**
Cragg Farm, Buttermere, 27
Cragg Farm, Colthouse, 36, 109
Craghouse Farm, Ireton, 36, 108, 119
Croft Foot, Colthouse, 26, 106
Crook, 33
Crop rotation, 113–4
Cropple How Farm, Ravenglass, Muncaster, 21, **22**, 67, 177
Crops *see* individual names

Crosslands Farm, Rusland, **140**
Crostenrigs, Troutbeck, 100, 147
Crow-steps, 63, 65, 155, 156
Crucks, roof, 52, 56, 61, 68, 97, 134, 165, 161–71, 187
Cunsey, 81
Cupboards (*see also* Spice Cupboards), 25, 37–42, 44, 47, 55, 58, 61
Curtains, bed, 50

Dale Head Farm, Martindale, 23, 65, **127**
Dalton, Richard, 176
Decorative motifs (in wood carving), 37–41, 43
Dennison, William, Low Yewdale Farm, Coniston, 165
Denny, Thomas, Newby Bridge Inn, 174
Detached kitchens *see* Downhouses
Dipping *see* Sheep dipping
Dixon, Christopher, 165
Dixon, Thomas, Scale Farm, Netherwasdale, 78
Dog-gates, 88
Dogs *see* Sheep-dogs
Doors, 19, 20, 37, 48, 59, 61, 99, 154, 165, 176–8
Double-pile plan, 60, 68–72, 172
Downhouses, 19, 32, 34, 35–7, 43, 48, 51, 60, 62–6
Dung *see* Manure
Dunthwaite, Setmurthy, 106, 119

Enclosures, 194
Entrances, 55–71

Far End Farm, Coniston, 58
Fearon, Agnes, Robinson Place, Great Langdale, 41, 58
Fearon, Thomas, Robinson Place, Great Langdale, 41, 58
Fearon, William, Robinson Place, Great Langdale, 89
Fell Foot Farm, Little Langdale, 21, 45, 49, 51, 53, 58, 187, **190**
Fell grazing, 12, 15, 16, 17, 78–80, 90, 91, 93, 94, 111, 112, 194
Fells, 12, 15, 16, 17, 76, 129, 196
Field barns, 99, 100, 130, **144**foll., 147
Fiennes, Celia, 23, 24, 25, 26, 105, 131, 149, 157, 158
Finsthwaite Church, 174, 185
Fire grates, 28, 29
Fire-cranes, 19, 23
Fire-windows, 29, 36, 46, 60, 65, 72, 167
Firebeams, 19, 20, 21, 29, 64, 68
Firehoods *see* Chimney hoods
Firehouses, 18, 19, 29, 30, 31, 35, 36, 37, 42, 43, 44, 46, 47, 48, 51, 52, 55–71, 167
Fireplaces, 19, 20, 21, 22–3, 28, 36, 37, 44, 47, 49, 53, 55–71
Firewood *see* Wood
Fisher, John, Furness, 164
Fisher, John, Townend, Grasmere, 193
Fisher, Nicholas, Furness, 164
Fisher, Robert, Furness, 164
Flag Street, Hawkshead, **189**
Flails, 115–16
Flax, 123–4, 125
Fleming, Fletcher, Fell Foot Farm, Little Langdale, 27, 45, 59
Fleming, Sir Daniel, Rydal Hall, Rydal, 21, 101, 102, 137, 139, 152, 165, 173, 174
Fleming, William, Rydal Hall, 101
Fletcher, Robert, Low Burnthwaite, Wasdale Head, 31
Floors, barn, 80, 98, 100
Floors, house, 37, 45–6

Fodder (*see also* Hay, Straw, Leaf fodder), 81–3, 96, 102–3, 117, 118, 131
Fold Head Farm, Watendlath, 23, 52, 57, 95, **144**
Food, 31–4
Forms *see* Benches
Forrest family, 17
Fountains Abbey, 76, 77, 85, 91
Funerals, 26, 32, 48
Furness Abbey, 73, 76, 77, 83, 90, 91, 131, 164

Gallowbarrow, Hawkshead, 30
Gatesgarth Farm, Buttermere, 90, 95
Ghyll Farm, Netherwasdale, 36, 68, 69
Gill Bank Farm, Eskdale, 79
Girdles, 23, 24, 25, 30
Glass, glazing, 46, 178–81
Glencoyne Farm, Ullswater, **19**, 43, 57, 65, 78, 93, 108, **144**foll., 155, **186**
Grain, 17, 52, 53, 97, 100, 105, 112, 114, 115, 117, 118, 127, 133–47
Granaries, 52, 122, 126, 139, 141, 142
Green End Cottage, Colthouse, 20, **48**foll., 72
Green End House, Colthouse, 29, 88
Greenhew, Law of, 163
Greenhow, Harry, Harry Place Farm, Great Langdale, 81
Grizedale, Mr, Baysbrown Farm, Great Langdale, 81
Grove Farm, Applethwaite, Windermere, 47, 52, 123

Hacket Farm, Great Langdale, 134
Hafodtai, 92, 94
Hair, for plasters, 163
Hall Bank, Rydal, 33
Hallan, 30, 48, 65
Harden cloth, 50, 124
Harrison, John, Great Langdale, 158
Harrison, Thomas, Glencoyne Farm, Ullswater, 108
Harrison, Thomas, Great Langdale, 158
Harrowhead Farm, Wasdale, 70, 103, 119
Harry Place Farm, Great Langdale, 45, 83, **99**
Hartsop Hall Farm, Patterdale, 80, 82, 99, **144**foll., 147, **151**, 155, 176, 187
Harvesting, 114–15
Hawes Farm, Broughton Mills, 122
Hawkrigg, Joseph, Grove Farm, Windermere, 47
Hawkrigg, William, Underhelm Farm, Grasmere, 45, 48, 49, 50
Hawkshead Church, 162
Haws Farm, Eskdale, 79
Hay, 133–47
Hayton, J., 118
Hazelhead Farm, Duddon, 147
Heafing/Heafs, 74–5, 79
Hearths, 19, 20, 21, 22, 23
Hearth fires, 20, 21, 22, 23, 26, 29, 30
Heather, 159
Hecks, 19, 20, 29, 61
Heelis Office, Hawkshead, 71, 72, 175, 191
Hemp, 50, 123–4, 125
Henhow, Martindale, 65
Hennery-piggeries, 108–9, 147
Herdwick sheep, 32, 46, **74**, 197
Heron Mill, Beetham, 173
Heron, William, Gosforth, 119
High Arnside Farm, Coniston, 20, 21, 60, 178
High Bakestone, 26
High Birk Howe Farm, Little Langdale, 21, 22, 32, **48**foll., 53, 57, 59, **67**, **159**, 176 179, 193

High Grigg Farm, Underbarrow, 141
High Hallgarth Farm, Little Langdale, 134
High Oxenfell Farm, Coniston, 41, **136**, **162**
High Park Cottage, Coniston, 46
High Park-a-Moor Farm, Coniston, 22, 112, 133, 158
High Snab Farm, Newlands, 69, **193**
High Wallowbarrow Farm, Duddon valley, 18
High Waterhead Farm *see* Boon Crag
High Wray Farm, Ambleside, 42
High Yewdale Farm, Coniston, 124, 167, **169**, **170**, **171**
High Skelghyll Farm, Ambleside, 62, 177
Hill Top, Near Sawrey, 31, 34, 47, 49, 51, 60, 62, 63, 110, 178, **180**
Hills, Robert, 33, 110
Hoathwaite Cottage, Coniston, 52, 154, 182
Hoathwaite Farm, Coniston, 46, 49, 167
Hodge Close Quarry, 152
Hodge Hill, Cartmel Fell, 128
Hodgson, Mrs, High Birk Howe Farm, Little Langdale, 32
Hogg houses, **48**foll., 80–1, **82**, 100, 147, 151, 152, 155, 171
Hole House, Troutbeck, **98**
Holehouse, Hawkshead, 56
Holeslack Farm, Helsington, 21, 51, 58, 178, 183
Holly, 81, 83, 102, 116
Holme Cultram Abbey, 76
Holme Fell, 26
Holme Ground Farm, Coniston, 110, 116 **140**
Holme, J., Ambleside, 108
Holme, John, Low Hallgarth Farm, Little Langdale, 41
Holme, John, Rydal, 137
Holme, Margaret, Low Hallgarth Farm, Little Langdale, 41
Holme, Thomas, 128
Honey, 109
Hops, 34
Hornyold-Strickland, Henry, Sizergh Castle, 154
Horses, 89, 97, 98, 100, 101, 103–4, 105, 106, 109, 114, 118, 119, 124, 131, 145, 183, 185, 196
House plans, 54–72
Houseboote, 164
Houseplace *see* Firehouse
Howe Green Farm, Hartsop, Patterdale, 23, **48**foll., 67, 109, **121**
Howe Farm, Troutbeck, 97, **156**
Howe Head, Ambleside, **189**
Howend, Netherwasdale, **193**
Hows Farm, Eskdale, 79
Hunter, Nicholas, Buckbarrow Farm, Wasdale, 113, 122
Hurdles, 83, 131, 132

Intakes, 79, 95
Ivy, 6, 83

Jack Scout Land, Silverdale, **184**
Jackdaw Cottage, Grasmere, 42
Jackson, William, High Wallowbarrow Farm, Duddon, 18
Joinery, 174–81

Kettles, 19, 30
Kiln Cottage, Troutbeck, 35
Kilns
    corndrying, 35, 121–2, 126
    lime, 182, 183–5
    malt, 34
Kilnstones, Longsleddale, 109

Kirkby, William, Blea Tarn Farm, Little
  Langdale, 89
Kirkland Hall, 185
Kitchens *see* Downhouses
Knipe Fold, Hawkshead, 108

Lambing, 83
Landlord's flock, 75
Lane Cottage, Troutbeck, 16
Lane End Farm, Sizergh, 109, 130
Lane Foot, Troutbeck, 154
Lane Head Farm, Patterdale, 37
Larder *see* Buttery
Laths, 21, 22, 52, 160, 161, 162, 165, 166,
  175, 190
Lawson Park Farm, Coniston, 22, 112, 133, 158
Lawson, Sir Gilfred, 164
Leaf fodder, 81–3, 102–3
Levens Hall, 118, 176, 183, 184, 185, 187
Lime, 27, 52, 53, 131, 153, 154, 163, 181–91
Lime kiln *see* Kilns
Limefitt Mill, Troutbeck, 122
Limewash, 67, 187, 189–91
Linen, 50, 124
Little Tarn, Newlands, 122
Lobby entrance plan, 62–3
Lofts, 18, 23, 36, 51, 52–3, 51–64, 67, 80, 99,
  108, 122
Longhouse plan, 66–7, 133
Longmire, 46
Longmire, James, Troutbeck, 31
Longmire, W. Taylor-, 74, **144**foll.
Low Bakestone, 26
Low Burnthwaite Farm, Wasdale Head, 31
Low Fold, Ambleside, 54, 155
Low Fold Farm, Crook, 33
Low Fold Farm, Grasmere, 36
Low Greengate, Near Sawrey, 72
Low Groves, Skelsmergh, 88
Low Hallgarth Farm, Little Langdale, 19, 40,
  41, 61, 134
Low House Farm, Troutbeck, 20, 45, 56, 160
Low Loanthwaite Farm, Hawkshead, 31, 178
Low Longmire Farm, Bouth, 33, 44, 102, 119,
  121
Low Millbeck Farm, Great Langdale, 194
Low Millerground, Windermere, 56, 57, 181
Low Park Farm, Rydal, 98, 137, 151, 152,
  165, 173
Low Park-a-Moor Farm, Coniston, 20, 36, 86
Low Tilberthwaite Farm, Coniston, 61, 141
Low Trock How, Hawkshead, 60, 191
Low Wray Farm, Ambleside, 110
Low Yewdale Farm, Coniston, 60, 110, 165,
  182, 189
Lowther family, 70
Lowther, Sir John, 183

Macon, 31, 32
Mains House Farm, Pooley Bridge, 119
Malt-houses *see* Malting
Malt/malted barley, 34, 35, 52
Mandall, Thomas, Tarn Foot, Loughrigg, 53
Manorial Courts, 79, 94, 95, 96, 102, 111,
  124, 128, 148, 158, 163, 164, 185, 197
Manure, 21, 22, 90, 96, 100, 103, 104, 131,
  182, 191, 197
Manure passages, 98, 99
Marriage, 41
Marshall, John, 165
Martindale, J. H., 25
Mattresses, 50, 115
Mawson, John, Silverhowe, Gosforth, 149
Meadows, 15, 17, 77, 90, 91, 96, 109, 149,
  196

Meat, 27, 30, 31, 32, 48, 52, 75, 81, 90, 95,
  96
  salted, 31, 48, 52, 96
  smoked 32, 33
Mell, 19, 56
Merry Neets, 47–8
Middlefell Place Farm, Great Langdale, 15, 80,
  194
Middlefell, Charles, Blea Tarn Farm, Little
  Langdale, 128
Middlefell, John, Wallend Farm, Great
  Langdale, 98
Milk, 32, 33, 48, 75, 77, 90, 95, 96, 101, 102
Millbeck Farm, Great Langdale, 56, 57, 66, 83
Millbrow Farm, Skelwith Bridge, 45
Miller, Mr, Troutbeck, 94
Mislet Farm, Windermere, 108, 109, 181
Monastic Houses, 14, 73, 75, 76, 77, 80, 90
Moor Farm, Keswick, 139
Moore, John, Whitehaven, 193
Mortar, 153, 154, 181, 185–7
Moss/Mossing, 53, 132, 162–3
Muncaster mill, 122
Muntin-and-plank panelling, 19, 37, 52, 53,
  56, 60, 61, 71, 175, 177
Mutton *see* Meat

Nab Scar, Rydal, 110
National Trust, 18, 173, 195, 196
Nether Levens Farm, Levens, 157
Netherwasdale mill, 193
Nettleslack, Martindale, 67
Nicholson, Nicholas, Cockermouth, 193
Ninesor, 183
Nook Farm, Rosthwaite, Borrowdale, 177
North Fold Farm, Troutbeck, 50
North Lonsdale magazine, 30

Oak, 102, 131, 163, 165, 171, 173, 175, 176,
  177
Oak Cottage, Rosthwaite, 38, 53, 67
Oatcakes, 23–6, 30, 32
Oat-flakes, 25
Oats/Oatmeal, 12, 23, 26, 30, 32, 52, 113,
  118, 121, 122
Old Dungeon Ghyll Hotel, Great Langdale,
  194
Old House, Hawkshead Fields, 167
Orrest Head Farm, Windermere, 29, 179
Out-kitchen *see* Downhouse
Outgangs, 79
Ovens, 26–8, 29, 30, 31, 34, 35, 36
Oxen, 89, 100, 101, 103, 113

Paddockwray Farm, Eskdale, 79
Pan-bread 26, 28, 31
Pannage, 15, 16, 107
Pantry *see* Buttery
Park End Farm, Brigsteer, 19, 21, 23, 29
Parlours, 20, 36, 37, 48, 49–51, 53, 55–71,
  190
Pastures, 16, 193
Pearson, John, Buttermere, 124
Peat, 17, 21, 22, 28, 30, 36, 84, 92, 128–31,
  183
Peat houses, 129–31, 147, 151
Peel, John, 76
Pegs, bone, 160–1
Pegs, oak, 160–1, 162, 163, 175
Pennant, Thomas, 94
Penny Hill Farm, Eskdale, 44
Pewter, 37, 48, 49
Piggins *see* Wooden vessels
Pigs, 17, 106–9 131, 196
Pigsties, 108–9, 139

Pinfolds, 94
Plank-and-stud partitions, 37
Plaster, 22, 52, 53, 154, 175, 181, 182,
  190–1
Plough/Ploughing, 89, 100, 103, 104, 113
Plum Green Farm, Finsthwaite, 49
Pollarded trees, 14, 79, 81, 82, 83
Pool Bank, Crosthwaite, 115, 128, 141
Porches, 14, 33, 61, 72, 154
Pot-crane *see* Fire-crane
Potash, 100
Potatoes, 123
Pottage, 32
Potter, Beatrix, 34, 40, 41, 43, 51, 62, 63, 72,
  110, 180, 191, 195, 196
Privies, 108, 109
Purlins, 69, 162, 165, 166, 167, 168, 169, 171,
  172, 173
Pye Howe, Great Langdale, 176

Quarries, 151–2, 158, 159, 160, 185

Rafters, 160, 162, 165, 166, 171, 172
Ranges, cooking, 28, 29, 30–1
Rannel-baulks, 23
Ratten-crooks, 19, 23, 25, 30
Raw Head Farm, Great Langdale, 84, 95, 129
Rawlinson, Leonard, Low Longmire Farm,
  Bouth, 44
Reckons *see* Ratten-crooks
Rectory Farm, Windermere, 36
Red Lion Hotel, Hawkshead, 72
Rendering, 66, 67, 154, 181, 185, 187, 189
Retting, 124, 125
Ridge tiles, 161
Ridges, 161–2, 165, 166, 167, 168, 171
Rigg, William, Hawkshead Fields, 118, 124
Rigge, George, High Yewdale Farm, Coniston,
  124
Ring-garths, 111–13, 148
Roberts, Mr, Oak Cottage, Rosthwaite, 53
Robin Ghyll, Great Langdale, 53, 55, 56
Robin Lane Cottage, Troutbeck, 189
Robinson Place Farm, Great Langdale, 41, 53,
  58, 89
Robinson, Elizabeth, High Arnside Farm,
  Coniston, 21
Robinson, Henry, High Arnside Farm,
  Coniston, 21
Robinson, John, Barton, 160
Roof coverings *see* Slate, Thatch, Shingles
Rook How Meeting House, 26
Rooking Farm, Patterdale, 187
Root crops (*see also* Potatoes, Turnips), 123
Root stores, 123
Rossett Farm, Great Langdale, 80
Rowhead Farm, Wasdale, 145
Royal Commission for Historical Monuments,
  42
Ruddle, 189, 191
Rum butter, 37
Rushlights, 47
Rydal Hall, 21, 88, 98, 101, 162, 165, 173,
  174, 175

Sadghyll Farm, Longsleddale, 92
Salted meat *see* Meat, salted
Salving, 85–6
Sand, for mortars, 153, 163, 185–7, 191
Satterthwaite, Benjamin, Townend Cottage,
  Colthouse, 25, 42
Satterthwaite, Charles, Wallend Farm, Great
  Langdale, 134
Satterthwaite, Edward, Townend Cottage,
  Colthouse, 42

Satterthwaite, Michael, Cragg Farm, Colthouse, 109
Satterthwaite, Robert, Wall End Farm, Great Langdale, 134
Satterthwaite, William, Beckside, Colthouse, 43
Sawrey, William, Boon Crag Cottage, Coniston, 170
Scale Close, Borrowdale, 93
Scales Farm, Netherwasdale, 151, 187
Scales (*see also* Shielings), 84, 92
Scots pine, 81
Scott, Walter, Ashness Farm, Borrowdale, 84
Screens *see* Settles
Scythes, 114
Seathwaite Farm, Borrowdale, 176
Seatoller Farm, Borrowdale, 20
Sedgewick, Adam, 125
Settles, 20, 43
Sheep, 17, 73–88, 90, 91, 92, 94, 95, 98, 102, 131, 196, 197
  dipping, 86
  granges, 14, 76, 77
  Herdwick, 73–5
  housing, 77–8, 80–1, 84
  meets, 79
  shearing, 86, 87
  washing, 85, 86
  wintering, 77
Sheep-dogs, 87–8
Sheets, 50
Shepherding, 84–5
Shielings (*see also* Scales), 84, 91–4, 148, 151
Shingles, 77
Shutters, window, 46
Sickles, 114
Sidehouse, Great Langdale, 193
Silver, 37
Silverhowe, Gosforth, 149
Simpson House, Low Hartsop, Patterdale, 63
Singleton, Isaac, Buckbarrow Farm, Netherwasdale, 44
Sizergh Castle, 130, 154
Skirwith Hall, 152, 176, 178, 185
Slates, roofing, 151, 155, 159–61
Sled tracks, 129
Sledges, 103, 104–5, 114, 115, 128, 129, 160
Sockbridge Hall, 92, 152, 160, 183, 185
Sods *see* Roof coverings
Spice cupboards, 20, 21, 29, 42, 58
Spinning galleries, 87, 88, 125–8, 141–3
Spout House Farm, Eskdale, 79, 94
St Bees Priory, 39
Stables, 100, 101, 104, 139, 140, 144
Staircases, 19, 36, 55–71
Stairs, 37, 46, 48*foll.*, 51, 52, 54, 178
Stangends Farm, Coniston, 141
Stangends Farm, Netherwasdale, 193
Statesmen, 11, 17, 192, 193
Staveley Park, Staveley, 60, 64, 109, 123, 178
Stepps End, Watendlath, **61**, 67, 179
⁓nton, Alan de, 107
⁓ale, James, 106

Stockholm Tar, 85–6
Stone, 148–57, 178
  quarried, 151–2
  surface gathered, 149–51
Stonethwaite Farm, Borrowdale, 36, 91
Stool End Farm, Great Langdale, 79, 86, 151, 194
Stools, 42, 43
Storeys, 85
Straw, 133–47
Swills, 117, 128
Swine *see* Pigs

Table-cloths, 44, 47
Tables, 42–4, 47
Talbert, John, 185
Tallow, 47, 75, 85, 90, 109, 189
Tanning, 128, 131, 165
Tarn Foot, Loughrigg, 51, 53
Taw House, Eskdale, **74**, 86, 130
Taylor, Agnes, of Penny Bridge, 50
Taylor, Clement, Finsthwaite, 52, 102
Taylor, Edward, Plum Green Farm, Finsthwaite, 24
Taylor, Ferdinando, Hawkshead, 71, 72
Taylor, George, Plum Green Farm, Finsthwaite, 49
Taylor, Miles, Penny Bridge, 50
Taylor, Rownson, 185
Tenants, 14, 15, 16, 17, 78, 163
Tester beds *see* Beds, Tester
Thatch/thatching, 77, 78, 81, 100, 105, 115, 132, 148, 158–9
Thorn House, Hartsop, **87**, 141
Thrang Crag, Martindale, 65
Thrang Farm, Little Langdale, **59**, 171, 191
Threlkeld, Sir Lancelot, 16
Threshing, 34, 52, 115–19
Threshing-floors, 103, 116, 134, 143
Threshing-machines, 118–19, 121
Tiering, 52, 53, 163
Timber (*see also* Oak, Ash, Holly), 131, 148, 163–5, 178
Tock How Farm, Hawkshead, 36
Tower Bank House, Near Sawrey, 193
Townend Cottage, Colthouse, 42, **67**, 175
Townend Farm, Colthouse, 119, 122, 135, **136**
Townend Farm, Finsthwaite, 107
Townend, Troubeck, **6**, 20, 23, **24**, 25, 26, 27, 28, 29, 31, 32, 35, 36, **42**, **43**, **44**, 45, 46, **47**, **50**, 51, 52, 74, 80, 88, 89, 102, 108, 109, 114, 118, 134, 141, **142**, **143**, 175, **176**, 178, **179**, **180**, 181, 191
Townhead Farm, Grasmere, 36, **64**
Transhumance, 81, 91–3
Trenchers *see* Wooden vessels
Troutbeck Park Farm, Troutbeck, 48*foll.*, 88, 103, 109, 144*foll.*, 153
Trusses, roof, 52, 60, 69, 165, 166–71
Turbary, 15, 128
Turn How Farm, Grasmere, 36
Turner, Nicholas, Coniston, 41
Turnips, 103, 123
Tyrer, Revd Ralph, 76

Tyson, Blake, 137
Tyson, Isobel, 51

Underhelm Farm, Grasmere, 45, 58, 50

Vaccaries, 14, 76, 90–1
Viccars, John, Eskdale, 101
Viking traditions, 39–40

Wads Howe, Longsleddale, 109
Waggons, 106
Waine, Jeremiah, Derwentwater, 164
Walker, Elizabeth, Underhelm Farm, Grasmere, 89
Walker, John, Fell Foot Farm, Little Langdale, 49
Wall End, Deepdale, 66
Wall construction, 153–5
Wall-paintings, 60
Wallacrag, 84, 93
Wallend Farm, Great Langdale, **48**foll., 58, **63**, 98, 102, 133, **134**, 151, **144**foll., 194
Wang cheese *see* Cheese
Watendlath Farm *see* Fold Head Farm
Waterside Park, Coniston, 112, 133, 158
Waterson Ground, Hawkshead, 15
Wha House, Eskdale, 94, 106, 123, 138, **139**
Wheat, 26, 27, 31
Wheat bread, 26, 27, 28, 32
Whitewash *see* Limewash
Wilkinson, Robert, Stangends Farm, Netherwasdale, 193
Willy Hill, Clappersgate, 15
Wilson, Dorothy, Ashness Farm, Borrowdale, 104
Wilson, John, Ashness Farm, Borrowdale, 104
Wilson, Miles, Ashness Farm, Borrowdale, 104
Wilson, N., 114
Wilson, Reginald, Wallend Farm, Great Langdale, 98
Windows, 44, 46, 47, 48, 57, 60, 61, 62, 90, 178–81
Windsor Farm, Wasdale, 86, 171
Winnowing, 34, 52, 115–18
Winnowing-cloths, 46, 118, 124
Wolves, 87
Wood Farm, Troutbeck, 60, 191
Wood, as fuel, 28, 30, 36, 183, 184
Wooden vessels, 48, 49
Woodland, 12, 15, 17, 103, 107, 128, 131, 163–5, 196
Woods of Warrant, 163
Wool, 75, 76, 86, 124, 125
Wordsworth, Dorothy, 193
Wordsworth, William, 11, 12, 33, 83, 156, 187, 189, 190, 192, 194, 195
Wrestler slates, 159, 161–2
Wyke, The, Grasmere, **186**, 187

Yanwath Hall, 16
Yatters Farm, Eskdale Green, **45**
Yew Tree Cottage, Stonethwaite, 31
Yew Tree Farm, Coniston, **68**, 88, **126**, 141, **144**foll., 172, 177
Yewbarrow Farm, Longsleddale, 151